Playing in the Cathedral

Currents in
Latin American
& Iberian Music

WALTER CLARK, SERIES EDITOR

Playing in the Cathedral

Music, Race, and Status in New Spain

JESÚS A. RAMOS-KITTRELL

OXFORD
UNIVERSITY PRESS

OXFORD
UNIVERSITY PRESS

Oxford University Press is a department of the University of Oxford. It furthers
the University's objective of excellence in research, scholarship, and education
by publishing worldwide. Oxford is a registered trade mark of Oxford University
Press in the UK and certain other countries.

Published in the United States of America by Oxford University Press
198 Madison Avenue, New York, NY 10016, United States of America.

Library of Congress Cataloging-in-Publication Data
Names: Ramos-Kittrell, Jesús A.
Title: Playing in the cathedral : music, race, and status in New Spain / Jesús A. Ramos-Kittrell.
Description: New York, NY : Oxford University Press, [2016] |
Series: Currents in Latin American and Iberian music |
Includes bibliographical references and index.
Identifiers: LCCN 2015050546 | ISBN 9780190236816 (hardcover : alk. paper) |
ISBN 9780190612672 (epub)
Subjects: LCSH: Music—Mexico—18th century—Social aspects. |
Church musicians—Mexico—18th century. |
Music and race—Mexico—History—18th century.
Classification: LCC ML3917.M4 R36 2016 | DDC 780.89/00972—dc23
LC record available at http://lccn.loc.gov/2015050546

1 3 5 7 9 8 6 4 2
Printed by Sheridan Books, Inc., United States of America

To the memory of María Elena Martínez and Robert Murrell Stevenson.
This book rests on their shoulders.

CONTENTS

LIST OF FIGURES

ACKNOWLEDGMENTS

While this book is the product of years of personal work, completing it would not have been possible without the help and support of several individuals. First, I would like to thank Professors Lorenzo Candelaria and Rebecca Baltzer for their guidance during the initial stages of my research. I would also like to express my most heartfelt gratitude to Professor Gerard Béhague† for inspiring me to move conceptually beyond historical musicology at this beginning point; his influence was "instrumental," as he would have said, on the methodology followed in this book. In this same breath I should mention Professors Susan Deans-Smith and Virginia Garrard-Burnett, whose comments made me push methodological boundaries even further.

From Mexico City I would like to express my most sincere gratitude to Lic. Salvador Valdés†, former archivist of the Archivo del Cabildo of the cathedral of Mexico. His passion for this church (or as he called it, this corporation and the center of social life in colonial Mexico City) permeated many conversations during my visits to the cathedral. My initial ideas and research trajectory benefited tremendously from his candor and openness to historical dialogue; he is certainly missed. I am also grateful to Lic. Salvador Hernández Pech for his continued assistance and for his great labor in the cathedral archives after the passing of Lic. Valdés. There are other people who greatly contributed to the development of ideas in this book and who cannot pass unnoticed. Special mention goes to Professor Aurelio Tello for sharing his knowledge on Manuel Sumaya and to Omar Morales Abril for commenting on my work as it was in progress. I am also thankful to Professor Raúl Torres Medina for his willingness to exchange research notes, and to Professor Rodolfo Aguirre Salvador for illuminating some aspects of the theoretical framework used in this study. Thanks to Yael Bitrán Goren and José Luis Segura Maldonado for their encouragement and for their many attentions during my visits to the Centro Nacional de Investigación, Documentación e Información Musical "Carlos Chávez" (CENIDIM). From the Archivo Histórico Banamex I would like to thank Lic. Héctor González Velázquez for helping me locate sources and for his conversation about the Palacio de Iturbide and the formation of the archive. Special thanks go also to Berenice Bravo Rubio and Marco Antonio Pérez Iturbe of the Archivo Histórico del Arzobispado de México. Their guidance, courtesy, and willingness to find me a place to work during busy hours were greatly appreciated. I will always be thankful to Professor Thomas Stanford for meeting with me several times for breakfast to share anecdotes about his research and cataloguing activity at different colonial archives, particularly at the cathedral of Mexico.

There are a number of people that I also need to thank for their input during the time when the ideas in this book were in a developing state. Thanks to Professor Susan Schroeder for her suggestions about the broader social landscape of Mexico City that I tried to piece together. Thanks are also due to Professors Alejandro L. Madrid and Leonora Saavedra for their comments on race and historiography, and for their continued support of this study. There are no words sufficient to convey my gratitude to Professor John Koegel, whose help with different aspects of this project went beyond the call of duty. Thank you for giving me a space to dissent and for being so receptive to that exchange, John. Many thanks also to Professor Craig Russell for his comments on a preliminary version of Chapter 3 of this book and for being so collegial about my observations related to some of his published work. I would like to thank also Professors Bernardo Illari and Tim Carter for their suggestions about the historical interpretation presented in this chapter. By the same token, I am most grateful to Professor William B. Taylor for his candid and supportive critique. His comments on *decencia* and *calidad* helped me to tighten some of the loose spaces in the narrative on these subjects. Likewise, I need to thank Professor Geoffrey Baker for his reactions to this portion of the book. John Swadley and Professor Javier Marín López should be acknowledged for their timeliness and generosity. Both individuals were extremely kind in sharing unpublished information regarding their research, as well as references to bibliographic and archival materials that enriched sections of this book (thank you for the pictures, John).

There are quite a few people at Southern Methodist University that must be mentioned. From the Department of Music History I want to thank Professors Andrew Greenwood, Peter Kupfer, and Zachary Wallmark for creating an open and productive environment of academic exchange. Their comments on articles, presentations, and some chapter sections were highly beneficial. I want to thank also Debbie Harvey, Melissa Keene, and Carole Harris, the people who make all things possible at SMU's Division of Music. Their administrative support facilitated in great measure the completion of archival work during the last stage of my research.

This acknowledgments section cannot conclude without recognizing the efforts of the best editorial team ever, Professor Walter Clark, Suzanne Ryan, Daniel Gibney, and Eden Piacitelli. I am very fortunate that Professor Clark believed in this project all along; thank you. At the same time, I must express my sincere thanks to Suzanne for remaining receptive to this topic, for her feedback about the book's title, and for inspiring quite a few thoughts in the introduction. I also want to thank Dan and Eden for helping me with all of the logistical aspects of publication, and for making the editorial process such a smooth experience.

This is the long list of individuals that, in one way or another, shaped the direction and form that this project took, and which now comes to fruition. However, any sense of personal accomplishment that this might entail is nothing but a humble and deep feeling of gratitude to the lights of my life, my beautiful wife, Agi, and my daughter, *mi niña*, Míra. Their endless patience, unrelenting support, and endurance (putting up with my bad mood, frustration, and seclusion) were the actual strength that sustained the writing process. I have no way to express to you both how overwhelmed I feel with the undeserved love and positive energy that you give me every day. This book is here ultimately thanks to you. *Nagyon szeretlek téged, Csillag! Te quiero mucho, Miri!*

Playing in the Cathedral

Introduction

> With the permission of your lordship and of the entire music chapel, as its most senior member, I would like to address two points:
>
> The first one is that the administrator of the chapel should not contract more than two events [for the chapel to perform in them], which can be covered without a problem. However, wishing to contract three or four, the administrator calls musicians from outside [to fill in] who are not our equals. They might be very good men, but not *decent* to so many white men and cleric gentlemen in the chapel (see appendix 1.1).[1]

Ignacio Pedroza, trumpet player, had joined the music chapel of the cathedral of Mexico in 1736 and by the time he wrote this letter he had been affiliated with the cathedral for close to thirty-two years.[2] The cathedral was one of the most important institutions in New Spain, and arguably the most important church in Spanish America. Its *cabildo* (chapter) made an effort to employ the most skilled and versatile musicians in the music chapel, as playing at this church was prestigious for a musician's social position. In the context of the racial *casta* (or caste) system that organized social and political life in the New World, membership within Spanish institutions certainly gave people advantages. One could claim benefits over other non-affiliated individuals dedicated to the same activity (especially if they were of a different race), which in itself was a reflection of one's status. Pedroza's letter is in good measure influenced by this scenario where *race* was central to status claims. The allusion to race seems to be straightforward with the mention of "white men." However, Pedroza's focus on "decency" (in relation to the skin color of individuals and their institutional—clerical—professions) suggests that status relied on a more nuanced view of a person's public profile, and that perceptions of race might have related to this complex social construction as well.

As I discuss in Chapter 2, "decency" was not necessarily defined by attitudes or behaviors (i.e., being a good person of virtuous customs). While personal conduct was important to an extent, the meaning of the term was far removed from the ways in which we might use it today. In eighteenth-century Mexico

City "decency" was an attribute of *gente decente* (decent people), a group characterized by the Spanish lineage and social privileges of its members. Proof of having Spanish lineage was required to join Spanish institutions (e.g., the military,
the royal administration, and of course, the church) in order to pursue careers.
Years of institutional service enabled individuals to develop public profiles in
relation to a series of attributes that reflected their *calidad* (literally translated as
"social quality"): an overall impression of their social reputation, byproduct of
their long-standing time of institutional service. Calidad, therefore, was defined
by elements such as place of employment, time of service, rank, acquired knowledge, and most important, the benefits and privileges that a person claimed as
a result. Due to their prominent social standing, and the prerogatives to which
they were entitled, nobles comprised the ideal of calidad in New Spain. Not all
Spaniards had the economic and political resources of nobles, however, which is
why Spanish institutions became avenues to procure the social luster that careers
and education could afford. For this reason, one could say that, more than skin
color, it was the perception of calidad that informed views of "Spanishness" and
what enabled individuals to define their social place.

As one might expect, "decency" encompassed a wide realm of social action
where people of different *calidades* claimed this condition. The calidad of nobles
certainly distanced them from "decent people," although that does not mean
that, as a social category, "nobility" was any less politicized. While there were
titled nobles in New Spain, the crown also granted the privilege of noble treatment (that is, enjoying the benefit of noble prerogatives) to individuals in specific lines of service. To aspire to such distinction, individuals had to prove their
merit by the type of service that they provided to the crown, their length of
service, their institutional affiliation, and their social connections. Just as with
"decency," this aggregate of qualifications (i.e., calidad) made nobility a highly
contested condition that defied strict definition. Employment in a Spanish institution was certainly an important factor, although a lot depended on the type of
institution where a person worked, his knowledge and education, and his rank.
Although there were indeed social differences in the designation of "decency"
and "nobility," both labels denoted dense fields of social contestation and relied
on different attributes for an individual to claim a place in them. Status and
identity were part of a single social *discourse* that individuals constructed, the
reason why the word *discourse* appears extensively throughout this book. The
Oxford English Dictionary defines discourse as a body of statements, analyses,
and opinions relating to a particular domain of social activity, characterized by
recurring themes, concepts or values. Moreover, discourse can also be a set of
shared beliefs implied or expressed in such domain of social activity.[3] In so far
as it is related to narratives of status, discourse alludes, therefore, to personal
modes of organizing knowledge, ideas, and experience in a specific historical

context. In this sense, one can say that in New Spain status was a fluid and highly discursive concept because it was based on subjective renderings of calidad that people claimed to secure a social place. Ultimately, it was the desire for privilege that informed the articulation of calidad among individuals, and that prompted them to envision ways of engaging with a social perception of what it meant to be "Spanish."

Thus, this book explores how musicians at the cathedral of Mexico claimed social status and privilege during the eighteenth century. In the tensions that brewed within the racial caste (casta) system of the time, low- and middle-class *criollos* (i.e., individuals of Spanish descent born locally) struggled to define their social position. This was not only because they ranked below Iberians but also because people of mixed race increasingly competed for the benefits of Spaniards. Amid these tensions, criollos claimed "decency" or "nobility" as attributes that, in the Spanish imagination, distinguished people with academic education, institutional memberships, and careers, among other things. Race was inextricable from these two imaginaries and many people in the low and middle classes strived to prove being Spanish so that they could have access to institutions, and thus, to opportunities for social mobility. Music—as an activity—was a key strategy for participating in this process, and affiliation with the cathedral was an important asset. While choir chaplains aspired to noble status, people in the music chapel (even non-Spaniards) used their membership with this institution to invoke "decency" as an attribute of their public images. Above all, musicians considered themselves to be *hombres decentes* (decent men), members of a Spanish body surrogate to the cathedral clergy, which was made up of individuals of proven Spanish lineage. In light of the social and political ferment that existed in eighteenth-century Mexico City, "decency" was an attribute that, just like nobility, enabled musicians to claim merit and privilege primarily based on race. This study addresses these cases by exploring how cathedral musicians constructed racialized perceptions of their status, the importance that institutional affiliation had in such constructions, and how music served as a strategy to articulate this phenomenon.

I first encountered cases related to decency and nobility in cathedral records while doing archival research on a different topic for my doctoral dissertation in 2004. Since then I have grown intrigued about how these labels intersected with music practices and how these specific cases connect with scholarly narratives of social status in relation to race. Considering that the structure of colonial society hinged on the administration of institutions by a Spanish political class, it is not surprising that the relationship between race and status has been studied through the lives of socially notable Spaniards, where decency and nobility surface as elite traits. Nevertheless, studies in history and cultural anthropology point out that race alone was not a marker of elite status, and that an aggregate of

elements (e.g., personal connections, accomplishments, and institutional affiliation, among others) largely informed perceptions of an individual's social place
(Kicza 1983, Cope 1994, Fisher and O'Hara 2009). These authors have shown
that this was the case among wealthy people who wished to enter and remain in the
circle of notable Spaniards in New Spain. Yet studies showing how people in
the low and middle classes engaged with this process are in the minority.
These types of analyses are important to understand how processes of status
construction worked for these individuals. On a more ontological level, these
studies can illustrate how those who were not Spanish (yet worked in Spanish
institutions) benefited from these racialized claims relying on activities (e.g.,
music) steeped in processes of "Spanish" identity construction.

Due to their discursivity, decency and nobility are elusive social categories: the phenomenon of status construction remains one of the most cumber-
some terrains of inquiry in New Spanish history. Aware of this challenge, the
present study frames the cases related to decency and nobility of cathedral musicians within a larger spectrum of status claims in these two categories prevalent
in eighteenth-century Mexico City. As a consequence, this framework decenters
the position of these labels from the activity of Spaniards in the upper classes
and thus questions any attempt to overgeneralize the Spanish race-status relationship. More important, the book positions music as a central element in
the construction of social profiles, lifelong projects of professional development through which individuals wrought their personal desires and carved a
social niche.

The role that music played in these efforts carried some aesthetic overtones.
This is why contrapuntal music in the so-called *stilo antico* (the style of composers such as Francisco Guerrero, Tomás Luis de Victoria, and Alonso Lobo, for
example) was important in cathedral music education for much of the eighteenth
century. The acquisition of the theoretical underpinnings in this music enabled
individuals to advance in a chain of ministries devoted to music and ritual. It was
after years of service that individuals developed careers as cathedral ministers,
which enabled them to claim different status discourses depending on their credentials (either as members of the music chapel or as chaplains). It should not be
surprising, then, that music in this style possessed institutional and social value,
and that the incursion of musicians proficient in new music trends (the *estilo
moderno*, as it was called) initially created political frictions. Although these tensions have been recognized in musicological studies (Dietz 2000, Davies 2006),
little has been done to shed light on their ideological and political underpinnings. For the most part, historical musicologists have addressed these reactions
as anachronisms, older biased Spanish views out of tune with the aesthetic sensibility and musical taste of modernity. These assessments have overlooked these
reactions and their social valence in favor of judgments of musical value. It is

possible that for this reason Spanish music culture of the eighteenth century has been approached in terms of the stylistic changes that influenced music practices in this period (Carreras 1998, Davies 2011).

There can be little doubt that the estilo moderno was one of the most important influences on approaches to music education, composition, and performance during the *Siglo de la Luces* (century of Enlightenment). To focus only on these changes, however, ignores aesthetic elements that, inherited from the time of Habsburg rule, also transpired in music practices until the middle of the century and that deeply shaped music culture. Musicianship (i.e., what it meant to "know" music) was one of such elements, and the rhetoric of traditional Spanish music theory treatises informed such a notion. This book shows that this theoretical grammar buttressed an understanding of musical knowledge similar to academic knowledge, which made cathedral musicians "erudite" in their profession, members of an important Spanish institution who defined their social place through these attributes. The disruption of this paradigm with the incursion of modern music, therefore, urges us to consider the eighteenth century in more complex terms: as a period of tension and negotiation, when cathedral musicians had to adapt to social and aesthetic transformations in order to retain their social position.

The fact that musicians could use their relationship with Spanish institutions to seek benefits has moved some scholars to look more closely at the Spanish race-power relationship. Quite recently, a few musicologists have sought not only to map the diverse social positionings that existed among musicians of different races and were marginalized in former studies of colonial music culture (Baker and Knighton 2011). They have also addressed the ways in which non-Spanish individuals engaged with a Spanish system of social and political order as a means of resistance (Irving 2010). These studies do not necessarily challenge the idea of Spanish hegemony as much as they highlight the ways in which individuals of different races interacted with it. The efforts of these scholars resonate with current views in social history, which stress the need to expand our understanding of how people related to the Spanish race-power ideology (Martínez 2012). Such interest becomes more pertinent if we consider the possibility that some individuals, who in the present are not perceived as Spaniards, might have considered themselves Spanish in the eighteenth century. For example, some people today refer to Manuel Sumaya (chapelmaster at the cathedral of Mexico from 1715 to 1738) as a Mestizo, even when he regarded himself as a Spaniard. Ignacio Jerusalem (chapelmaster from 1750 until 1769) is another interesting case: he was an Italian, but in all probability he wanted his children to be considered Spanish. That is possibly why he intended for his son, Salvador, to join the cathedral Colegio de Infantes (for which being Spaniard was required), and why his daughter, María Michaela, joined the Convent of Capuchin nuns.

Historian María Elena Martínez has raised important questions that relate to these cases: did the possibility that people could "pass" as Spaniards generate desires and political loyalties that were crucial to the maintenance of the hierarchical racial order? If so, how did the construction of "Spanishness" transpire in intimate domains of social life and experience for these people?

This book departs from these queries in order to assess "Spanishness" in relation to the activity of cathedral musicians. Although this might seem at first a case study about Spanish individuals (and therefore, not interested in the lives and doings of musicians of other races) its intentions are deeper. Considering that the operation of Spanish hegemony was connected to a hierarchical racial system, the study traces the lives of musicians who relied on Spanish perceptions of status to claim merit and privilege. The analysis might seem straightforward in the case of people who proved having Spanish blood, but the narrative becomes more politicized in the case of non-Spaniards; members of the music chapel (some of whom were either Italian or French) are a good example of this. They claimed status not as Spaniards but as "decent men" based on their membership in a Spanish institution, as well as their knowledge of music and their careers in the church. The possibility that these individuals could subscribe to decency (a trope of belonging in the Spanish imagination) prompts us to consider race in terms of its social dimensions and its cultural effects, and not necessarily its purported biological character. This study, therefore, approaches "Spanishness" as a highly fluid social construction and considers the act of making music as a vital strategy in the construction of its meaning. In this regard, the act of making music is resonant with Christopher Small's notion of *musicking*. Musicking refers to taking part, in any capacity, in all activity connected to music performance (performing, listening, rehearsing, practicing, or composing). This concept recognizes that the social meanings of music-making do not necessarily have to be separated from the properties of sound, as both contribute to an overall understanding of music as an activity.[4] This means that performance renders conceptual applications (e.g., learning music theory) relevant to musicking, especially if the latter is imbued with social meaning. Performance denotes a metaphor for the ways in which individuals present themselves and their activity to others. In this sense, musicking is a type of social performance that attempts to play with the elements that inform an impression of the performer in the public eye and relies on those elements to sustain the performance itself. The ultimate objective of the performer (or in this case, group of performers) is to sustain the social impression that their performance fosters.[5]

The notion of "playing" acquires a unique and liminal character in this context. On the one hand, it refers to the act of performing music, which enabled musicians to affiliate themselves with the most prominent ecclesiastical institution in Spanish America, and arguably with the leading music ensemble in

New Spain. On the other hand, playing refers to a course of conduct and a social maneuver that cathedral musicians performed with this affiliation. Playing in the cathedral (of Mexico) meant more than just the act of music performance or the possibility of a salary for this service (although that was surely a motivation). It was in itself a social action, which implied the possibility of negotiating one's position upward in the colonial social hierarchy of Mexico City. Race was a central component of such a move, and in this regard "playing in the cathedral" refers to the creative ways in which individuals integrated this element into their social and political identities. Musicians, therefore, relied on music to "play" (to make a move, to maneuver) in the highly pageant and contested environment of eighteenth-century Mexico City.

Such an environment resonated with the creative ways that individuals used to construct their social positions in New Spain at large, where institutional affiliation and race were key elements in any attempts to advance socially. It is mainly for this reason that this book does not specify "eighteenth-century" or "Mexico City" in the second portion of its title. Doing so would restrict the relevance and operation the conceptual framework hereby presented, geographically and historically. The phenomenon of racial status construction in New Spain (from the late sixteenth through the eighteenth century) has been abundantly documented by historians such as María Elena Martínez and Rodolfo Aguirre Salvador, both of whom are cited extensively in this work. Perhaps the same cannot be said about analyses of music-making during the colonial period, and one study alone cannot account for such a large historical and geographical terrain. Cases studies by Omar Morales Abril and Alfredo Nava Sánchez, however (both cited in this book), give reason to believe that music did operate as a strategy to articulate racialized discourses of status beyond Mexico City and the eighteenth century, and the work of Geoffrey Baker in Cuzco, Peru, suggests the possibility that this conceptual framework might be extended beyond New Spain. The present book is the product of ten years of data collection and analysis. I hope that the historical and institutional specificity of this study will open avenues of inquiry among scholars interested in how other institutions and groups of individuals participated in this social phenomenon. More analyses of this type are still needed in Latin American colonial music studies.

Thus, the present book concerns itself with what was arguably the most important religious institution in New Spain during the period of highest social commotion in New Spanish history. Considering the transformations that occurred during the eighteenth century and the economic and political challenges that the increasing instability of the caste system produced, one must ask: how important was race to musicians in pursuit of social desires and ambitions? What were the racialized identities that these individuals were able to produce, and how did music participate in these processes? How was institutionalized musical activity—and more important, ways of thinking about music—linked to these processes? How did new aesthetic trends in music intersect with this phenomenon and what changes did they generate? These are some of the questions that this book attempts to answer.

A few words regarding the genesis of this project are pertinent before delving into an account about the methodology used. Research work for this book began in the summer of 2003 during my first visit to the Archivo del Cabildo of the cathedral of Mexico. Although I cannot say that I was deeply influenced by the work of scholars like Robert Stevenson, Craig Russell, and Steven Barwick, I was, nonetheless, interested in contextualizing the substance of their scholarship regarding this important cathedral. At that time, I was particularly interested in learning about the liturgical and institutional backdrop of musical activity in this church. Which types of religious services called for music by the music chapel? How and when did services occur? How did the liturgical calendar (in the way that it was observed at this cathedral) structure the work of musicians, musical instruction, and musical texts? Which political and/or economic factors influenced or affected this arrangement? After all, was the music life of the most important cathedral in the New World really "splendorous" during the eighteenth century? These were the queries that fueled my initial visit to the archives while I looked for a theme for my doctoral dissertation.

It took close to six months to find a topic after searching through books of chapter acts, folders of miscellaneous documents without chronological order, boxes of payment records, service attendance, inventories, rosters, letters, and manuscript volumes describing cathedral ritual customs, religious endowments, and changes in musical and liturgical practices at the behest of private donors. After one and a half years of archival research I was ready to begin an in-depth analysis of the records that I had found before attempting any type of historical interpretation. Eventually, I had the chance to distance myself from the dissertation and to allow some ideas and concepts to mature. I also was able to pursue further research on themes that surfaced in some of the documents that I consulted, which I did not have the opportunity to approach initially. As a result, the present book is radically different from my doctoral research in significant ways. The topics explored in this study take into account the latest contributions in musicology and social history, and connect musical activity to a larger panorama of social life in colonial Mexico City. Moreover, the critique of some of my work (i.e., articles and the proposal for this book) by colleagues in musicology, history, and art history has expanded the breadth of the historical contextualization that the study aims to present. Finally, this case study is richly documented with archival references taken from a database that holds more than one thousand records at the moment (all inspected for this study, although not all are included) and that has grown after later visits to the archives.

This book does not attempt to follow a traditional model of historical causal narrative based on references to facts, events, ideas, and individuals described in primary sources. Rather, my intention is to present this information within a theoretical framework of social and historical interpretation. Here, it is important to point out that this approach sometimes bypasses our current modern views of some concepts (race and music theory are good examples) in order to shed light on how eighteenth-century individuals (specifically, those who lived in Mexico City, who were part of the low and middle classes and worked in the cathedral) possibly understood them. It is also pertinent to add that this study neither departs from nor focuses on the historical assessment of music texts. The main purpose of the book is to explore the social dimensions of musical activity in order to identify the elements that made institutionalized music-making politically relevant. The study of music culture (a particular music culture) lies at the core of this purpose, and it would be helpful to explain upfront how the book approaches the concept of "culture." It has been mentioned that a frustrating aspect of studying New Spanish music culture outside religious institutions is the absence of notated music.[6] This view considers the written score an important means for deriving an image of the soundscape that the performance of that music produced, which in turn would enable us to learn something about the musical activity of a place. In recent studies, this notion of music culture has provided an invigorating platform to contemplate how sound interacted with epistemologies of colonial power. The theoretical backdrop of these studies considers the urban soundscape a sphere of contact, which, within the context of urban geography, aims to map the position that musics of different racial origins occupied in a city.[7]

Inspired by this scholarship, the present study seeks to contribute to an ongoing dialogue about productive ways of envisioning music culture in Spanish America. While it might be true that certain musics (indigenous, African, Mestizo) found a niche in relation to their racial underpinnings, this book does not attempt to learn about the social place that musicians occupied (or claimed) by focusing on the discursive properties of sound alone. Race was an important component in efforts of social positioning, but a focus on the racialization of sound cannot account for the creative ways in which individuals attempted to position themselves, and for how race was actually constructed. This does not necessarily mean that we should ignore music if we are to study the efforts of cathedral musicians to define their social place. Music, as a cultural product, was not neutral; it was created, performed, and received to deploy meanings, and in that regard music's discursive properties have to be acknowledged. In New Spain, music (as part of musicking) gave rise to subjective orientations and to efforts of social mobility in which readings of race (and the elements that informed it) were relevant. This phenomenon is extremely important to an understanding of "culture," and the consideration of sound alone cannot describe the affectual traces of the subjectivities that produced it. The present study, therefore, builds on the efforts of current scholarship in musicology and social history by approaching music culture as an arena articulated by dynamics of social exchange among individuals and institutions. This activity was steeped in a historically and geographically situated structure of values and ideologies in which race was important, and that influenced the activity of musicians. Considering that musicking—in reference to the social dimensions of music-making—was central to the generation of music culture, this book does not focus on how music was interpreted (although that point will be touched on) but rather on *how it was used* both by musicians and the institutions that employed them.[8]

While the theme of this book has been inspired by some of the writings of musicologists Geoffrey Baker, Tess Knighton, David Irving, and Bernardo Illari, its theoretical approach is indebted to historians William B. Taylor, Rodolfo Aguirre Salvador, and María Elena Martínez. Taylor's observations were extremely helpful in defining and conceptualizing the operation of elusive concepts such as calidad, "decency," and "nobility." The work and commentary of Aguirre Salvador provided valuable insight into the social value that the relationship with the cathedral (conceived as a Spanish corporate institution) had for musicians. In turn, Martínez's work on *limpieza de sangre* has been central in the organization of these elements to form a conceptual framework for this study. As a result, the book seeks to contribute to the efforts of these musicologists and historians in specific ways. While broad concepts such as "Spanishness," "decency," and "nobility" have been discussed before, this study addresses their manifestation in one activity (music) within one single institution. My aim is that the institutional specificity of this analysis will enable us to see decency and nobility as hierarchical levels of political identity based on calidad, which in turn invites us to think about the different hues and complexity of that concept in relation to perceptions of "Spanishness."

The piecing together of individual lives (in a general way, without going into any type of biographical analysis) such as Manuel Sumaya's, Martín Bernárdez de Rivera's, and to a lesser degree those of Miguel de Herrera, José González, Martín Vásquez de Mendoza, Ignacio Jerusalem, and Antonio Rafael Portillo y Segura (all cathedral musicians) sheds light on how institutional music-making enabled these men to claim either "decent" or "noble" status for themselves, and how those claiming the first benefited from interacting with the latter. Thus, I hope to draw original conclusions about the operation of calidad as part of Spanish identities in ways that might not have been contemplated before (see the Epilogue). To do this, the book presents archival information relevant to (1) the trajectory of individuals through years of cathedral service, and (2) references to this activity from individuals seeking recognition for merit and privilege. The sources for the first category are largely drawn from the Archivo del Cabildo of the cathedral of Mexico and encompass minutes from cathedral chapter meetings, payment records, cathedral chapter decrees, and personal correspondence between chaplains, musicians, and the members of the cathedral chapter. Other records pertinent to institutional promotion and status claims (such as information about university studies and clerical advancement) encompass lawsuits, descriptions of university examinations, graduations, and the recording of ecclesiastical ranks attained by individuals, which make up the second category. The sources in this second category were located at the Archivo General de la Nación and at the Archivo Histórico del Arzobispado de México. Other archival information relevant to the lives of notable individuals (like Miguel de Berrio y Zaldívar, marqués de Jaral de Berrio, and conde de San Mateo de Valparaíso, for example) come from either the minutes of cathedral chapter meetings and correspondence located at the Archivo del Cabildo of the cathedral, the Archivo Histórico Banamex, or from secondary sources.

All of this information has been used to map the institutional upbringing of individuals—from the moment they became choirboys to their final appointment as either musicians in the chapel or as chaplains—describing in detail the proficiencies (e.g., knowledge of music, having a good voice, knowing how to play an instrument, knowledge of Latin) and positions (e.g., choirboy, acolyte, instrumentalist) that they claimed as *calidades* to secure higher appointments. For the second category, I refer to personal correspondence and lawsuits to describe situations when musicians and chaplains claimed privileges over other individuals. The study pays special attention to the lives of the individuals named above mainly because cathedral records document their trajectories quite thoroughly. The lives of these men serve as reference points to which to compare others for whom information is more fragmentary. This approach should help to flesh out a broader narrative about the activities of musicians at this institution.

Before giving an outline of the book's structure, I will describe briefly the sources used. As mentioned above, archival references derive from research at primarily four repositories. In the Archivo del Cabildo the following branches were consulted: Actas de Cabildo, Acuerdos de Cabildo, Archivo de Música, Canonjías, Capellanías, Correspondencia, Edictos, Fábrica Espiritual, Fábrica Material, and Ordo. At the Archivo General de la Nación, research focused on the branches Inquisición and Universidad. Although I spent a lot of time at the Archivo Histórico del Arzobispado de México, this book only used information from the Fondo Cabildo. The Fondo Marqueses de Jaral de Berrio was the only branch consulted at the Archivo Histórico Banamex, and only one source from the Fondo Reservado of the Biblioteca Nacional de México was inspected. Documents related to limpieza de sangre and to claims of nobility were found at the DeGolyer Library of Southern Methodist University and are used only for illustrative purposes. For more in-depth research on these topics, the reader would be advised to consult the work of Rodolfo Aguirre Salvador, María Elena Martínez, and Doris Ladd cited in the bibliography.

Transcriptions of original Spanish sources appear only when English translations are provided in the text. I have done this for reasons of space. No changes have been made to the original Spanish wording; only accent marks, punctuation marks (commas, semi-colons), and the modern spelling of certain Spanish first names (e.g., José instead of Joseph) have been added. In some cases the transcriptions are partial, given that documents can be quite lengthy. In all instances the folio number in the citation indicates where the narrative on a given topic or fact begins in a primary source.

To approach the phenomenon of status construction, its relation to colonial racial ideology, and its expression in music practices, I thought it pertinent to begin the book with an overview of musicological literature in colonial music studies. Chapter 1, therefore, begins by positioning this case study within the breadth of scholarly work done so far. This review of scholarship aims to show how the treatment of colonial music culture has changed in music historiography. The chapter addresses particularly how the book seeks to build on the efforts of these scholars, especially of those who have addressed the concept of music culture lately. It is at this point that the issue of *race* makes its first proper appearance. The chapter stresses how archival evidence urges us to consider race in more nuanced ways within musicological studies so as to understand the elements that constructed it and how music participated in this process.

Chapter 2 gives a broad description of musical activity in Mexico City during the eighteenth century, showing how certain places colored the social views of musicians active in different urban spaces. This chapter introduces the phenomenon of status construction and relates it to perceptions of a person's profile (in terms of race, occupation, education, affiliations, but also of customs and demeanor). The panorama presented here serves to contextualize the case study of cathedral musicians on which the book centers, mentioning its particular components. The chapter shows that for Spaniards without political or financial resources, institutional affiliation was a way to define their social status. For cathedral musicians, affiliation with the church served this purpose, as they used it to claim a place of respectability. Such status raised them above the perceived vices and low behaviors prevalent in the environment of the low and middle classes in the city, entitling them to certain privileges. Chapter 3 goes into more depth. It addresses the activity of cathedral musicians who chose to become priests. The chapter stresses that proving one's purity of blood was critical for following this path because Spanish blood was required to join Spanish institutions. It also illustrates how individuals used music as a strategy to climb through the ranks with the goal of being ordained. Ultimately, this trajectory entailed a certain type of "noble" status in light of the erudition, institutional career, and clerical rank that individuals acquired.

Chapter 4 departs from the framework laid out in Chapters 2 and 3 to address the tensions surrounding the tenure of the cathedral chapelmastership by the Italian composer Ignacio Jerusalem. While much has been written about him, as well as about the need for a historical assessment of Italianate music within Spanish music culture, little has been done to interpret the position of this composer—and the changes that he brought to cathedral musical activity—in the social context of eighteenth-century New Spain. This chapter, therefore, considers Jerusalem's activity in relation to the institutional and social role that music had for Spanish cathedral musicians, and to the epistemology and aesthetics associated with that role. Chapter 5, then, departs from the political tensions caused by Jerusalem's appointment in order to understand the corporate transformations that transpired in the music chapel and how these changes affected claims of status and privilege among musicians. The chapter discusses how these individuals relied on their institutional affiliation to claim decency as a racialized discourse of status that entitled them to specific benefits. In light of significant changes that occurred during the eighteenth century (i.e., the destabilization of the caste system, shifts in music aesthetics, and the loss of corporate integrity by the music chapel) the chapter focuses on how cathedral musicians adapted to a landscape in transformation in order to continue claiming decency as part of their status.

The book concludes with an epilogue that advocates new ways of seeing how Spanish discourses (i.e., "decency," "nobility") interacted with music as an intimate realm of experience. This section shows that such notions—which departed from ideas of knowledge and erudition—influenced ways of thinking about music, and that this understanding enabled musicians to follow paths of social mobility. The epilogue reminds the reader of the different discourses of status—based on levels of achievement—that individuals claimed using music as a strategy. By doing this, the epilogue frames music as an activity that, by forging close relationships with institutions, generated political loyalties and social desires among musicians.

Studying Music Culture in New Spain

Introduction

Approaches toward the study of New Spanish music culture have changed considerably since the 1930s (when Gabriel Saldívar's book *Historia de la música en México* first appeared), so it seemed appropriate to get a historiographic glimpse of literature pertinent to this field. While some of the scholarship addressed below does not deal necessarily with New Spain, it is still worth mentioning it because its view of colonial music history resonates with narratives that have focused on this area. The chapter closes by addressing how the present book contributes to recent work in the field of colonial music studies, with a particular emphasis on New Spain.

Rupture and Continuity

Although a lot has changed since the 1950s in colonial music studies, the figure of Robert Stevenson still looms large in this field. Either in the spirit of guidance or criticism, his work—and that of scholars influenced by him—continues to inspire dialogue and new directions in research, to the extent that a word about him could not be overlooked in this chapter. During the summer of 2003, while I was conducting archival research for my doctoral dissertation in Mexico City, I received an invitation to attend a meeting of the Seminario de Música en la Nueva España y el México Independiente (seminar of music in New Spain and independent Mexico) at the Universidad Nacional Autónoma de México (UNAM). The main objective of this research community was (and still remains) "the study of cathedral musical activity (*el fenómeno sonoro*, or the sonic phenomenon, to be exact) in order to understand New Spanish society during the period of 1525–1858."[1] The seminar functioned as a collaborative network of scholars from different disciplines, which made the prospect of the meeting quite exciting. The agenda featured two presentations addressing ambiguities and inaccuracies in some of Stevenson's writings, particularly in relation to two well-known polyphonic pieces with Nahuatl texts. These examples of colonial polyphony were part of a miscellany of manuscript vocal music that Father Octaviano Valdés acquired in 1931, allegedly from a group of Indians planning to use its contents as kindling paper.[2] The two Nahuatl pieces in this music collection—known today as the Valdés Codex (or Códice Valdés)—became the focus of the meeting, which was not short of opinions about Stevenson's inconsistent interpretation of these works in two of his books. In *Music in Mexico: A Historical Survey* (1952), he had referred to them as hymns for the Virgin Mary, whereas sixteen years later he called them chanzonetas in his book *Music in Aztec and Inca Territory* (1968).[3] The discussion proceeded with a scrutiny of Stevenson's framework of analysis to find probable reasons why he had used mismatching labels. In the end, the presenters outlined a series of errors in his interpretation and suggested a revised historical assessment of this music based on their own observations, which departed from a critical reading of Stevenson's work. Although the interdisciplinary environment of the seminar proved to be stimulating, much of its intellectual substance on that occasion had derived from Stevenson's scholarship, even if from the vantage point of critique. That evening I realized that the meeting had not necessarily proposed new directions in research as much as it had laid the groundwork for a better understanding of Stevenson's contributions and his position in colonial music studies.

Following the pioneering efforts of Gabriel Saldívar (*Historia de la música en México*, 1934) and Jesús Bal y Gay (*Tesoro de la música polifónica en México I*, 1952), Stevenson's *Music in Mexico* was the first book on the subject in English. *The Music of Peru: Aboriginal and Viceroyal Epochs* (1960) followed after that, a book that fulfilled the author's interest in presenting the musics of the two "high American cultures."[4] *Music in Aztec and Inca Territory* aimed precisely at highlighting the importance of both musical legacies to an English readership, for which the author felt compelled to approach again the two Nahuatl pieces: testimonies of indigenous cultural presence in the midst of the conquest. This monograph offered a revised edition of the two previous publications (namely, *Music in Mexico* and *Music in Peru*) and it was not spared from the criticism that the members of the seminar voiced thirty-five years later. Specifically, critics said that *Music in Aztec and Inca Territory* offered no conclusions "simply because no real issues were ever tackled," which made the revision and synthesis of earlier material ineffectual.[5] It was not only the inconsistent reading of the two Nahuatl pieces that seemed problematic to Gerard Béhague, who reviewed the book in 1969, but the complete absence of evidence to support any interpretation of either Aztec or Inca music culture (before or during the conquest) also made the book lack substance according to him. Béhague, nonetheless, pointed to the author's impressive bibliographic knowledge and thorough documentation, which he recognized as one of the major strengths of his work.

Even if informally, scholars today voice similar opinions about Stevenson's approach to colonial music culture, which has inspired new directions in research in the last ten years. Some of the latest work in this field has sought to move beyond ecclesiastical centers to gain a broader understanding of colonial musical life. Geoffrey Baker was among the first scholars to focus on this line of inquiry. In his book about music in Cuzco, Peru, he states that by mainly approaching cathedrals—institutions that blocked opportunities for indigenous advancement—previous studies "[have] reduced the role of indigenous musicians in urban institutions to that of permanent underlings."[6] This approach, Baker notes, has also marginalized these individuals from narratives of colonial music culture, giving privileged attention to Spanish musicians.[7] Likewise, Tess Knighton has brought attention to the need for considering different types of documentary evidence (diocesan, notarial, and municipal records, instead of relying entirely on cathedral sources) that can reveal a more holistic account of colonial music culture and the place of diverse musics (e.g., indigenous, African, and European) and individuals in it.[8] This line of research grew out of an interest in considering music practices beyond the activity of cathedrals, privileged loci of study in early colonial music literature. By and large, Stevenson spearheaded these initial efforts in which exhaustive documentation was the main concern. After 1968, his next large monograph (considerably more substantive than *Music in El Paso* and *Philosophies of American Music History*), *Renaissance and Baroque Music Sources in the Americas* (1970) served that very purpose, being the most comprehensive listing of archival colonial music sources at that point. This fervent interest in documenting was not Stevenson's alone; he was working within the academic momentum of his time to provide indispensable research tools for those embarking on the study of Latin American colonial music.[9] It was because of their surviving music archives that cathedrals received central attention with the hope of revealing their "renaissance and baroque music treasures."[10] Stevenson's concern for recording the existence of Spanish polyphonic music in the New World started with a series of articles previous to this volume, the first of which appeared in 1954.[11] In the first of these articles, the author mentions the work of Steven Barwick and Alice Ray Catalyne on polyphonic music at the cathedrals of Mexico and Puebla, which spurred academic interest in the music holdings of other major ecclesiastical centers in Mexico (the cataloguing work of Thomas Stanford at the cathedral of Mexico in 1966, and Spiess and Stanford's *An Introduction to Certain Mexican Musical Archives*, 1969, merit mention here).

It would be misleading to label the reaction of scholars like Baker, Knighton, and others to these studies as revisionist. In fact, they recognize the strong influence that this scholarship has had in the field, which ultimately led them to consider unexplored directions in colonial music studies. One such direction concerns the lives and social position of musicians, an area still in need of more attention. For Baker, non-Spanish musicians are of particular interest because their activity has been addressed mostly in relation to Spanish ecclesiastical music practices, without considering how racial and other class-related factors influenced music practices for them, through which they wrought their own political intentions.[12] Stevenson's appraisal of Juan Mathías, for example, is a case in point, given that the cathedral of Oaxaca was the main arena to assess his activity, independent from the highly racialized sociopolitical environment in which he lived.[13] There is much more that past scholarship could have said about colonial musicians and their place in society. To call this a deficiency, however, would be to ignore the issues and context that surrounded this research.

During the first decades of the twentieth century, an exoticist enthusiasm for pre-Hispanic culture fueled interests in Latin American artistic expressions, which could have possibly influenced approaches in music scholarship by Stevenson and others. In Mexico, the idea of an "Aztec Renaissance" was taken as the basis of what was "profoundest and deepest in the Mexican soul," said Carlos Chávez in 1928. This view emerged parallel to a cultural project of nation building that gained strength in Mexico after the civil war of 1910. According to some scholars, this project promoted the idea that the Spanish colonial past had no bearing on modern notions of cultural identity, for its "roots" lay in the legacy of pre-Hispanic societies.[14] Based on this idea, the press promoted Mexican artistic expressions in the United States, postulating that Mexican art had reached a cultural apogee in both the pre-Hispanic and modern periods.[15]

To some extent, this fascination with pre-Hispanic culture lay at the center of a nationalist discourse about history that measured cultural development by means of comparison with Europe. In this regard, it should not be surprising that narratives of music history aligned with such discourse, and that readings of colonial music had to adapt accordingly. For example, Saldívar's *Historia de la música en México* and Stevenson's *Music in Mexico* open up by addressing the state of pre-Hispanic music before the conquest, after which they glide into the colonial phase by pointing to the unproblematic European acculturation of indigenous people. Other Latin American scholars followed the same tendency, emphasizing how indigenous individuals easily adapted to the musical activity of Spanish institutions. Seemingly, these natives openly adopted European liturgical music "and greatly enjoyed Gregorian chant and polyphonic singing."[16] Scholars also stated that there was not a lack of original (i.e., national) symphonic music in modern Latin America, where opera productions could be compared to those at La Scala.[17] According to Stevenson, cultural nationalists were not necessarily opposed to the idea of colonial music, but he did realize that for some the notion itself was anti-national, and this troubled him. In his experience, some nationalists felt that all music before 1821 "belongs to Spanish history, and is therefore of secondary importance to the truly patriotic historian."[18] The main concern for Stevenson was that this attitude could dispose of a rich musical legacy, much like the bones of conqueror Hernán Cortés, which the Mexican Congress ordered to be dug up and burned right after independence.[19] Quite possibly, this was an incentive for Stevenson to document extant colonial music sources at different repositories in Latin America and abroad and the reason that ecclesiastical centers became a priority for him.

Nevertheless, historical contexts are hardly so clear-cut and schematic. In Mexico, nineteenth-century attitudes toward music were also responsible for the neglect of colonial music. Historian such as Gustavo Campa and Alba Herrera y Ogazón were not necessarily enthusiastic about colonial music. An engagement with European romantic music had priority during this time, and tensions between the church and the nation-state only fueled the dislike for what was perceived as being culturally "Spanish." Anti-clerical sentiments intensified in the 1920s and 1940s (during the presidencies of Plutarco Elías Calles and Lázaro Cárdenas), when colonial music lay dormant in ecclesiastical archives. It would be fair to say that the problems between the church and the government largely affected the state of colonial research during the early twentieth century, but one must not forget that theft (sometimes by scholars) only worsened things. This author was told more than a handful of accounts (occurring at the Archivo General de la Nación, the Archivo del Cabildo of the cathedral of México, and the Archivo Histórico del Arzobispado de México) of scholars mutilating documents, taking music scores, or cutting illuminations from chantbooks. In light of this history, the church became suspicious not only of government initiatives to approach (or expropriate) ecclesiastical holdings but also of the scholarly community that failed to fulfill the ethical obligation of publishing and truly researching these sources.

One might disagree with Stevenson's approach today, but it is hard to argue that his efforts were not influenced by historically specific conditions. If he (and probably others, like Saldívar) focused their attention on the church, and more specifically on cathedrals, it was in part because of this context. Access to archival holdings was hard to obtain, and documentation, unsurprisingly, was a priority. Also, during that time, the musicological community paid little attention to Latin America unless an unknown masterwork by a European composer was found hidden in some church.[20] For Stevenson, introducing Latin America in Western narratives of music history was also important because of the central position that this territory had in the development of Western culture on the continent. Regarding music, Stevenson wrote, it was there where the first opera was written, where the first music was printed, and where the first attempts at music criticism appeared.[21] It might be true that Stevenson's efforts were not thorough if one considers the sociocultural richness of the colonial past that awaited exploration, but then again, one must remember the context in which he worked. Perspectives have changed considerably among colonialists today (inside and outside Latin America), although it is hard to deny that the position of Latin American colonial music remains the same within Western narratives of music history. It was only recently that George Buelow and Peter Burkholder incorporated New World music in their respective texts. However, the *Oxford History of Western Music*, arguably one of the most authoritative texts on music history in the United States, omits the topic altogether in the first and second volumes. In a way, Stevenson's approach toward colonial music was a way of engaging with different mentalities, and his interest in documenting extant sources was perhaps a way to qualify this area of study. After all, he thought of New World cathedrals as the "last musicological frontier," probably the reason he was so diligent in seeking out information about composers active in these centers.[22]

Like the work of any scholar, Stevenson's writings are not immune to criticism, especially if one considers the work done by others who came after him. Needless to say (but it better be said anyway), decades of scholarly endeavors can give one the advantage of historiographic perspective. In this respect, one must remember that any disposition toward criticism entails a willingness to approach Stevenson's scholarship, which offers the possibility of better understanding the position of his work in the study of colonial music culture. His indefatigable and keen capacity to document was extraordinary, and his endeavors should be gauged in that context. Only by engaging Stevenson can we establish a productive critique in pursuit of new terrains of inquiry. Or, as Gerard Béhague once told this author, "one must go through him in order to go beyond him."

New Approaches to Colonial Music Culture

Following Stevenson, other scholars produced more nuanced studies of music sources and activity in Spanish America. Steven Barwick's *Two Mexico City Choirbooks of 1717* (1982) and Paul R. Laird's *Towards a History of the Spanish Villancico* (1997), for example, revealed previously unknown sources and provided information about musicians and composers in relation to this repertoire. Later publications by Craig Russell, Grayson Wagstaff, William Summers, Lester Brothers, Mark Brill, Aurelio Tello, and Bernardo Illari expanded our knowledge of colonial music practices in regard to stylistic issues, genre development, and performance approaches. More recent scholarship, however, has made new inroads in the mapping of colonial music culture. In 2009, Russell's *From Serra to Sancho: Music and Pageantry in the California Missions* addressed how music performance related to religious practices, and showed that the music of New Spanish composers was disseminated throughout different regions in northern New Spain. Russell suggests that these interregional connections had a considerable impact on local musical life, making California missions active spots within a colonial network of music circulation and performance.

Javier Marín López's work on choirbooks has shed further light on this line of study. His publication *Los libros de polifonía de la catedral de México* (2012) is not only the most detailed catalogue of Mexico City cathedral's choirbook collection; it is also an extensive codicological study that shows how the music in these volumes relates to a common set of music practices that existed among different ecclesiastical centers in New Spain, and even across the Atlantic. Other Spanish musicologists, like María Gembero Ustárroz and Emilio Ros-Fábregas (*La música y el Atlántico: Relaciones musicales entre España y Latinoamérica*, 2007), also have shown interest in this area of research, and in their scholarship they allude to transatlantic connections between colonial Latin America and Europe in terms of repertoire and performance. These recent studies have contributed to an understanding of music culture in which sound acted as a sort of connecting tissue, which in a way demarcated an epistemologically coherent area in terms of musical and religious practices. Issues related to style have also been addressed within this framework, especially in consideration of a large body of music from the eighteenth century that awaited proper attention. After Russell's publications dealing with music by Ignacio Jerusalem (arguably one of the most important composers from this period), Drew Edward Davies's dissertation "The Italianized Frontier: Music at Durango Cathedral, *Español* Culture, and the Aesthetics of Devotion in Eighteenth-Century New Spain" (2006) became the first in-depth study focusing on matters of style in sacred music of the *estilo moderno* (modern style). For Davies and others (e.g., Juan José Carreras), a historical assessment of this music was clearly needed to scrutinize prior judgments of musical value that had marginalized extant eighteenth-century Spanish repertoire. Davies's publication of the complete opus of composer Santiago Billoni (active in Durango cathedral from 1749 to 1756) in 2011 was a further step in that direction.

While the work of these musicologists constitutes an important effort to redress historiographic problems in previous scholarship (of a rather nationalist tinge, in which eighteenth-century Italianate music did not feature prominently), their approach to style has recognized sociocultural concerns that need careful examination and reveal that the study of music culture should be approached with even more nuance. One of these concerns pertains to the reactions of Spanish individuals to Italianate trends in sacred music of this period. Scholars have mentioned that negative responses to the incursion of Italian-influenced music and musicians possibly reflected an anxiety about modernization (in reference to music in the *estilo moderno*). While for pundits like Benito Jerónimo Feijóo y Montenegro this music represented an attack on (Spanish) ecclesiastical tradition, for musicians (who were proficient in this new music, by the way) these trends produced different sorts of political tensions that have to be gauged in their respective social and political contexts. For cathedral musicians in Mexico City, for example, the incursion of Italian players and composers brought an end to a paradigm of music thinking and pedagogy that formed the basis not only of ecclesiastical tradition, but also of these musicians' institutional and social identities. In some cases, as Davies has pointed out, these political interests elicited judgments of value against Italianate music and musicians that, today, are problematic at best.[23]

From the vantage point of sound (and here I refer to the structural and aesthetic appreciation of this music today), there is little room for argument. One cannot but agree with Davies that the perpetuation of these reactions in music historiography affected the study of a repertoire that, indeed, formed part of Spanish musical life. For the purposes of studying colonial musical culture, nonetheless, there is something about this anxiety among Spanish musicians that is deeply relevant to the sociopolitical and economic factors permeating their lives. Assessing such reactions in their own historical context offers the opportunity to learn about the social environment that kindled desires and sensibilities among musicians, which without a doubt shaped music culture as well. One of the most important contributions by recent scholarship in colonial music has been the study of music practices in relation to localized systems of values and behaviors, in which race largely defined how people operated in society. Work by Baker, Knighton, and lately, David Irving, has addressed the ways in which people of different descent (indigenous, African, Mestizo) interacted with a Spanish framework of social and political organization. If these studies advocate a less cathedral-centered approach to music studies, it is out of an interest in showing that, beyond the music and activity of Spanish individuals and institutions, colonial music culture was a complex arena of interaction defined by the presence of people and musics from different racial origins. The activity of non-Spanish individuals has received special attention from these scholars, on the one hand, to learn how music enabled them to define their place in a highly stratified society, and on the other, to consider to what extent this process (sensitive to perceptions of race and class, among other things) questions the privileged position that previous scholarship has assigned to Spanish musicians.

In the last seven years, Baker and Irving have provided the latest scholarly examples of how race, class, and religious culture shaped the lives of non-Spanish musicians in relation to their activity in Spanish institutions. Baker's book *Imposing Harmony: Music and Society in Colonial Cuzco* (2008), for example, considers the efforts of indigenous individuals to become involved with the

Spanish church in order to claim a prominent place in society. Whereas previous scholarship focused on the music and doings of Spanish musicians, Baker sheds light on how Andean natives used a Spanish system of social and political order in an empowering way. Yet, the book is thought provoking in its approach toward race, given that indigenous people remain "indigenous" throughout the narrative. This makes one wonder to what extent was race important in the intentions of these people to assert their social position within the Andean elite. Was the issue of Andean "purity" relevant to these efforts? Were people of mixed descent part of this landscape, and if so, what was their position in relation to those considered of "pure" indigenous descent? Baker's argument for a center-periphery approach is quite compelling in the sense that it shows how Spanish hegemony (as a system of social operation) was contested and negotiated. But given that the book focuses on how individuals positioned themselves in society and how their relationship with institutions, and more importantly, race, were part of this process, one wonders if this binary framework does justice to such a complex sociopolitical and cultural landscape. This observation is most pertinent if we consider that sound (more specifically, polychorality) has been used to gauge social interests (whose?) to establish Spanish difference.[24] Most recently, David Irving used counterpoint as an analogy to address this dual division (i.e., Spanish hegemony vis-à-vis the indigenous periphery). In his book *Colonial Counterpoint: Music in Early Modern Manila* (2010), Irving explores the juxtaposed positions that native Filipinos and Spaniards held in the colonial Philippines. Irving's take on counterpoint as a music metaphor of colonialism is set within a narrative of strict control by a power structure over indigenous "others." The author's impressive theoretical backdrop to this analysis considers the ways in which Filipino individuals absorbed and adapted to European music in ways that imply resistance to a Spanish system.[25] It would be hard to argue that no such thing as a colonial sociopolitical structure existed in Spanish territories; the documented activity of individuals in this framework only corroborates that. This interaction, however, invites closer scrutiny of labels such as "Spanish" or "indigenous" not as set categories in relation to individuals, but as highly discursive identity constructs that problematize strict modes of racial classification.

The landscape of musical activity in colonial Spanish America (to use Tess Knighton's words) suggests an arena of contact, conflict, and negotiation within a rich racial spectrum, where efforts to define one's social place were highly politicized. While it is true, as Irving observes, that a Spanish system of social and political control was rather strict, this was probably symptomatic of the plurality of strategies that individuals used to negotiate their social and political positions. The discursive nature of this phenomenon suggests the possibility that race was not closed and impermeable, but rather fluid, and therefore, a highly political realm of action. It is possible that the state-sponsored dual form of organization that existed in colonial society—the Spanish and Indian republics—has informed research in colonial music studies to some extent. This classification indeed had important repercussions—at least in New Spain— well into the eighteenth century. Among other things, the *república de indios* (republic of Indians) promoted the survival of native communities with their own hierarchies and recognized Indian purity. However, studying colonial society according to this division poses significant problems. The number of laws compiled in favor of indigenous rights notwithstanding, Spain did not produce a body of legislation during the seventeenth century that dealt with the rising number of people of mixed descent. Moreover, the state also did not define the status of criollos as natives of a particular jurisdiction either. Colonial legislation was vague at best during the Habsburg regime, and this prompted people to redefine their classification and status. These efforts produced a variety of identity constructs that cannot be contemplated in the scope of a Spanish-indigenous binary.[26] The increasing number of people of mixed race triggered state initiatives to control colonial subjects with regulations based on perceptions of *calidad* (see Chapters 2 and 3) and race. However, beneath this illusion of social orderliness was a racial ambiguity that indicated the chaotic and diverse exchanges and behaviors among individuals in society, challenging any possibility for strict racial categorization.[27] The discursive nature of race is something that characterized colonial identity in New Spain and that made the system of castes (castas) a fluid system of classification as well.

This scenario not only urges us to approach race with more nuance; it also invites a more careful assessment of privilege in relation to readings of "Spanishness," a very murky construction in itself. Issues of class, social environment, and connections had a decisive influence on perceptions of what it meant to be Spanish, largely affecting the position that people could claim as Spaniards. That means that while proving *limpieza de sangre* (purity of blood) surely offered possibilities for advancement through a network of contacts and affiliation with Spanish institutions, it would be mistaken to say that this condition bestowed a de facto elite status on individuals. This was especially true during the eighteenth century, when people of mixed descent with financial means increasingly claimed Spanish ancestry to have access to these benefits. In what has been unproblematically categorized as an elite group, limpieza de sangre was a very politicized condition: it was supported by birth records, oral accounts, and ancestral lineages required from those claiming to be Spanish. In all possibility, the oral and subjective character of this process produced a significant number of fictitious renderings, especially because "Spanishness" opened possibilities for social mobility. These administrative and archival practices, nonetheless, fostered the creation of a historical consciousness that identified individuals with a broader community of kinsmen, ratified by their trajectories in a Spanish network of social and professional operation. Inclusion in this group generated desires, political loyalties, and identity imaginaries, which, although they rested on the reproduction of a hierarchical racial order, derived from creative strategies that people used to negotiate their place in it. As a sociopolitical concept, limpieza de sangre was closely related to the creation of the system of castes (as a hierarchy of dissociation, and thus, a system of social classification based on blood), so it should not be surprising that in New Spain race was a very fluid social construction as well, which calls for careful historical study.[28]

In the context of New Spanish social life, declaring blood lineage was inescapable for individuals. From the very moment of birth, blood lineage assigned one a category of social belonging with fiscal and judicial implications. It was blood lineage that settled a person's position within the system of castes, which organized social, economic, and political endeavors. Given the rise in the population of mixed race, limpieza de sangre became an important and sought after condition among Spaniards, especially to allow them to dissociate from other racial groups. But while limpieza entailed a mechanism through which Spanish individuals understood their identities, it would be problematic to contemplate limpieza and race as separate categories. These were concepts with initial religious undertones, strongly connected to notions of lineage (blood and religious lineages; see Chapters 2 and 3). Moreover, both labels gained historical currency at the same time (in certifications of limpieza, blood and race appear side by side),[29] and the first influenced the latter, as limpieza became a discourse of racial difference. In light of the connection that existed between both terms, this study considers *race* in reference to the different identity imaginaries, which, based on constructed lineages (genealogical, religious, of blood) positioned individuals in distinct social niches. The study pays particular attention to how individuals used music as a strategy to articulate identity discourses in which affiliation with Spanish institutions was important.

The setting of this study (Mexico City) makes it pertinent to issue a precaution. Given the social importance that blood and lineage had in New Spain, one should remember that race ought to be studied within the bounds of a historically situated sociocultural context. There is always the danger of reading history backward (that is, of interpreting concepts, ideas, and phenomena according to our own way of thinking in the present), and that is why one must be aware of how meanings of race not only change over time but also across geographies. In this respect, although there were certainly points of connection with Spain in the way in which limpieza de sangre was recognized, it is not possible to achieve a complete understanding of race and the way it operated in the early modern Hispanic world. The shifting meanings and uses of race in different contexts only underscore its social constructed nature, which means that there is no single unequivocal way to approach it historically. Our task as scholars is to recognize the factors that produced (as well as challenged) its valence in a specific histori-cal setting. Therefore, this case study departs from current views in social history to show how individuals from the low and middle classes used music as a means to claim a status of distinction and respectability, something that characterized social perceptions of what it meant to be Spanish in New Spain. In light of the diversity of claims of "Spanishness" that existed in eighteenth-century Mexico City, and of the different social positionings that such claims enabled, this study problematizes the notion of Spanish privilege by considering status as an eco-nomically and politically situated, and thus, highly fluid social construction.

The line of research by musicologists like Baker, Knighton, and Irving has broken new ground in exploring the richness of colonial music culture, thus shedding light on musics and peoples that had not received attention in former studies. Their efforts highlight the racial diversity that existed in colonial societ-ies, where being Spanish had considerable advantages. This study seeks to con-tribute to the state of current research by exploring the complex connections that existed between readings of race and the activity and behaviors of musicians within a prevailing political and economic context. Specifically, the book seeks to understand how cathedral musicians in eighteenth-century Mexico City used music as a means to claim a racialized discourse of status. This social analysis focuses on the activity of a very particular group of people to show that race and status were not rigid categories of belonging in colonial society, and that assum-ing that cathedral musicians held an uncontested elite position is problematic (although that was certainly their interest). The intention of this study is not to propose new ways to understand the relationship between Spanish racial ideol-ogy and power. Instead, it considers that flexibility—more than rigidity—was intrinsic to this relationship, given the different strategies that individuals used to engage with it. The book also emphasizes the important role that institutions played in articulating these claims, and that this was a salient phenomenon in New Spanish music culture of the eighteenth century. This phenomenon has motivated this author to approach the cathedral of Mexico not solely as a place where music practices happened, but as a site in which musicians hoped to real-ize their social and political goals.

Music, Race, and Social Status

Introduction

The aim of this chapter is to give the reader a broad glimpse of social life in eighteenth-century Mexico City and of the diverse spaces where musical activity occurred. The chapter argues that perceptions of status relied on a person's social image. Even among Spaniards, elements such as institutional affiliation and occupation influenced views of someone's social condition. In this light, the chapter shows that cathedral musicians used music as an activity to seek membership with the cathedral of Mexico so as to claim Spanish status. The chapter also highlights the importance that such activity assumed during the late eighteenth century. This was a time when social, political, and aesthetic transformations affected New Spain's racial order and also its musical culture. The chapter closes by addressing how cathedral musicians coped with these changes and how they are explored in this book.

Music and Social Life

The eighteenth century stands out as a fascinating period of social, economic, and political transformation in the history of New Spain. The century started with a change in monarchies (the Bourbons succeeding the Habsburgs), which altered the relationship between the Spanish crown and the church, brought about a series of initiatives for economic and social reform in the viceroyalty, and led to new ideologies in music, art, and literature. It became known as the *Siglo de las Luces* (Age of Enlightenment) due to the impact that enlightened thought had on approaches to education, ways of thinking about religion, and perceptions of the involvement of the church—arguably the most important social institution—in economic and political affairs. The advance of the "torch of reason," however, is just one factor active in the ferment of this period. After almost two centuries since the arrival of the *conquistadores,* the structure of New

Spanish society hinged on the administration of institutions (e.g., the church, the high court, the treasury, the university) by a Spanish political class, a group that was positioned at the top in the racial system of *castas*. As some scholars have noted, this structure served to organize the material and social environment of the New World, which was necessary to establish Spanish hegemony in urban centers where race was an important element of social and political organization.[1] Yet the actual operation of this structure, and the ways in which individuals moved in it, was far from this civic ideal given the tensions that existed in New Spain's racial order.

During the eighteenth century the "City of Palaces"—as the capital, Mexico City, came to be known—boasted a social life marked by opposites, to the extent that scholars have called this the "era of paradoxes."[2] A society rife with widespread poverty existed behind the opulence and splendor that has characterized New Spain in the historical imagination. The city did indeed improve its appearance during the eighteenth century and there was impetus to enhance cultural life in the urban space. Policing in the streets increased, the appearance of journals and newspapers promoted intellectual curiosity and literacy, and the establishment of hospices, orphanages, colleges, and fine arts academies (e.g., the Academia de San Carlos) reflected an interest for the well-being of society. This interest by the state to improve living conditions fostered the growth of more socially active and cultivated lifestyles; people tended to dress better when going to the theater, and among the upper classes there was a tendency to attend *saraos* and *tertulias* at the viceroyal palace, or to engage in conversation at the cafes that appeared toward the end of the century.[3]

This activity, however, reflected an effort, if not to address, perhaps to mask more pressing realities. Overall, the city streets and squares were nothing short of filthy. It was common to walk through dirt roads filled with ponds of sewage. From the windows in the second floor of private houses people usually threw trash, dead animals, and even the content from chamber pots into the streets. Squares functioned as market places where people milked cows, killed goats, and kept pigs in pigsties that added to the stench of excrement, blood, and rotten food. Beggars—either because of their age or a physical impediment—were a common sight: dispossessed old men and women, the blind, mutilated people, either on crutches or crawling and showing leg ulcers and open sores, roamed through the city in extreme poverty. Amid this scenario, clerics in frocks and capes—secular, Franciscans, Dominicans, Carmelites—noblemen on horses or in ornate coaches, merchants, tradesmen and tradeswomen, and black slaves were all part of a dense landscape of activity.[4]

The hoarding of money by a rising class of miners and merchants, the consistent extraction of capital by the monarchy to cover the costs of war, and the effects of agricultural crises were some of the factors that polarized the distribution of wealth and resources in New Spain, contributing to this landscape. Scholars assert that this contrast gave the city a dual character in terms of how the sensory feeling of the urban space projected social tendencies and attitudes that were in conflict with desired principles and ideals. On the one hand, the majesty and splendor of the city's architectural design contrasted with the vice, delinquency, and lack of public-spiritedness caused by urban filth, natural disasters (floods, fires), poverty, and hunger.[5] On the other, the ideals of decorum and propriety zealously guarded by the church were offset by the realities of drinking, gambling, adultery, and overall permissiveness permeating public life. While the economic imbalance fueled anxieties over wages and employment, the tug of war between raucousness and sobriety, vulgarity and urbanity in everyday life created tensions among castes in the middle classes, where views of race, class, and demeanor, among other things, influenced perceptions of social status.

Against this backdrop, music transpired in a variety of settings, and professionals and amateurs competed for income as they strived to define their place in society. Musicians tried to find a job, for the most part, in one of the ecclesiastical centers in the city (e.g., parishes, convents, or the cathedral), as no other place offered the stability that individuals found in the church. This is not to say that good musicians—and good music, for that matter—could only be found there, and that church musicians did not look for opportunities elsewhere. Music-making thrived in private as well as in public spaces, and it would be a mistake to think that European-styled music dominated the city's soundscape. For example, during the eighteenth century, viceroyal authorities remodeled and encouraged visits to canals, parks, and *paseos* (walks), where people walked, chatted, and ate at leisure. These places included the famous water canal called Canal de La Viga, the avenue known as Paseo de Bucareli, and popular parks like the Alameda or the Bosque de Chapultepec. In the second half of the eighteenth century, these sites were remodeled largely through the efforts of viceroys Juan Francisco de Güemes y Horcasitas (first count of Revillagigedo, 1746–1755), Carlos Francisco de Croix (1766–1771), Matías de Gálvez y Gallardo (1783–1784), Bernardo de Gálvez y Madrid (1785–1786), and Juan Vicente de Güemes y Pacheco (second count of Revillagigedo, 1789–1794); as a result, the areas became a common gathering place for people. Pestilent creeks that had run through the city were drained to enable pedestrian access to the Alameda. The canal that pierced downtown from east to west was cleaned, and it was typical to see the viceroy navigate through it in his way to the theater.[6] Streets were also paved with stones and lit with lamps. Figures 2.1 and 2.2 show that even the main square, the place where all levels of society met, was radically reconditioned. Although these urban improvements began to develop in the late 1730s,[7] only in the second half of the eighteenth century were they finished. These efforts intensified after 1789, when news of the French Revolution could likely

Figure 2.1 Plaza Mayor, Mexico City (ca. 1695), by Cristóbal de Villalpando. Lord Methuen. Photo credit: Art Archive at Art Resource, New York.

ignite anti-royalist sentiments.[8] In all these locations people could hear singers and military bands (who either competed for attention or performed during the holidays) amid the sounds of town criers and their trumpets to make public announcements; vendors yelling to announce their sale of fruit, drinks, or candy; public invitations to competitions or examinations at the Royal University; and music from religious processions going to small churches and convents.[9]

Music could also be heard at the houses of notable individuals during elegant and socially exclusive gatherings in the afternoon or evening. Figure 2.3 shows that these saraos (outdoors) or tertulias (indoor) showcased music and dances (sometimes performed by church musicians) and were quite popular among civil and ecclesiastical officials.[10] For moral pundits, paseos and saraos were spaces that fostered the ideals of order and urbanity of *gente decente* (decent people) and represented an effort to organize the physical space of the city according to rationalist principles in order to cleanse society—so they hoped—of undesirable behaviors. The interest in remodeling public spaces like the Alameda, for example (shown in Figure 2.4), was a step in that direction: its geometrical design and ordered vegetation reflected a concern for uniformity and control, which served as conceptual backdrop to enlightened ideals of social order and regularity promoted by the Bourbons. The elite considered paseos an antidote

VISTA DE LA PLAZA DE MEXICO NUEVAMENTE ADORNADA PARA LA

ESTATUA EQUESTRE DE NUESTRO AUGUSTO MONARCA REYNANTE

CARLOS IV, *que se coloco en ella el 9 de Diciembre de 1796 cumple años de* la Reyna Nuestra Señora MARIA LUISA DE BORBON, *su amada Esposa a*

por Miguel la Grua Marques de Branciforte Virrey de Nueva España, quien solicito y logro de la Real Clemencia erigir este Monumento para desahogo de su

spiritual y consuelo general de todo este Reyno, e hizo grabar esta Estampa, que dedica a Sus Magestades, en nuevo testimonio de su fidelidad, amor y respeto.

Figure 2.2 Vista de la Plaza de México, lithograph by José Joaquín Fabregat, 1797. Nettie Lee Benson Latin American Collection, University of Texas Libraries, The University of Texas at Austin.

Figure 2.3 Garden Party on the Terrace of a Country Home, anonymous artist, Mexico, ca. 1730–1750. Denver Art Museum Collection: Gift of Frederick and Jan Mayer, 2009.759. Photograph © Denver Art Museum.

Figure 2.4 View of Alameda park as background of a casta painting. *Casta: Alvina y Español produce negro Torna Atrás.* Óleo sobre lámina, 44.5 x 55 cm. Colección Banco Nacional de México.

to the presence and diversions of plebeian people, and they sought these places to escape the presence of all those who were naked, dirty, barefoot, indecent, and homeless.[11] This was the spirit that the French Enlightenment and the Bourbon reforms introduced in New Spain, which, just as with the organization of physical space, hoped to transform society according to the norms of reason and refined sociability. Metaphorically, such reforms aimed at making the city a grand paseo, in which the appearance of elite lifestyle and wealth could outshine the material problems and anxieties of the lower classes.

In the end, this did nothing but accentuate the bipolar character of society. If authorities promoted such values it was in hopes of mitigating the widespread popularity of *pulquerías, tepacherías,* and *jamaicas,* as well as events in private houses such as *coloquios* and *oratorios.*[12] These spaces were considered hubs for iniquity and vice that encouraged men and women to engage in questionable behaviors and that contradicted social initiatives by the viceroy and the church to rid society of vulgarity and immorality. Here, individuals of different races— for whom music was more a hobby of necessity than a profession—provided entertainment, although church musicians (some of whom were of European origin) could also be spotted on occasion; sometimes even cathedral musicians rehearsed popular dances like fandangos or zarambeques to play at these venues.[13] It was in these places where indigenous and African sounds likely combined with Spanish *coplas, décimas,* and *seguidillas* to create a musical landscape of rich diversity. Pulquerías were open-air stalls that sold *pulque*—a fermented beverage made out of maguey juice—where musicians with harps and guitars played songs on request from patrons inviting people to dance in the middle of the street.

Pulquerías were quite popular in Mexico City, although censorship and taxes applied to pulque by the end of the eighteenth century made people go instead to clandestine tepacherías (places that sold a fermented beverage made out of the flesh and rind of the pineapple).[14] Drunkenness would take over in some occasions, and this led to lewd exchanges between men and women that caused the indignation of moralists. Jamaicas—public open-air dances—were specifically targeted for this reason. According to critics, "the lascivious nature of the songs' lyrics, the dance moves and gestures, and the touching of naked bodies" is what created a "scandalous and sacrilegious" environment.[15] Censorship also extended to private homes that hosted events featuring such indecencies. One of these was the coloquio, a theatrical representation that took place in a private home and that was based on religious subjects and events of the season. After the play was over, the hosting family usually served cake and lemonade—although people also brought their own alcoholic beverages—while musicians animated people to dance. By the end of the century coloquios became known as places where "profane songs (*sones*) and cantatas were invented to instigate sensuality" among people from all classes.[16] The oratorio, however, was the private space that caused the most concern to ecclesiastical and civil authorities. Ideally (although not always), this was a designated room inside a home where people set an altar on a table with a sacred image on it. The church had clear rules for establishing domestic oratorios: they had to be inside a home without a public entrance, as these were supposed to be rooms for prayer.[17] In theory, oratorios were allowed only in the houses of affluent people—preferably nobles—with a valid excuse for why they could not attend Mass or other services in the church. There were instances, nonetheless, in which men and women after long days of work could not go to church either, and therefore, felt that they had a good reason to set their own oratorios. By the second half of the eighteenth century oratorios were seemingly common at all social levels, and sometimes even outside of the house. For ecclesiastical authorities this was a problem not only because these spaces compelled people to not go to church, but also because they had become sites for socialization rather than prayer, as Figure 2.5 shows:

> It is a custom among different people, especially among the common people, to have an oratorio inside their homes with altars, many candles

Figure 2.5 DeGolyer Library, Southern Methodist University, Casimiro Castro, *México y sus alrededores*, 1862. "Trajes Mexicanos, un fandango." DeGolyer Library Collection.

devoted to San Francisco, San Nicolás, Santa Rosa and other saints with the celebration and noise of harps, guitars, and dances that they make in the same oratorios, with men and women dancing all night, and with a lot of people procuring houses with these celebrations (see appendix 2.1).[18]

During the night, oratorios could also feature coloquios where people enjoyed wine, hot chocolate, and pastries. Largely, black, Mestizo, and Mulatto amateur musicians formed informal itinerant ensembles to play at these gatherings. These were usually workers from different trades (e.g., carpenters, knitters, metalworkers) who learned to play guitars, harps, or bandolas to make some money on the side.[19] All in all, the church was not concerned so much with the veneration of imperfectly or erroneously painted images at these oratorios (some of which could feature saints wearing revealing clothing, or images from stories that were more fiction than scriptural inspiration). It was the food, music, and sensuous dancing that made these places inappropriate for piety and devotion, and conducive to indecent behavior. Therefore, regarding musical life in the city, popular entertainments found in the streets, squares, and private houses also contrasted with the "well-ordered paradise" projected by the activity of churches and palaces. For musicians, to consider these contrasting environments was extremely important because they influenced views of the musicians' social condition at a time when occupation, credentials, connections, and context of operation defined a person's status.

Given the wide range of musical activity that colonial cities had and the plurality of social contexts that featured such activity, recent scholarship has brought attention to the relationship of musicians to such contexts, the ways in which this relationship defined their position in society, and the role that music played in that process. In this scenario, music culture appears as a complex arena that contextualizes the activity and experiences of musicians within a historically situated system of ideals and behaviors. For musicians, the phenomenon of social positioning related to the ways in which music—as an activity—enabled them to define their place in this dynamic social context. For this reason, ecclesiastical venues (such as convents, parishes, and cathedrals) cannot be studied as isolated places where music practices simply happened. Their historical importance lies in their being centers that, along with other private and public spaces, formed networks of operation sensitive to socioeconomic and political factors, through which musicians carved a social niche.

This backdrop offers a way to understand how cathedral musicians in Mexico City claimed status during the eighteenth century, and why considering confessional institutions (e.g., the university, the church) is important: they offered opportunities to musicians for professional development which became central in the construction of social profiles. Many children applied to be cathedral choirboys for this reason; in addition to the social significance of pursuing higher education and a clerical career, association with the cathedral allowed them to enjoy the benefits of Spanish corporate employment. It is true that not all cathedral musicians were Spanish and that not all started as choirboys, much less that all were clerics. However, for these individuals their affiliation with the cathedral was not socially unimportant. For members of the music chapel their institutional affiliation was a credential that would allow them to claim social status as church ministers, something that entitled them to specific privileges over other musicians. During the eighteenth century these claims became more contrived not only because Mestizo and Mulatto individuals increasingly competed for these benefits, but also because shifts in music aesthetics challenged the institutional paradigm through which cathedral musicians articulated their status claims. As it will be shown, race and institutional affiliation became key assets that musicians used to negotiate these tensions in order to define their place in a landscape steeped in competition and social change. Ultimately, this study shows that while the caste system described a racial hierarchy of sociopolitical organization, its instability makes problematic any attempt to overgeneralize the status of Spaniards and complicates assumptions about their social position as all-around "elite." In this light, the aim of the present chapter is to give a broad view of how race and institutional membership allowed individuals to articulate a discourse of status. The chapter shows that music was a strategy through which individuals procured employment with the cathedral of Mexico in their process of status construction. The chapter also addresses how shifts in aesthetic trends altered this paradigm of social positioning, the tensions that cathedral musicians faced in light of these changes, and how race remained at the core of their efforts to negotiate this conflict. With this overview, the chapter sets a contextual stage to outline events, situations, and concepts central to this case study, addressed in later chapters.

Race and Calidad

For quite some time, the *race* and *class* categories have permeated debates about the structure of New Spanish society.[20] It is because both concepts were sensitive to a diversity of factors (e.g., biological traits, economic standing, occupation, credentials, connections) that testing their relative weight in particular situations is rather difficult, and why any attempt to neatly define the structure of the colonial social map poses a challenge. On the one hand, the phenomenon of social mobility that characterized the eighteenth century complicates this assessment because class (in part determined by socioeconomic position) became a driving force in efforts to define one's place in a racially stratified society. This was particularly significant among people of mixed race in the middle classes who, in aiming to secure for themselves the benefits that Spaniards received (such as access to higher education and the possibility to develop careers in institutions), negotiated their positions across racial groups. Race, on the other hand, remains a fluid category in New Spanish historiography because it was a concept that acquired contextual definition. The situation is no less complicated in a study that focuses on Spaniards given that "Spanishness" was a self-reflexive condition that acquired different hues.

As addressed in Chapter 3, Spaniards by and large subscribed to the concept of purity of blood (*limpieza de sangre*) to articulate a sense of group belonging derived from a person's lineage. Initially, the concept of limpieza de sangre had religious origins, although in the New World it came to acquire racial overtones. It was due to these origins that the term *raza* (the opposite of limpieza) was initially deployed against Jews and Moors, whose lineage was considered impure or defective because of their religious histories.[21] This was in part the reason why in New Spain the term raza was applied to individuals of mixed blood, and why primary sources refer to Jews and Moors as *malas razas* (bad races). It should be mentioned, though, that Mestizos (the offspring of Spanish and indigenous people) were encouraged to be a part of the republic of Spaniards during the sixteenth century. This measure, however, prompted others to do the same by relying on their light skin color, and why authorities started to distrust complexion as a sign of "Spanishness." From this it followed that, in order to confirm limpieza de sangre, people had to possess attributes showing that, socially, they were part of "Spanish" society. Such attributes encompassed the Spanish lineage of a person's parents, but also the individual's education, institutional affiliations, corporate memberships, and circle of social connections. The official recognition of "Spanish blood," therefore, came to rely on perceptions of an individual's social profile rather than on exact knowledge of his or her origins.

Narratives of "Spanish blood" encompassed a diversity of claims from people who exhibited different attributes according to their socioeconomic position. This made "Spanishness" a highly perceptual category, which ultimately complicates any attempt to draw generalizations about the status of Spaniards. Unlike race or class, *calidad* (literally translated as "social quality") was a more inclusive contemporary concept that referred to occupation, credentials, and socioeconomic standing. Calidad was an aggregate of attributes that defined one's status among Spaniards and that gave an all-encompassing impression of a person's social reputation.[22] Being "Spanish" did not automatically make anyone part of the social elite. Factors such as wealth, credentials, institutional rank, and connections positioned individuals at different levels, for which one could say that calidad functioned as a hierarchical indicator of Spanish belonging. Those born in the upper echelon were not so concerned with proving their "Spanishness" as with preserving their advantageous social position. Personal allegiances in business and strategic marriages with notable people ensured the continuity of important office appointments, the accumulation of wealth, and the longevity of credentials. These qualities or *calidades* informed views of an individual's overall calidad, and renewed the position of the entire family in the elite circle.[23] The calidad of these individuals projected an image of distinction and respectability considered exemplary of the customs and lifestyle of gente decente (decent people), a milieu characterized by the Spanish lineage and social privileges of its members.[24] No single criterion or attribute defined gente decente; at best it was not so much a class as a conglomeration of groups that enjoyed legal exemptions and benefits.

In large part it is the perceptual nature of "decency" that makes it an elusive and ill-defined category in colonial studies, and a label that continues to baffle historians. It is true that not all Spaniards were wealthy, educated, and "respectable," although all those who were wealthy, educated, and privileged were likely Spanish. Only the racialized dimensions of this perception were clear: no Indians were recognized as "decent," nor were Mestizos and Mulattoes. Those who considered themselves gente decente, therefore, emphasized the importance of social appearance in terms of the credentials and accolades that composed their profile. These were calidades that they used to dissociate from the remainder of the Spanish caste, especially because people of mixed descent increasingly claimed to be Spanish during the eighteenth century. It is for this reason that this book approaches status as a subjective endeavor and considers it a discourse: It was a personal and subjective way of claiming a social place according to self-purported attributes, the value of which was context-specific, and thus, historically situated.

A system of castes organized New Spanish society primarily into five racial groups, namely, Spaniards (composed of people from the Iberian peninsula and *criollos*, that is, those from Spanish parents born in New Spain), Indians, Mestizos, Negroes, and Mulattoes. Each group denoted not biological distinctions but fiscal and judicial categories of belonging (established at the moment of birth) that assigned specific rights and duties to each person.[25] This categorization, however, reflected more an ideal of social order than an actual framework of operation because these groups were not so closed in definition.[26] It was the *social perception* of race—more than its physical characteristics—that determined social difference and enabled individuals to establish a claim to status.[27] "Decency" was one of such claims; it was a trait that distinguished individuals in light of their calidades (such as wealth, education, occupation, legal privileges, and lineage), given that these attributes informed an idea of what it meant to be Spanish in colonial society.[28] There is evidence that Spaniards in the middle classes (like cathedral musicians, for example) strived to relate to this perception, although they struggled to define their status due to sociopolitical and economic factors that destabilized the caste system in the eighteenth century.

For one, changes in marrying patterns accelerated the growth of the population of mixed descent, something that led to the blurring of boundaries among castes.[29] Threats of excommunication by the church to all those living in informal unions had a direct influence on this: they increased rates of legitimacy among Mestizos and Mulattoes, and compelled them to claim Spanish ancestry; in some cases, they claimed being Spanish altogether.[30] The growing efforts by people of mixed descent to climb the social ladder—in part aided by the expansion of mercantile capitalism—also made socioeconomic boundaries more fluid, especially as people found themselves at the same economic level of middle-class Spaniards.[31] This moved the Spaniards to seek in institutions the social luster that degrees, careers, and other credentials could add to their social profiles.[32] By law, only persons of proven Spanish lineage could attend and work in Spanish institutions and corporations. These encompassed certain artisan guilds, municipal groups, the royal administration, the military, the university, and of course, the church. Proof of limpieza de sangre (purity of blood) was an essential requirement to join, and people of mixed descent were not shy to claim this condition.

Today, scholars recognize limpieza de sangre as a complex concept with different interpretations in Spanish historiography.[33] While in mid-fifteenth-century Spain limpieza might have referred to an absence of Moorish and/or Jewish ancestry, in New Spain it alluded to a Spanish lineage of impeccable orthodoxy that invariably influenced views of a person's status.[34] To this end, institutions asked individuals to provide witnesses who could give testimony of their legitimate birth from Spanish parents—preferably "old Christians"—and of their virtuous and decent customs. However, it was not uncommon that the oral nature of this process inspired genealogical fictions among those with financial means. As efforts for social mobility intensified in the middle classes, Indians, Mestizos, and Mulattoes began to contemplate academic degrees and the clerical path as possibilities for advancement as well. These individuals increasingly applied to the Real y Pontificia Universidad de México (Royal and Pontifical University of Mexico) in the second half of the seventeenth century, to the extent that in 1688 Bishop Juan de Palafox had to add a new rule to the bylaws. Palafox drafted *Constitución 246*, a rule that specifically banned Negroes, Mulattoes, and those in other castes from the university (but also those with an "infamous" background, such as being born out of wedlock or having been tried by a religious or civil court).

But this did not necessarily safeguard the university from racial diversification. Indigenous individuals, for example, were admitted given that they were the sons of *caciques* (indigenous men who ruled over principalities or towns outside a major city). Moreover, Mestizos argued that *Constitución 246* did not exclude them specifically, while Mulattoes always tried to prove their Spanish ancestry.[35] Seemingly, economic growth in the middle sector opened new possibilities for other castes. While Mestizos and Mulattoes were born with the social stigma of their impurity, those who moved economically upward tried their best to "prove" or buy testimonials of their Spanish ancestry and thus to dissociate themselves from their original racial group.[36] The church experienced a similar situation, although never to the extent witnessed in the university. It was not uncommon for find Mulatto and Mestizo priests in the parishes of small towns (even while these clerics did not openly admit their mixed ancestry). Bishops considered the "low spirit" of these men to make them unfit for priesthood, and it is possible that this stereotype marginalized them from more distinguished appointments closer to the city, such as those given to criollos (who largely composed the clergy).[37]

Ultimately, it is because fluidity increased among castes that the term "Spanish" became highly contested and ambiguous, and why social and economic connotations were more relevant to its definition. This made Spanish institutions extra-zealous of their racial exclusivity and Spanish individuals obsessed with proving their lineage, to the extent that limpieza de sangre became the basis of honor, distinction, and of the very quest for "nobility" during the eighteenth century.[38] If "decency" alluded to an image of distinction and respectability among Spaniards, then it is not hard to see why limpieza was central to the construction of "Spanishness": it was a currency that allowed one to enter Spanish institutions, which offered the possibility to define one's status in light of benefits and privileges that one could claim with this corporate membership.

To a good extent, scholars in social history have focused on the lives of notable individuals to show how institutional affiliation played a role in processes of status construction among Spaniards. Similar studies addressing the lives of people in the middle and lower classes are needed in order to understand how they engaged in the same process. For those in the upper classes, the seemingly bipolar social environment of Mexico City (one in which ideals and behaviors were in a constant state of conflict) did not necessarily affect views of their calidad. The credentials and wealth of people in this stratum (composed by owners of large estates and mines, merchants, high-ranking royal officers, and clerics) established their status as notable Spaniards for whom moral and behavioral laxity could always be permitted. For people in the lower classes (which included poor Spaniards, and uneducated, unskilled indigenous, black, and mixed-race laborers with little chance for advancement), lack of skills, money, and education made it impossible to brush off perceptions of raucousness, vulgarity, crime, and other social vices attributed to their living environment. It was in colonial society's middle sector where tensions between decency and impropriety, shabbiness (sometimes shoddiness) and respectability transpired in efforts of social advancement. In this stratum (comprising Spanish guild and retail workers, and artisans of different trades; people of mixed-race with a learned trade, and indigenous people acculturated to Spanish social customs, also known as *gente de razón*), individuals did not just try to earn a living; they tried to position themselves in niches where they could claim benefits and privileges according to their profiles. In lieu of wealth, these individuals did not necessarily disregard good social manners and behavior because their calidad was also sensitive to perceptions of their demeanor and customs. It is here that cathedral musicians provide an illuminating case study showing the complexities involved in processes of status construction. As members of a Spanish institution, cathedral musicians articulated a racialized discourse of status based on attributes that informed their calidad, such as limpieza de sangre, institutional affiliation, and occupation. It was because of these calidades that they claimed benefits over other musicians in the city. However, social, economic, and political changes occurring in the middle classes highlight the challenges that cathedral musicians confronted as this discourse of status became undermined.

On the one hand, problems in New Spain's economy triggered initiatives among some cathedral musicians to capitalize independently from these benefits. On the other, itinerant groups of musicians of mixed descent increasingly competed for these same opportunities, sometimes aided by independent cathedral "contractors." This activity aimed to debase the position of the music chapel as a Spanish corporation that entitled its members to specific privileges. Shifts in music aesthetics during the eighteenth century (i.e., the favoring of Italianate trends in music of the *estilo moderno* vis-à-vis the continued practice of renaissance-style polyphony) became directly relevant to this scenario. Changes in notions of musicianship (i.e., what it meant to know music and to be a musician) altered views about the music profession, and this prompted some to compete with the music chapel relying on a music paradigm different from the one endorsed by the cathedral. Amid the tensions caused by these changes (specifically, the increasing competition for benefits by musicians from different castes, and changes in views of music as an activity that enabled social advancement), "decency"—a trope of "Spanish" belonging—became a label that cathedral musicians used to hold their stakes. Music, as an activity, was central to this process because it enabled musicians to articulate a racialized discourse of status to negotiate these tensions.

In their customs and lifestyle, nobles and other notable people represented the ideal of distinction and respectability among gente decente. Nevertheless, not all Spaniards had the political and economic resources of notable people, and this might explain why those who aspired to a spot in this milieu emphasized the importance of social appearance. Issues pertaining to personal conduct—ways of carrying oneself, staying away from scandals and activities that could stain one's reputation, like gambling, adultery, and physical confrontations—were especially relevant, for which context of operation (socially and professionally) was as important as lineage, credentials, and occupation to define one's calidad. Regarding cathedral musicians, it is true that some played at jamaicas and dances at private homes to procure extra income. But there is little evidence that, as a corporate group, the music chapel actively competed with other musicians for these venues. The canons considered the chapel an extension of the cathedral's clergy, even if some of its members were not men of the cloth. Chapel musicians were a reflection of this institution not only in their occupation but also in the way they lived their lives. In fact, the chapel was considered to be a corporation governed by the same rules as the chapter—as long as these were applicable— which required its members to live with the decorum that their institutional affiliation demanded.[39]

The canons had no objection to musicians playing at the houses of notable people, and even taking leaves of absence to travel with them out of the city.[40] The concern was for those places and activities that unfavorably colored perceptions of their image due to the behaviors that transpired in the city's public life, especially at the socioeconomic level in which musicians lived. For this reason the chapter urged members of the chapel "not play with musicians from the Teatro Coliseo nor attend profane functions or other things that might not be decent, and to attend only venues in circumstances of respect and urbanity" (see appendix 2.2).[41] If the Coliseo was mentioned it was not because of the music performed there but because of its notorious environment. As efforts to clean up the city from social vices and disreputable customs unfolded during the eighteenth century, authorities aimed to revitalize the image of the theater as a medium for social education. It was mostly because of its favor among the lower classes that viceroyal authorities saw the theater as an optimal platform to disseminate the attitudes, values, and ideas of the Enlightenment among the population of Mexico City. Nevertheless, financial constraints and deficits often prompted theater administrators to feature comedies and plays suited to the tastes of the paying public, even if these entertainments were not in tune with enlightened ideals. It was not unusual to hear popular airs and dance tunes in between acts, which aroused improper behaviors during the presentation of comedies that were already frivolous by themselves.[42] It is possibly for this reason that the theater continued to host many of the vices and excesses that authorities aimed to curb.

During the eighteenth century, theater troupes—including its musicians— performed in different parts of the city in addition to the Teatro Coliseo. Locations encompassed anywhere from improvised stages (called *corrales*) to the theater of the viceroyal palace, which the social elite frequented.[43] On the stage different publics saw at play the bipolar character that permeated social life: "the ideas and beliefs of society, its myths and its hopes, the folk (*el pueblo*) and the elite, the power of money and the traditional hierarchies . . . morality and scandalous behavior (*desfachatez*), order and mayhem."[44] While, on the one hand, the lower classes attended performances at improvised corrales, the Coliseo, on the other, showcased the wide spectrum of society: dignitaries and individuals in high office, gente de razón aspiring for social attention dressed in their best attire, guild workers, and peasants, all looking for a night of loud entertainment.[45] Scholars consider that this mix of people led to the relaxation of customs and manners, and that this intensified frictions between social classes.[46]

Its raucous atmosphere is what made the theater a particularly notorious place in the social imagination, to the extent that some writers mentioned how "the sole word of 'comedy' elicited horror and was unthinkable among honorable families."[47] While scholars recognize that there were exceptions, overall, it is very possible that such an environment tinged social perceptions of actors and musicians. Royal decrees and local regulations reflect ongoing efforts to change the conduct of these individuals throughout the eighteenth century. People were often reprimanded for exhibiting lewd behavior on stage through dances and provocative movements, and scandals involving sexual affairs or marital infidelity were quite common. This, in addition to the emotional instability and confrontational temper of some personalities, painted an image of the theater as a vulgar social milieu that lacked a serious and sober character.[48] Such an image informed views of Coliseo personnel as individuals of dubious moral values, the reason that scholars suggest that these people were very unlikely to be seen as gente decente.[49]

Possibly for these reasons, the cathedral chapter discouraged chapel members from playing or fraternizing with Coliseo musicians. This is not to say, however, that the chapter was aloof to talented musicians from the Coliseo orchestra, and that all members of the music chapel were men of impeccable conduct. There were cases when the canons had to dismiss people due to their actions. One such case was that of bassoon player Francisco Javier Cerezo. The chapter dismissed him on June 9, 1751, for living in adultery (a crime punishable by law) and for confronting the chapelmaster with a *trabuco* (a hand firearm), thinking that the chapelmaster had reported the adultery to the authorities.[50] Vicente Santos was another case. Santos entered the cathedral as a choirboy and grew up to become a cleric. Records show, however, that he had been in trouble since early in his career. Santos missed grammar and music lessons repeatedly, reasons that his education was less than ideal for a cathedral minister; it was only because of his voice that the canons were so lenient with him.[51] Due to his vocal abilities the canons chose Santos to be a succentor upon leaving his post as choirboy, but his continued absenteeism (this time from liturgical services) made this a short appointment.[52] As an adult, Santos accrued substantial debts from gambling, and although the canons made efforts to convince him to mend his ways (at some point he was kept from leaving the cathedral and only allowed to come out of his quarters to sing in the choir), Santos did not change. Eventually, he attempted to get loans from the chapter under false pretenses (either to cure himself from some fictitious disease or to help his poor widowed sister feed her five children), possibly to pay his debts. The canons denied him the money and lamented the poor judgment of this minister, who by then seemed irredeemable.[53]

If demeanor was so important for cathedral authorities, it was because it influenced perceptions of a person's status. It was a reflection of one's social image, which together with institutional affiliation and other credentials informed notions of what "decency" was in the Spanish imagination. Musicians complied with these expectations—even non-Spaniards—not least because of the material benefits associated with this "Spanish" perception. At the cathedral of Mexico, music was an activity through which individuals articulated such discourse to claim a social place and its corresponding privileges. Notions of musical knowledge and aesthetics were especially important for two reasons. On the one hand, "knowledge" denoted a sense of professionalism that distinguished cathedral musicians from amateurs, and that entitled them to corporate benefits. On the other, shifts in music aesthetics altered the parameters that defined musical knowledge by the second half of the eighteenth century. These changes not only produced tensions and transformations within the music chapel. They also posed challenges to the social claims of cathedral musicians given that new aesthetic trends enabled other players (regardless of race) to compete for performance opportunities and even for status. As a response, members of the chapel continued to endorse "decency" to retain their position. In light of this scenario, the next section shows how music culture was impacted by the tensions and changes transpiring in the caste system during the eighteenth century.

Shifting Trends in Music and the Benefits of Corporate Membership

As new stylistic trends in music started to become more pervasive, the canons also began to look favorably at Coliseo musicians. This is why the chapter hired Ignacio Jerusalem and Gregorio Panseco in 1746 and 1761, respectively.[54] Although more evidence needs to be gathered to make an assertion, it is possible that the musical proficiency of these individuals made them stand out in the eyes of the cathedral chapter at a time when the art of music was in such an "advanced and exquisite state."[55] For example, the canons thought that Jerusalem would be an important addition to the chapel because of his "intelligence in all music and composition" and because of his dexterity in playing the violin.[56] The canons knew that Jerusalem was mostly experienced in writing arias and music for the theater, and although they felt that he needed more practice writing polyphonic music, they did not see his theater experience as a shortcoming (*no le perjudicaba*).[57] The canons also hired Panseco because they considered him a "perfect musician" (*músico perfecto*) in light of his skills in violin as well as his experience as chapelmaster of the parish at the Casa Profesa, and as conductor of the Coliseo orchestra.[58] The chapter did have reservations about Panseco's demeanor, nonetheless. When he met with the archbishop to discuss his cathedral appointment, clerics noticed Panseco's arrogant behavior. They felt his talent was necessary, but they also warned him about "the way in which he had to live his life, and the way in which he ought to treat the archbishop, the canons, and society" upon being hired.[59]

Coliseo musicians did not hesitate in approaching the cathedral either, mainly because working in the music chapel offered attractive benefits. Outside of the church, musicians had limited choices for earning income. These could be either freelancing to play at services and events in different convents (outside cathedral jurisdiction), at the houses of notable people (if one had connections), at private houses, or playing for a modest allocation at pulquerías, tepacherías, and other public events. Also, the Coliseo orchestra offered contracts that were only seasonal. In reality, very few jobs offered musicians the stability that they found in the church. Of these, the cathedral was the most sought after institution, especially because, in addition to a steady annual salary, musicians also enjoyed other benefits. If the person had the desired knowledge and skills (and if the treasury could afford to pay another salary), he became part of a corporate group (i.e., the music chapel) that gave its members important privileges. Among these were the allocation of loans without interest and *derechos de gracia* (rights out of grace). The latter were a series of favors granted at the discretion of the chapter. Among such derechos, musicians could request alms or "help with costs" (*ayuda de costa*) to cover expenses for things like clothing and medicine, for example. *Patitur* was another derecho that allowed musicians to be absent from work with pay during illness. In addition, the chapter allowed leaves of absence to those who needed to attend to personal affairs out of the city without withholding their salaries.[60]

Perhaps the most important benefits cathedral musicians had were *obvenciones*. According to bylaws, chapel members were not allowed to work for hire freely at any event happening at convents and parishes surrogate to the cathedral's jurisdiction. The hiring person had to contact the chapelmaster to make the proper arrangements for the performance. After the event, the chapelmaster collected payment, from which the cathedral chapter taxed a portion for the treasury. The rest, then, was divided among the musicians (these payments called obvenciones) and the chapelmaster usually received one *real* out of each peso paid to the chapel.[61] As it was, the Real Audiencia (the high court) had granted the music chapel the exclusive right to perform—and charge for the music played—at services in these parishes and convents.[62] This right was also applicable to civil and religious processions in the city, such as the general processions that occurred on Corpus Christi and Easter, or when newly appointed viceroys and archbishops arrived in the city.[63] That meant that no other music ensemble could play at any of these events unless the cathedral agreed to it.

The designation of these privileges was not arbitrary; they stemmed from a racialized corporate mentality that was an integral part of the cultural baggage that Spain brought to America.[64] In this respect, the music chapel was primarily a corporation with a specific political and juridical character. The ensemble was homologous to the royal chapel in Madrid, and as such it was entitled to prerogatives that its members sustained through merit and service.[65] It is true that not all musicians in the chapel were Spanish, as the examples of Jerusalem and others show (like Italian violinist Benito Martino and French organist Juan Baptista del Águila, to name a couple).[66] Yet evidence suggests that for these musicians their affiliation with the chapel was important because of the benefits and privileges that they could enjoy as affiliates of a Spanish corporation. If, as historians say, limpieza de sangre was the basis of status and privilege for those in Spanish institutions, it should not be surprising that institutional membership was a key component of racialized status claims that people used to support their social aspirations. Accordingly, it was this affiliation what made the music chapel a group of

> *decent men*, fifteen of them criollos of known lineage, all alumni of the Colegio de Nuestra Señora de la Asumpción, who before being admitted gave testimony of their legitimacy, purity of blood, and of their ancestry from old Christians . . . from which five are presbyters and two more are on their way to this rank. The other fifteen are European who have found accommodation [in the chapel] due to their proficiency and ability, having passed previously through a rigorous examination and scrutiny of their lives and customs (see appendix 2.3).[67]

Seemingly, foreigners were included in this group of "decent men," although the document suggests that this calidad derived in good part from the limpieza de sangre and ancestry of its criollo members, and not the least because seven of them were in fact clerics (emphasizing specifically how many had the rank of presbyter, or full priest). These attributes are set strategically at the top of the document to highlight the "Spanishness" of the corporation, which legitimized the chapel's claims to all the privileges that musicians carefully outlined in two folios. The mention of Europeans in the letter is interesting in that it shows that they were admitted only after a close scrutiny of their lives and customs, and after a rigorous examination of their musical skills. While the occupation of these individuals enabled them to join the cathedral, their preparation and study in music is what ultimately made such occupation an important attribute of their calidad. It is true that the cathedral hired only those with instrumental proficiency (hopefully in more than one instrument). Nevertheless, knowledge of music is something they had to demonstrate if they wanted to keep the appointment.

Cathedral records show that the chapter made a clear distinction between performance skills and knowledge of music when gauging an individual's musicianship, and that they used the word "music" when referring to the latter.[68] In case a musician proved deficient in music (see Chapter 5) he was asked to attend the *escoleta* (music school). This oversight was even more strict for choirboys, who could be dismissed if they did not show improvement in their music studies.[69] Such knowledge was a requisite for appointments that boys pursued to move up in the hierarchical ladder on their way to becoming priests (see Chapter 3). More likely than not, Spanish families attempted to position their children in the cathedral so that they could pursue a career in the church. After years of service, youths considered themselves "professionals" because, as part of their occupation, they had devoted most of their lives to the study and practice of music at a venue known for its elaborate music activity. Their preparation encompassed not only years of practice and performance but also of academic study, attributes that placed them above other musicians who were not considered "professionals" and who did not have such an important affiliation.

Although more research needs to be done on music education in New Spain, surviving evidence shows that the cathedral was not the only institution that taught music in the capital city. For example, we know that the orphanage for girls of San Miguel de Bethlen [*sic*] had a music school because in 1746 Archbishop Juan de Vizarrón y Eguiarreta published a document in which he set an endowment for such school. The document shows that the school had existed since 1740 and that the archbishop had funded it from its beginnings.[70] Possibly for this reason, in 1747 Ricardo de la Main (who had worked as conductor of the Coliseo orchestra) published the preface and index of a music treatise for that orphanage.[71] It would be fair to speculate that, with the treatise, de la Main was hoping to become music instructor at that place, but as no copies of the treatise are known to exist, possibly it was never published and he did not receive the appointment after all. Some authors have mentioned that he did in fact teach orphan girls at San Miguel, although there is no actual evidence of that.[72] Moreover, Vizarrón y Eguiarreta's endowment document clearly indicates that music instructors should be appointed from among those serving the church, as they had been until that point. This is corroborated by the document cited above from around 1768 (see appendix 2.3), in which musicians mention that the cathedral chapel was in charge of this duty.[73] The foundation document for San Miguel de Bethlen (shown in Figure 2.6) says that this school was established to train girls so that, with their music skills, they could enter a convent in

Figure 2.6 Cover of published foundation document of the music school of San Miguel de Bethlen, photographed by the author. Archivo del Cabildo, Catedral Metropolitana de México, Correspondencia, book 30, fol. 300r.

the city to become nuns.[74] This point in itself is important because it shows that, at ecclesiastical institutions, music education served a specific social purpose: to enable individuals of scarce means to join the church. The music school of San Miguel was an example of that. Its main goal was to help

> the innumerable poor girls of the capital city . . . to find an application and aptitude (music) . . . always choosing those with inclination to become nuns (*religiosas*) . . . and in case that a convent asks for a girl to enter as musician nun (*religiosa música*) the appointed instructors shall make a rigorous examination of the girl . . . and after notifying the prelate they shall take such girl to the convent.[75]

The cathedral's Colegio de Infantes (the college for the teaching of choirboys) was created in 1725 with this aim in mind as well. Specifically, the Colegio sought to recruit from among poor Spanish children in the city so that they could become ministers of the church.[76] Just as in convents, music education was an important strategy to this end at the cathedral, for it not only gave youths a craft with which to make a living. It also provided an intellectual basis for advancement in a hierarchy of ministries that required different levels of knowledge related to music and ritual. The Colegio prepared children with the basics of a liberal arts education, emphasizing grammar, music, and philosophy. Only after boys showed proficiency in these subjects could they be considered for higher positions with the goal of attending the university. This was an important step: a degree was a requirement for priesthood, and clerical rank ultimately enabled individuals to pursue a career in the church.

Scholars suggest that Spaniards lacking prospects in mining or trade or without noble lineage or distinguished connections supported their social aspirations with the possession of knowledge, especially because academic study enabled them to join Spanish institutions to develop careers.[77] Careers were in themselves avenues to claim status in light of, first, a person's years of service and rank within an institution, and second, the body of knowledge accumulated after a lifetime of service in a line of appointments. Music was central to this process in the cathedral: It made individuals not only music professionals after years of training and study but also members of a corporate group within the most important religious institution in New Spain. In this context the chapelmaster acquired special significance at different levels. He was the highest-ranking individual in the music chapel and the main liaison between musicians and the chapter. He was also a financial administrator and a representative of this corporation in society. Musically, he was a pedagogue, composer (although this was not a rule), instrumentalist, and conductor, and as such he was expected to know the "science of music" better than any other musician in the group (see Chapter 4).

The word "science" is especially significant here because it alluded to knowledge of music as the product of rigorous theoretical study that distinguished between those who played instruments and those who "knew" music.[78] For this reason the word *maestro*, according to theoretical writers, was reserved for those who knew music beyond the practical aspects of performance and composition.[79] Although there is evidence that music treatises addressing these points reached New Spain, more research needs to be done about the extent to which they were actually used in music education, especially at religious institutions. Nevertheless, there is evidence showing that approaches toward music education in the cathedral—and the understandings of musicianship derived from these approaches—were highly resonant with the outlook of writers like Pedro Cerone, Andrés Lorente, and Pablo Nassarre, whose treatises are known to have circulated in New Spain. As a concept, these authors considered counterpoint to be the cornerstone of musical knowledge and the basis of a theoretical grammar that informed notions of musicianship in Spanish ecclesiastical institutions.[80] The canons indeed believed that "counterpoint was needed in order to know how to make music."[81]

The importance of this theoretical basis in actual music practices started to wane, however, not the least because of the incursion of Italianate trends. In 1710, chapelmaster Antonio de Salazar mentioned that singers did not really need to learn counterpoint in order to perform their duties, and that he reserved the teaching of this subject only to those interested in composition or in becoming succentors in the choir.[82] This statement was possibly prompted in part due to Salazar's poor health at that time, but also by the fact that he had problems enforcing attendance at counterpoint lessons. Records show that Manuel Sumaya (apprentice of Salazar and chapelmaster after his passing in 1715) faced the same issue, much to the canon's dislike. Singers, specifically, grew disinterested in principles that had little relevance with current music trends.[83] The lack of a theoretical apparatus for the study of modern music eventually changed views of "musical knowledge" as an academic component in the formation of a professional musician, and practical aspects acquired more weight instead.

These changes had deep implications in views of music within the music chapel. There were people for whom music, based on an older paradigm of musical knowledge, had been a strategy for developing a career by advancing in a hierarchy of ministries since they were choirboys. Their institutional membership was not merely a credential: it was the product of a lifetime of service that gave them social status in light of their rank as church ministers, even if they were not clerics. But there were others who did not subscribe to this paradigm. The cathedral chapter was aware that music was changing and that the music chapel needed individuals proficient in modern music trends. Talented performers (and composers, as we will see) considered their practical skills just as important as traditional parameters of musical knowledge to justify their membership with the chapel. New music trends emphasized practical ability over traditional principles of musical knowledge and this produced hierarchical tensions between musicians and the chapelmaster. The activity of Ignacio Jerusalem (chapelmaster from 1750 to 1769) shows this.

Jerusalem entered the cathedral in 1746, although he did not apply for the post of chapelmaster until three years later. Information about the appointments of the two chapelmasters previous to him (Salazar and Sumaya) is for the most part declaratory. In both cases, documents outline the process of their selection by a majority of votes. Jerusalem's case is quite different in that records are filled with vexing opinions about his capacity to occupy this position. Documents relevant to his examination mention that he was tested according to the guidelines used for Sumaya's exam in 1715. According to these guidelines, candidates had to be able to write contrapuntal music, most likely in a style similar to that of composers like Tomás de Victoria, Cristóbal de Morales, and Francisco Guerrero, whose music Salazar had used to teach members of the examination committee. This was also the model that Sumaya inherited and the one that he used to teach when he was appointed Salazar's assistant in 1710.[84]

As Jerusalem was not proficient in this type of music, committee members were unsure about the extent of his musical capacities, something that triggered doubts about his being the right person for the job. Moreover, the chapter also felt that musicians did not see Jerusalem as an authority figure. On the one hand, some canons thought that his chummy and roughhouse rapport with chapel members was a probable cause for this, especially considering that his musical proficiency could be compared to that of other talented people in the group.[85] Moreover, his compositional skills were not necessarily a credential. The canons had originally hired Jerusalem to help with composition, but only because the cathedral needed someone to write new music and because he was the only composer in the city at that moment.[86] Compositional craft did not define the profile of a chapelmaster, and the cathedral had precedents of hiring people to help with composition previously. In 1669, for example, the canons appointed Guillermo Carvajal to assist chapelmaster Francisco López Capillas with this task; the same happened in 1710 with Sumaya, due to the illness and blindness of Salazar.[87] Furthermore, musicians did have direct access to written music already, even aided by Jerusalem himself who handed the key of the music archive to whoever needed it.[88] Due to these reasons the canons thought that the relationship between Jerusalem and the chapel was bound to be less hierarchical and more on equal terms.

On the other hand, the chapter also feared that Jerusalem's apparent lack of musical knowledge could accentuate this situation.[89] It would not be far-fetched to think that, in the minds of clerics—individuals for whom academic study and degrees were important credentials to earn institutional appointments—the position of chapelmaster at the cathedral of Mexico required a type of knowledge supported by a body of music treatises dealing with the theoretical rules of counterpoint. This erudition was important in that it reflected rigorous study, which made a person eligible for a distinguished position in a Spanish corporation, attributes that ultimately informed views of a chapelmaster's calidad. However, as some canons had originally recognized Jerusalem as "intelligent in all music and composition," it is hard to see how this suddenly became a factor. In truth, the music chapel was undergoing a period of transition and the chapter's reservations were in part a response to conflicting views about Jerusalem among musicians. It is quite possible that for people who grew up under a music paradigm buttressed by principles in treatises of the seventeenth and early eighteenth centuries (Cerone looming as the most likely direct influence), musical knowledge was indeed important.[90] For others, performance proficiency had more weight, especially considering that trends in music of the estilo moderno had introduced pedagogical needs that these treatises did not address.[91] These aesthetic differences possibly played a part, but there is evidence that also points to other political issues.

The chapel had been operating without a leader since Sumaya had left the cathedral in 1738. It is possible that some musicians were uneasy about welcoming someone who could undermine efforts of free enterprise that had developed during this time. Prior to Jerusalem's arrival, Domingo Dutra de Andrade had been assigned to lead the ensemble. His appointment, however, was merely to have him conduct musicians—to "keep the beat" (hechar el compás)—and records show that in his duties Dutra acted mostly as an administrator.[92] Notices of cathedral musicians freelancing their services—something that the chapter did not allow—tend to be common in cathedral records. Although there were additional financial factors, the main instigator was that other ensembles (either from convents or parishes, and even made up of amateurs) started to compete for performance benefits that belonged to the entire music chapel. After eleven years without leadership and oversight, musicians had grown accustomed to arranging performances on their own—either independently or in small groups—and some convents even got used to dealing with some of the musicians directly (perhaps to ensure a lower cost for the performance). This activity undermined the corporate integrity of the music chapel and its claims to these privileges.

By the time Jerusalem arrived, musicians were accustomed to acting as independent contractors and it would not be surprising that the claims of the new chapelmaster to a percentage from these performances (to which he was entitled as head of the chapel) was troublesome for some, not the least because they had secured only for themselves an attractive corporate benefit. The aftermath of the appointment was a tense relationship between Jerusalem and some members of the music chapel, which led to political divisions in the group. A number of musicians openly showed their dissent and followed some of their colleagues, instead of obeying the chapelmaster. Antonio Portillo was one. He had earned fame as a talented singer, but also as a swindler and a cheat who used his affiliation to his own advantage. Portillo and his followers began to disregard their cathedral duties after Jerusalem became chapelmaster. The canons blamed Jerusalem for this insubordination, mainly because of his lack of leadership skills.[93] This view became more poignant as Jerusalem complained about the disrespectful attitude of musicians and about how some failed to obey him when he asked the chapel to perform in functions outside of the cathedral. Seemingly, the group led by Portillo did not join the rest of the ensemble in these events and only showed up to mock the chapelmaster.[94] They continued to contract obvenciones for themselves without sharing in the profits, much to Jerusalem's outrage, as he emphatically denounced that he was being robbed of the compensation to which he was entitled as *maestro de capilla por erección* (appointed chapelmaster according to bylaws).[95] In 1754 the chapter finally decided to fire Portillo, although not because of these altercations but because he was caught stealing from the treasury.[96] Portillo's dismissal created further problems for Jerusalem and the music chapel, nonetheless, as he recruited musicians (Spanish, but also Mulattoes and Mestizos) to create his own group, and thus, compete with the cathedral for performance privileges.

While it is true that efforts for socioeconomic mobility became rampant during the eighteenth century it is possible that factors affecting the local economy in part fomented such entrepreneurship among musicians. These efforts derived from an economic anxiety pervading New Spain at large, an anxiety to which the cathedral itself was not immune. In this period, the cathedral treasury was severely impacted by the effects of recession and mismanagement, which jeopardized religious practices in the first half of the eighteenth century. Although primary sources emphasize that ritual services were surrounded by an aura of solemnity and splendor, the cathedral was, in fact, trying to cope with a very different reality. The chapter no doubt aimed to project its desired image through elaborate ritual and musical activity, and this explains why the notion of "splendor" has become a common trope in studies of music and ritual in New Spain.[97] This idea, however, stands in stark contrast with the condition of an institution on the verge of bankruptcy, struggling to pay salaries, and in some cases, forced to cancel services altogether. More specifically, the financial condition of the cathedral's treasury through the first half of the eighteenth century relates to factors that weakened New Spain's economy.

On the one hand, the agricultural crisis of 1710–1714 (which ran parallel to fluctuations in the growth of crops and an inflation of grain prices in the international market) made it impossible for the cathedral to rely on the annual collection of tithes—a key source of income—to cover expenses. Documents from 1700 show that political problems with the high court regarding the collection of tithes also played a role, at least at the beginning of the century.[98] During this period, the payment of salaries posed a financial burden and the chapter contemplated reducing personnel in the music chapel in 1700, 1709, 1711, and 1712.[99] On the other hand, the hoarding of hard cash by merchants, in addition to the export of coined metal to Spain, halted the circulation of currency in New Spain, which made liquidity a scarce and valued asset.[100] In the cathedral the inadequate administration of the treasury by *mayordomos* (head accountants) such as Antonio Robles and Manuel Roman (the first during the last quarter of the seventeenth century, the latter from 1737 to 1745) aggravated the effects of this recession.[101] Robles's administration was the reason that choir chaplains, for example, worked without pay from 1689 to 1691, why the chapter reduced their annual salary from 200 to 175 pesos, and ultimately, why two chaplaincies were canceled altogether—in addition to other positions to which musicians usually applied, such as that of choir assistant.[102] Roman's administration, however, dealt a more severe blow to the treasury in 1745. The cathedral almost went bankrupt that year, and for a moment the chapter struggled to pay salaries to musicians, chaplains, and even the canons themselves.[103] The result of this recession was a widespread reliance on credit in New Spain, the reason musicians frequently approached the chapter for loans or charity only to be turned away at this specific time.[104]

Under these conditions, it is not surprising that some musicians looked for opportunities outside the music chapel on their own to supplement their incomes. This economic scenario, in addition to the competition posed by other ensembles, fueled a concern for wages that eventually compromised the corporate structure of the music chapel. Even though cathedral musicians were not allowed to freelance their services, archival records show that they did so repeatedly, notwithstanding reprimands from the chapter. These situations in which musicians worked for hire without the chapelmaster's knowledge or the chapter's approval were called *zangonautlas* (roughly translated as "moonlighting"). Although cathedral records show that these illicit activities were common in the seventeenth century, they were seemingly not as rampant as in the first half of the eighteenth. By the 1740s they had become so pervasive that at some point the chapter had to penalize the entire chapel.[105] Zangonautlas were not only detrimental to ritual practices (when musicians missed services or arrived late); they were also a revenue loss for the treasury, which paid salaries to absent musicians and did not receive any tax income from their work elsewhere.[106]

Due to the state of New Spain's economy, obvenciones also declined in number, and so did the payments that musicians could expect from these events.[107] It is possible that the increasing competition posed by other ensembles—especially itinerant groups made of individuals of mixed race—motivated Portillo and others to team up and sell the services of the "cathedral's chapel" on their own. He and other recruited colleagues would arrive at these events and perform in front of the group wearing their cathedral frocks, a tactic that convinced paying patrons that they had hired the actual cathedral ensemble.[108] As a corporation, the music chapel faced challenges on two fronts. First, some of its members were independently arranging performance opportunities that belonged to the entire group. Second, itinerant ensembles were also trying to compete for these performances. For example, there were times when events conflicted with cathedral duties. In these instances, the chapter allowed ensembles from other convents, parishes, or colleges to perform. Such was the case in 1662 when the ensemble from the Colegio de San Juan de Letrán (a religious school) performed in the Easter procession. It was these situations—when the cathedral chapel was absent—that actually lured other makeshift groups to compete for these apparently "leftover" opportunities. Antonio Visencio, music instructor at San Juan de Letrán, complained about this in a letter to the chapter:

> During Easter different music groups come out to play in processions when music is not their occupation, as these groups are made of young lads who are stockings tailors, goldsmiths, dancers, comedians, fruit vendors, blacksmiths, and others of broken skin color, all of whom are subject to mockery because of the ridiculous things they say during such [acts of devotion], in addition to the scandal they cause when they fight about the concerts with people that do not know what they are doing, all of which is public and goes in detriment of us, humble priests and other virtuous persons, who have been in service of the church since childhood without any other occupation to sustain ourselves and our obligations but this one [music], which we practice the entire year, and the ones mentioned above only do it during this time (see appendix 2.4).[109]

It is clear that for Visencio these individuals were competing in a corporate turf that did not belong to them, neither socially nor judicially. Judicially, these opportunities belonged to the cathedral chapel and to those allowed by the chapter to partake in them, individuals who, unlike these other amateurs, were trained in music. Socially, the interlopers were workers from lower trades trying to take over the benefits of "humble priests and other virtuous persons" who had spent their lives in service of the church devoted to music as their main occupation. Furthermore, these were people of "broken skin color" competing for the rights and benefits of clerics, who were Spanish. By 1752, the situation had been aggravated by the willingness of a rising number of Mulatto musicians to play for rather low fees, enticing patrons to hire them instead of the chapel. These situations—in which itinerant ensembles not only took over these benefits but also devalued the work of musicians at large—were also prompted by "the scarcity of commerce as well as by the universal poverty of Mexico" in the mid-eighteenth century.[110] To avoid others from snatching obvenciones, the chapel had to regroup and regain its corporate structure (see Chapter 5). It also had to divide into three groups so that one group could be present at every venue and event in addition to fulfilling its cathedral obligations. Problems occurred, however, when musicians were missing due to illness or travel and people from outside had to be hired to fill in services while the other two groups performed elsewhere. In some of these cases cathedral musicians, like Ignacio Pedroza, complained that hired individuals were of inferior calidad ("they are not our equals"—*no son de nuestro igual*), which could taint their image as church ministers. According to Pedroza, these could be good men, but not "decent to so many white men and cleric gentlemen in the chapel."[111]

These tensions derived from a competition for wages during a period of economic turmoil. However, both Visencio and Pedroza show that institutional membership and occupation were calidades that musicians used to establish racialized claims to specific privileges. This fact is important as it shows that musical proficiency was part of a social construct ("decency") that musicians used to navigate a sociopolitical landscape in a state of ferment. This fact is more significant if we consider that changes in notions of musicianship introduced an alternate paradigm for procuring institutional membership, and thus, for seeking social mobility. For Jerusalem, these changes enabled him to secure support from influential people—like canon Francisco Jiménez Caro—to help him secure employment in the cathedral. Jerusalem's skills earned him the endorsement of Jiménez Caro, who proposed that his son—Salvador—be admitted as a choirboy for these same reasons.[112] The new aesthetic trends in music were gaining favor among influential individuals, and Antonio Portillo relied on this preference to secure their patronage, thus allowing him to compete for status and privilege with cathedral musicians. As we will see in Chapter 5, Portillo was avid enough to catch the ear of important personalities in Mexico City after his departure from the cathedral. One of them was the viceroy Carlos Francisco de Croix, marqués de Croix, who on one occasion told a member of the chapter of "a great voice and ability that there is in Mexico . . . someone called Portillo, that people say sings divinely."[113]

Portillo's connection with Croix's circle of acquaintances led to other opportunities, mainly because of the performance talent that some personalities perceived in him. Miguel de Berrio y Zaldívar, marqués de Jaral de Berrio and second conde de San Mateo de Valparaíso, was one of such individuals.

Berrio y Zaldívar was a good violinist and a keen collector of music and instruments. It was well known how much he enjoyed spending time playing among
musicians (some of them from the cathedral's chapel). Even at events that did
not take place in his palace people asked Berrio y Zaldívar to show his abilities,
as viceroy Croix did on January 6, 1758:

> In the evening of this day, by invitation of His Excellency to attend
> the terrace, many distinguished ladies came to the royal palace. And
> knowing His Excellency the dexterity of the conde de San Mateo de
> Valparaíso in the violin, they asked him to show his ability, which he
> did with great air, and once he concluded, the festivity began with great
> music, which lasted until midnight.[114]

It was Berrio y Zaldívar who, along with Ambrosio Eugenio de Melgarejo
Santaella (mayor and judge of the supernumerary crime court of Mexico) advocated in Portillo's favor at the Convent of Capuchin Nuns in the city, where
they hoped the singer would find employment.[115] It is not known whether
Portillo profited from this inquiry. It is well known, though, that Melgarejo's
son (Antonio Eugenio Melgarejo Santaella, rector of the university) kept him
as protégé in the parishes of San Miguel and the Hospital Real.[116] It was through
him that Portillo attempted his most audacious move: to write directly to the
king requesting his permission to establish a music chapel at the university, so
that Portillo—as chapelmaster—and the whole ensemble could be considered
equal to the royal chapel of his majesty in Spain, and thus, could play anywhere
without the impediment of the church.[117] The response by the cathedral's chapel
was immediate, and in their letter they outlined their merit to their privileges in
light of their calidad as "decent men" (see appendix 2.3). With this status, the
music chapel claimed specific rights, such as playing at special occasions honor-
ing civil authorities, at annual festivities in the city, in military functions, and
in processions organized by corporate groups (e.g., guilds, confraternities) and
convents surrogate to the cathedral. But more important was the emphasis that
chapel members placed on their lineage and institutional membership as calidades that put them above Portillo's group, which seemingly was composed by
"all types of musicians: good and bad, white and black, and none affiliated to the
cathedral."[118]

The examples of Jerusalem and Portillo suggest that aesthetic changes produced shifts in views of music. They also show that, despite these changes, music
remained an important strategy through which to seek institutional affiliation.
In Portillo's case, the interest in creating a music chapel in the university (a confessional institution) was an initiative to compete with the cathedral's chapel for
status. For Jerusalem, his appointment as chapelmaster possibly represented

an opportunity to move socially upward as well. Considering that he arrived to New Spain as a theater musician, it is not far-fetched to think that he was inspired more by an interest to distance himself from a notorious environment than by ecclesiastical vocation. Membership with Spanish institutions was an important asset for social mobility, and erudition continued to be an avenue for procuring this credential throughout the eighteenth century.[119] If the accumulation of knowledge remained central to the corporate and social aspirations of many Spaniards it was because being fit for letters and professions was an attribute inherently related to notions of Spanish blood (and therefore, to claims of "Spanishness"; see Chapter 3). In this regard, it is not surprising to find that understandings of musicianship (i.e., what it meant to know music and to be a musician) at the cathedral of Mexico were permeated by views of counterpoint as the theoretical basis that gave musicianship an academic character. Less surprising is the fact that this basis was the cornerstone of a music style that, for some musicians, reflected a sense of Spanish identity (see Chapter 4).[120]

However, it would be problematic to say that Spanish musicians disfavored modern music for social and political reasons. As mentioned before, ecclesiastical authorities considered the incursion of trends that characterized the estilo moderno to be a sign of the "advanced and exquisite state" in the art of music. The social elite welcomed these changes, and cathedral musicians endorsed them in the same way that other musicians—affiliated to religious institutions or not—did. As Chapter 5 shows, aesthetic transformations also made people re-evaluate what music erudition was. Notions of music as a "science" started waning after 1750. Practical ability in modern trends became more relevant and it enabled musicians like Jerusalem to procure institutional affiliation. This shift also enabled non-affiliated groups to compete for status as well; Portillo's case is a good example of that. This was because notions of music erudition became permeated by secular attributes such as grace and good taste. These ideals positioned erudition within the realm of Spanish sociability, which made it possible for musicians not affiliated with an institution to compete for status by appealing to elite sensibilities.

By the second half of the eighteenth century the cathedral music chapel was facing competition from ensembles that increasingly featured better skilled performers. It is true that in most litigation cases or institutional disputes the music chapel came out on top. However, the fact that cathedral musicians confronted this situation so often suggests that conflict, more than uncontested privilege, is what characterized the professional life of these individuals. This was the main tension that they struggled to negotiate in the second half of the eighteenth century as they continued to rely on their institutional affiliation to articulate a social profile in which race was important. Like other institutions (e.g., the university, and the church itself), the music chapel had to cope and adapt to the incursion

of social changes. Above all, the survival of the corporation was the most important preoccupation of cathedral musicians, especially because it was central to
the articulation of their institutional and political identity. As the social position of the music chapel became affected by issues transpiring across the racial
spectrum, cathedral musicians frantically recoiled to invoke "decency" in order
to hold their claims. It was a racialized status claim through which they sought
privilege over other individuals. In the following chapters, this book explains
that "decency" and "nobility" were Spanish identity imaginaries in which limpieza de sangre was central. Chapters 3 and 5 consider the ways in which limpieza
informed the construction of status discourses in these two categories and how
music enabled cathedral musicians to subscribe to them. Chapter 4 addresses
how the incursion of aesthetic music trends influenced this process. Chapter 5
also explores the tensions produced by these changes and how the music chapel
adapted to them.

3

Music, Letters, and the Clerical Path

Introduction

This chapter focuses on the activity of musicians who entered the cathedral at childhood and chose the clerical path. The chapter shows that, for these individuals, *limpieza de sangre* (purity of blood) was a currency allowing them to enter the cathedral in order to pursue higher education and the rank of presbyter, *calidades* (or social qualities) that led to a specific status. *Nobleza* (nobility) was a particular social condition that these musicians sought, an aspiration which they also shared with people in other institutions. Finally, the chapter emphasizes that music was the main strategy these individuals used to claim nobility as a mark of Spanish belonging.

Limpieza de Sangre as Social Currency

When Manuel Sumaya was ready to audition for a choirboy position at the cathedral of Mexico, his father, Juan Sumaya, was probably shocked to learn that the boy's record of baptism was missing. Cathedral authorities required this document as part of the audition process not only to verify that the child had been baptized but also to demonstrate that he was in fact Spanish. The record was eventually found, but much to Sumaya's dismay, as he learned that the baptism had been recorded in the wrong book. As blood lineage became more important in defining identities, rights, and privileges during the course of the seventeenth century, royal decrees ordered the church to log separately birth, baptism, marriage, and death records of Spaniards, Indians, Mestizos, Mulattoes, and Negroes. For Spaniards, such records were key to proving their limpieza de sangre, a condition that assigned to them specific fiscal and juridical rights and duties. The social importance of the concept of purity of blood can be traced back to religious concerns that arose in fifteenth-century Spain. Its centrality in the American system of *castas*, however, was tied to a colonial concern for restricting the political and economic claims of non-Spaniards, or rather, for delimiting who could claim to be Spanish.[1] The rhetoric of limpieza de sangre established during the Habsburg regime originally based this delimitation on the religious lineage of individuals, which meant that a person had to prove that his or her descent came from "old Christian" Spaniards, not stained with blood from "new Christians" (i.e., converted Jews and Moors). As the population of mixed race increased in New Spain, more people claimed Spanish descent in order to enter institutions. This was because affiliation with the university or the church, for example, entitled individuals to privileges such as exemption from base punishment and the payment of tribute. Aware of this tendency, authorities grew suspicious of skin color as a factor that could determine the "true origin" of people, for which proof of limpieza became increasingly peppered with references to aspects of social appearance. Attributes related to a person's profile (like education and occupation, but also customs and behaviors) informed views of "Spanishness" and largely defined the position of individuals in New Spanish society. For this reason, notions of being "Spanish" became highly politicized in the eighteenth century, as claims of Spanishness came to depend more on the assessment of a person's credentials rather than on his or her true descent.[2] In Juan Sumaya's case (as he probably contemplated the cathedral as an avenue of social mobility for his son), the predicament was how to prove the "Spanishness" of his family in a way that would show that the baptism of his son had been entered by mistake in the logbook of Mestizos, Negroes, and Mulattoes. For this he would have to find honorable and credible individuals who could give testimony about the Sumayas' virtuous customs, their "old Christian" descent, and their Spanish standing in Mexico City's society (judged by the marriage and baptism records of Juan and his wife, Ana)—that is, if he wanted his son, Manuel, to enter the cathedral.

The increasing importance of social appearance in eighteenth-century New Spain derived from a protocol that institutions used to determine limpieza de sangre, something that contributed to the destabilization of the caste system. It was because physical traits were an unreliable proof of Spanish descent that an individual's purity came to be established mostly from the social weight that oral testimonies had, that is, from "public voice and fame" (*pública voz y fama*).[3] For the most part, such testimonies stressed that witnesses (who previously established their own credentials) knew the individual in question to be born legitimately from Spanish parents, who were old Christians and of virtuous and decent customs. Testimonies of purity of blood, therefore, were not meant to assess the physical characteristics of a person but rather his or her general reputation in terms of behavior, character, moral conduct, political standing, and honor. Scholars point out, however, that such oral testimonies tended to be formulaic, and that the rigidity of institutional questionnaires gave little room for respondents to define their own understanding of what limpieza—and more importantly, "Spanishness"—was. Figure 3.1 shows an example of the set of questions asked to individuals; the printed format indicates that this was a sort of standardized process. This suggests that Spanish institutions were in charge of constructing and maintaining a cultural model that projected specific religious, social, and political values, and that influenced claims of Spanish blood.[4]

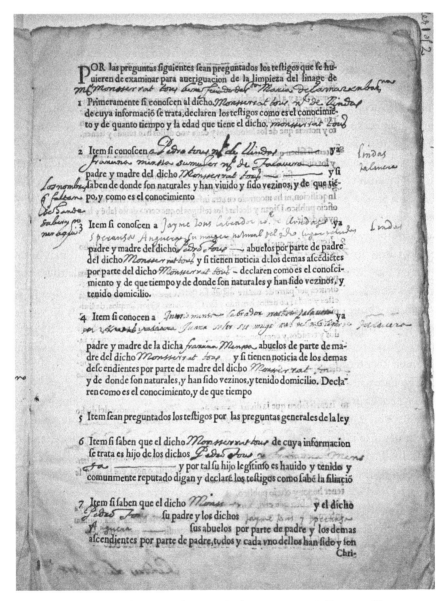

Figure 3.1 DeGolyer Library, Southern Methodist University, Collection of documents regarding *limpieza de sangre* and *renuncias*. DeGolyer Library Manuscript Collection.

Considering the relationship of individuals with the cultural role of institutions, therefore, is central to an inquiry about the subjectivity for which oral testimonies cannot account and that are relevant to a historical understanding of what it meant to be "Spanish" in New Spain. While it is true that *calidad* (informed by the social appearance that lineage, behavior, education, and other credentials projected) was an important component of Spanish identity, it is possible that Spanish identity imaginaries (such as decency or nobility) were also identified with the institutions that helped to construct them. Juan Sumaya (aided by the priests of the metropolitan sacrarium, where his son Manuel was baptized) eventually fixed the mishap by proving that the record had been accidentally misplaced, and the document was transferred to the logbook of Spanish baptisms.[5] Whether this incident left an impression on Manuel Sumaya as a youth is hard to know. However, the fact that thirty years later—already a chapelmaster—his assessment of musicians looking for a job in the cathedral included his observations about their social appearance suggests that these values were projected on the very institution through which musicians articulated their profiles. Sumaya's assessment of violin player Antonio Rodríguez in 1730 is a good example:

On a previous occasion I made a report about this candidate where I said that he is proficient in playing the violin and Italian music, which is the music that this type of instruments usually play, and now I say my opinion: I only add that the decency of the cathedral choir, and of a chapter so illustrious [as this one,] demands that its ministers do not occupy themselves in activities that can mar the church (see appendix 3.1).[6]

The document does not mention the activities Sumaya was referencing, and from the writing itself one cannot tell whether Sumaya acted from a personal bias. That does not mean that the document is any less relevant. With this statement the chapelmaster was not necessarily rejecting Rodríguez (who was actually hired by the chapter). Rather, he stressed that certain issues pertaining to an individual's social activity were connected to the values and principles encoded in the social image of the church, and therefore, were projected onto the image of the ministers who served in it. This is further illustrated by the cases of Francisco Cerezo, Gregorio Panseco, and Vicente Santos addressed in Chapter 2, in which demeanor and behavior were important attributes of a church minister's profile. For the chapter, musicians were an extension of the cathedral's clergy and a reflection of the cultural model that this institution promoted. It should not be surprising, then, that Sumaya (who was the highest authority of the music chapel) virtually identified the cathedral with the social character of that model.

From the vantage point of institutional operation, this case study of cathedral musicians does not break new ground in social analyses of blood, race, and
caste in New Spain. Proofs of limpieza in cathedral records are for the most part
similar to the testimonies found in other institutions, something that, at best,
places the cathedral on an equal plane with the university or the Inquisition, as
examined in historical studies. Nevertheless, a series of inquiries stemming from
this institutional concern for "Spanishness" promises a more original contribution. These are questions related to the ways in which individuals infused aspects
of lived experienced with the cultural model promoted by the church (specifically, the cathedral). Did the possibility that musicians could be affiliated with
the cathedral generate identities that relied on a hierarchical racial order?[7] How
did these identities enable people to claim a position in New Spanish society? At
the core of these inquiries lies the most important question: how did music, as
an institutionalized activity, articulate this phenomenon?

In Chapter 2 we mentioned that if claims of "decency" tend to be prominent
in cathedral records it is because this became a trope of belonging in the Spanish
imagination during the eighteenth century. More specifically, "decency" was a
discourse of status directly related to the social appearance and reputation of
individuals (i.e., their calidad) in terms of the attributes that informed such a
perception. As addressed below, institutional affiliation was an important component in establishing a person's Spanish status. In this regard, the claims of
cathedral musicians were not very different from those of people who joined
other institutions. For musicians, specifically those who entered the cathedral
in their childhood, proving their limpieza was essential to being accepted into
this institution, which in addition to a salary offered the possibility to pursue
higher education leading to a career in the church. Once admitted, their musical
activity enabled them to advance in a hierarchy of ministries devoted to music
and ritual, a process through which they elevated their profiles in light of the
attributes (calidades) that they earned along the way (e.g., musical and liturgical knowledge, skills writing music and playing different instruments, ability to
teach, education, and their ultimate rank). The cathedral chapter considered
this aggregation to be merits that entitled a person to higher positions and to
benefits that resulted from these appointments. In the end, musicians established racialized status claims that were not based on limpieza de sangre as an
unquestionable proof of their "Spanishness." Rather, their claims derived from
their achievements and from perceptions of how these aligned with institutionally based discourses of status (such as "decency" or "nobility"). In this light,
the present chapter addresses the activity of musicians who chose the clerical
path as an avenue of professional and social advancement that the cathedral
offered. The chapter focuses on a case study about cathedral chaplains to show
that the desires and aspirations of low and middle-class individuals rested on the

maintenance of a hierarchical racial order during a time of social and political transformation.

Nobility: The Desired Calidad

If the nobility represented the ideal of calidad among Spaniards it was probably because a pervasive emphasis on social appearance derived from an interest by the elite to display their customs and behaviors, possibly to cleanse the city from the pervading images of poverty and hunger. During the eighteenth century, many Spaniards strived to attain noble status, and limpieza de sangre was key to realizing their aspirations. In New Spain, the concept of *nobleza* became highly convoluted in the eighteenth century due to the increasing claims of Spaniards to this condition.[8] Whereas these claims reflected a desire for inclusion in a European category of social privilege, the colonial designation of "nobility" departed from the recognition of one's limpieza de sangre. The recognition of limpieza was originally informed by religious concerns in the sixteenth century, although it became increasingly infused with secular concepts of self-industry and achievement. As limpieza started to be defined by aspects of social appearance, reference to merits gained from serving in activities thought to be "noble" in nature also infused notions of "nobility." These references made "nobility" a quality derived from efforts in personal growth, which enabled people to exercise noble prerogatives even if they did not have a noble title. "Nobility," therefore, became a much sought condition among individuals seeking social advancement in particular fields. Financial and political factors surely defined one's position among the "nobility," and they created a hierarchy among those dedicated to noble endeavors. Many Spaniards claimed noble status in different ways and always according to their level of accomplishment, which in the end made "nobility" a category that defied strict definition. The following section provides an overview of how perceptions of limpieza changed after the sixteenth century and how such changes enabled limpieza and nobility to become intertwined in the Spanish imagination.

Back in the sixteenth century, the ideals of the aristocracy in Spain maintained that noble qualities could only be inherited, for true nobility ran in the blood. Nevertheless, this notion came under threat with the incursion of limpieza de sangre as a concept meant to prove an individual's Christian ancestry. The titled nobility saw this as an attack on aristocratic honor because such understanding opened the door to the infiltration of newly converted people (i.e., Jews and Moors) into a realm that prided itself in a lineage "from time immemorial."[9] As a result, the focus of limpieza shifted from an interest in religious beliefs to a preoccupation with true religious origins. That meant that, to prove limpieza, it was not enough for a person to demonstrate that his or her parents were Christian. Ultimately, the person had to show that his or her religious lineage went back for generations, that is, that his or her descent was "from old Christians" (*cristianos viejos*). In the New World proofs of limpieza became especially important not necessarily because of the possible infiltration of Jews and Moors (who were initially barred from the Indies) but because of fears that the offspring of Spanish-Indian parents could become a political threat.[10] Although early policies in the sixteenth century encouraged the incorporation of Mestizos into Spanish society, the caste system appeared parallel to the establishment of the Inquisition in response to an anxiety over the persistence of pre-Hispanic religious ideologies among the population of mixed race. While in principle the implementation of proof of limpieza was driven by religious concerns, its racial overtones informed the way this condition came to be perceived in New Spain.

Scholars mention that this was possibly influenced by the displacement of Iberian status categories (noble, commoner, and slave) onto the three primary colonial groups (Spaniards, Indians, and Negroes) in the sixteenth century.[11] This observation, nonetheless, calls for a word of caution because contemporary European class distinctions cannot be applied to New Spain without distortion; after all, New Spain did not have a clearly defined class system.[12] If for the sake of strict comparison Europe and Spanish America are at odds, historically situated subjectivities make us wonder to what extent such displacement influenced perceptions of limpieza in relation to the social aspirations of individuals. Research shows that claims of "nobility" proliferated among Spaniards as a sort of syndrome, sometimes based on mere skin color. This was particularly acute among Europeans, for even the most "miserable ones without education or cultivation, [believed themselves] superior to whites born in the New Continent . . . a white man, although mounted barefoot on a horse, believes himself to constitute nobility of the country . . . a barefooted fellow with white skin is often heard to exclaim: 'Does that rich man think himself whiter than I am?'"[13] Chapter 2 mentioned that for individuals of mixed race, their light skin color was an asset to their claim of being "Spanish" and authorities began to distrust a light complexion as proof of Spanish origin. It is nonetheless possible that even those in the lower social ranks could establish the Spanish lineage of their children (i.e., their limpieza). After all, the oral testimony of "witnesses" could confirm their birth from "Spanish" parents, who were old Christians with no connections to Jews, Moors, Mestizos, or Mulattoes. Even if untrue, these testimonies could be fixed through a previous arrangement with the parish priest, the only person who, in the end, was the final arbiter of such "facts" in the church registries.[14] Once recorded, the public recognition of limpieza positioned an individual among Spaniards, which opened up possibilities—more than certainties—for social mobility.

Advancement was not necessarily guaranteed, and this was because limpieza was a very mercurial condition, mainly for three reasons. One, physical appearance was not a reliable proof of Spanish descent, especially with an increasing number of people of mixed race claiming to be Spanish. Second, the most important part of determining an individual's limpieza (the oral testimony) was also the most problematic because, in the end, the whole case depended on the presumed impartiality of oral witnesses.[15] Finally, the interests of different institutions to decide over matters of limpieza hindered the implementation of a unilateral process to determine such a condition. This corporate mentality, in addition to the factors outlined above, made limpieza highly unstable, "accessible but easily lost, depending on one's reputation within the community, personal relationships, and the outcome of the next *probanza*."[16] It is likely for this reason that a baptism certificate was not enough to sustain one's claim of Spanish blood over a lifetime. A person had to undergo a new process to determine his lineage each time he desired to enter a guild, confraternity, the university, the church, or the military, or to receive a high office appointment. Each time the process was repeated, more elements were added to the evaluation, such as marriage records, the limpieza of the spouse, education, occupation, credentials, personal connections, and other merits, for which one could say that, by the eighteenth century, proofs of limpieza incorporated religious origins into an overall perception of an individual's calidad (social quality) among Spaniards. For this reason, nobility claims also became increasingly supported by assessments of social appearance. As mentioned before, calidad alluded to an overall impression of a person's reputation, which encompassed attributes (or calidades) like education, occupation, institutional affiliation, and rank.

In contrast to *nobleza de sangre* (nobility of blood), *nobleza de privilegio* (nobility of privilege) was a designation derived from efforts in self-accomplishment and social advancement. Of these two categories of nobility, the latter became the one to which individuals most commonly subscribed in the eighteenth century. Scholars have mentioned that rampant claims of nobility derived from concerns among Spaniards to preserve their social rank during a time when many kinsmen sank into the lower ranks of the gente decente, mostly because of the state of the economy in New Spain (see Chapter 2).[17] The crown never really gave noble titles to anyone in New Spain based on their service to the monarchy. It did, however, bestow the privilege of noble treatment to those who developed careers in certain occupations. If this recognition was passed within the family—something that required a new process to determine the limpieza of the interested individual each time—it could come to represent nobility of blood by the third generation, which was the most sought after distinction among Spaniards because it implied being part of a lineage "from time immemorial."[18]

Records related to the genealogy of the Hurtado de Mendoza family in
Mexico City show how the process unfolded over generations. These documents contain copies of petitions that Cristóbal Leonel Hurtado de Alcocer
Mendoza y Castilla (of the family's third generation) and his wife and sons
made to royal authorities for confirmation of their limpieza de sangre and
nobility in 1700 (see Figure 3.2). For this, Don Cristóbal Leonel relied on

Figure 3.2 DeGolyer Library, Southern Methodist University, *Carta de Hidalguía, 1743–
1744.* DeGolyer Library Manuscript Collection.

testimony that his uncle (Luis Hurtado) drafted in 1639 about the genealogy of the Hurtado family, which he traced back to the Middle Ages in Spain.[19] Along with this testimonial, Don Cristóbal Leonel included an account of the honors and promotions that his father received in the military, including his right to noble treatment.[20] The certification obtained by Don Cristóbal Leonel ultimately passed to José Teodoro Hurtado de Mendoza in 1743, and he used it to certify at that time his purity of blood and noble claims. These documents illustrate that while an actual title was not involved, the prerogatives recognized by nobility of privilege enabled a growing Spanish gentry to acquire a much desired sense of self-definition in relation to the nobiliary image that limpieza de sangre had in this milieu.[21] There can be little doubt that financial considerations played a critical role. However, the fact that nobility of privilege made it possible for families to sustain their status due to the privileges and possessions that a *mayorazgo* entailed, explains how social appearance related to the recognition of calidad, and why the latter became such an important component in efforts of social mobility.[22]

Noble prerogatives (such as the *fuero* or judicial immunity) were awarded to military officers, academics, and clerics for their service and careers, although in the eighteenth century the crown especially favored contributions to economic development. These were considered to be distinctly noble in nature, explaining why metallurgy, for example, was made a noble profession (and miners, by default, "nobles") in 1783. As a result, "all of those dedicated to this important study and occupation [could] be admired and treated with all the distinction that this noble profession [entailed]."[23] It was the economic needs of the Bourbon monarchy that apparently led to the sale of titles to rich miners and merchants in the 1700s, mostly because of the tax revenue that could be collected from newly appointed nobles.[24] But wealth was not the only requisite for acquiring a title. Individuals also needed to be supported by institutional appointments and corporate memberships that reflected their political standing. These calidades, in addition to the genealogy and limpieza of a person's family, were carefully outlined in documents declaring the social quality of the individual, and presented to the king. By the turn of the eighteenth century, therefore, Bourbon economic interests made it possible for a growing criollo aristocracy to develop, obtaining titles on the basis of their wealth and land ownership, but also on their merits and credentials.[25] For this titled nobility, however, a dilemma remained in having to share noble prerogatives with the shabby gentility of a lower Spanish class of judges, lawyers, military officers, clerics, and university students.[26]

Scholars have observed that shifts in perceptions of limpieza (from religious concerns to an interest in social appearance) represent a sign of the impact that secular narratives were having in the reappraisal of blood as an element of Spanish identity imaginaries in the late seventeenth and eighteenth centuries.

In New Spain, other proofs than evidence of Spanish descent became increasingly important to claim having Spanish blood as a consequence of a scientific rhetoric that attempted to disenfranchise American Spaniards. This rhetoric rested on the notion that the natural environment of the New World corrupted the virtues of Spanish blood. Specifically, European theories of colonial degeneration held that the American environment made people lazy, superstitious, and prone to social vices. According to these theories, the climate of the new continent changed the physiological makeup of Spaniards, making their temperament, intellect, and rhetorical wit prone to decay.[27] From this, it followed that not only the influx of Europeans slowed down during the course of the seventeenth century, but appointments to high office were also given mainly to Iberians.[28]

The spread of these theories intensified as notions of impurity started to be associated with American Spaniards due to the proliferation of casta paintings. Prominent in the first half of the eighteenth century, casta paintings became popular visual representations of the different racial mixtures found in the Spanish colonies (see Figure 3.3). Some casta paintings were more than mere physical illustrations; they depicted people in environments that contextualized races in terms of their perceived social attitudes and surroundings. Figures 3.4 and 3.5 show that, in some cases, these depictions even included music as part of such contextualization. Casta paintings presented musical activity as part of particular settings. In the process, these images racialized and localized music practices in the social map.[29]

It was because of their depiction of different castes that these paintings promoted the idea that the impurity of American Spaniards resulted from their lascivious encounters with or their breeding from individuals of impure blood. American Spaniards strived to be seen as anything but impure, especially those interested in debasing the notion that in New Spain there was a lack of intellectual potential. These individuals reacted against caste representations because they portrayed an image of "useful minds but not noble ones, what harms us, not what benefits us, what dishonors us, not what ennobles us."[30] Today, scholarship shows that the term *criollo*, as a derogative connotation, surfaced precisely in the context of tensions that this rhetoric of impurity created between Iberians and those born and raised in America. It was because intellectual capability was the measure of such alleged degeneration that criollos focused on it as they competed for public and religious employments to restore the dignity of their blood. Calidad, an important construct for assessing a person's limpieza de sangre, became intrinsic to claims of nobility. For if true nobility ran in the blood, the true nature of nobility, then, could be inferred from the attributes that supported claims of Spanish blood. Sure, there were noble lineages "from time immemorial," but there were also noble minds, noble efforts, and noble professions that enhanced the position of Spaniards in terms of the privileges that they received.

Figure 3.3 Human Races (Las Castas), anonymous, eighteenth century. Museo Nacional del Virreinato, Tepotzotlán, México. Photo credit: Art Archive at Art Resource, New York.

Figure 3.4 Casta painting. *De castizo y española, español*. Museo de América.

In the realm of nobility of privilege the application of intellectual aptitude is what distinguished "noble spirits" and is the reason education and knowledge became so important in efforts of social mobility.

The interest in education in New Spain was driven by two related elements: first, after years of study, an individual could receive an important post according to his level of accomplishment; second, these credentials could greatly increase his social standing. Even elementary school instructors considered their profession worthy of recognition because of the social possibilities that education offered. In 1601 they formed a guild, the Gremio de Maestros en el Nobilísimo Arte de las Letras (guild of instructors of the very noble art of letters), which required proof of limpieza de sangre for membership. Among other

Figure 3.5   Casta painting. *De castizo y española, español.* Museo de América.

things, guild members were allowed to carry arms, as well as to have "armed horses like those of hidalgos (titled nobles) . . . [they are also] exempt from incarceration by civil authorities."[31] These noble prerogatives distinguished men of letters from the rest of the king's subjects as being among the most subordinate and loyal to the crown.[32] Not surprisingly, an important part of the Bourbon agenda for social reform was the renovation of colleges, which included the Real Colegio de Santa Cruz and the Real Colegio de San Juan de Letrán (both in 1728), and the Real Colegio de San Ildefonso in 1740.[33]

Spaniards in the middle and lower classes, therefore, supported their social aspirations through academic study and the possession of knowledge, as these enabled them to claim nobility of privilege after years of service in Spanish institutions.[34] In New Spain, the concept of "career" did not relate to a mere sum of appointments but rather to a lifelong project of professional growth with several stages of development in an institution. Through these stages, individuals acquired and refined knowledge that was necessary for higher positions, which in turn enhanced the calidad of a person in terms of his acquired erudition and institutional rank. Intrinsic to the character of a noble mind was the pursuit of intellectual endeavors, which distanced individuals from any aspect of manual labor.[35] For, although Charles III had declared that even the work of skilled craftsmen could be "noble" (i.e., blacksmiths, tailors, masons), people "preferred genteel poverty to the 'disgrace' of learning a craft or practicing a mechanical trade."[36] For this reason, the acquisition of academic degrees became an avenue to seek "noble" status. In a report to Phillip V, a New Spanish lawyer, Juan Antonio de Ahumada, addressed this fact in his advocacy for the recognition of nobility among American Spaniards:

> The prerogative of nobility cannot be denied to American Spaniards because they have their origin either from those who, having lost their lives and spilling their blood in the conquest of the New World, stamped with their own red color the best execution of loyalty to their sovereigns; or from those that, being born second in their noble families and not having enough to maintain with decency their legacy, came to the Indies to flee from poverty; or, finally, from those that, because of their virtues, erudition, and distinctions, deserved the political and military employments that your majesty and his glorious ancestors granted them, for which cause, and from their roots, they ought to be considered noble (see appendix 3.2).[37]

Although vast and general, the concept of nobility outlined by Ahumada is resonant with the concept of nobility of privilege mentioned above. This categorization was widely acknowledged in New Spain, especially among those who saw the university as a means of social advancement.[38] As it was, many Spaniards considered themselves noble by the sole fact of proving their limpieza.[39] They thought of themselves as "raised and educated in the same splendor as [Iberians]. . . . They are ignorant of manual work and dedicate themselves to their studies; mechanical jobs neither agree with the luster of their birth nor offer a decent subsistence."[40] It seemed apparent that being fit for letters and the professions was an important attribute of a person who wished to move up in the Spanish political hierarchy, especially among American Spaniards.[41] It was exceptional, one must say, for the son of a titled noble family to continue his father's business trade. As part of a political oligarchy, the titled nobility groomed their children for careers in government, as well as for the management and continuity of their *mayorazgo*. Those without political and financial resources rarely sought to enter business; rather, they aimed for public employment. These Spaniards (American in their majority) populated confessional institutions such as colleges, the university, monasteries, parishes, and cathedrals, for the church was the main institution that offered the possibility of attaining political standing in New Spanish society.[42] Higher education and the clerical path went hand in hand because a university degree (the degree of *bachiller*, to be precise) was a requirement for priesthood.[43] With this degree a person could advance through the hierarchy of the lower clergy, which encompassed the ranks of subdeacon, deacon, and presbyter. Promotion to higher appointments (such as a cathedral canonry) required a doctoral degree, which gave individuals a notable status in light of their rank and long-standing ecclesiastical careers.

While it is true that secular concepts such as personal industry and self-achievement were central in rampant claims of nobility, such claims departed from a desire for privilege attainable through institutional memberships only. The corporate advantages that the titled nobility had as a political class, such as the right to carry arms, not paying tribute like the rest of the king's subjects, and judicial immunity, could only be secured by being a member of a Spanish institution like the military, the university, or the church. Of these privileges, the *fuero* (judicial immunity) was by far the most important. Accordingly, the fuero was "the Magna Carta of a noble condition and of liberties among individuals. . . . The right to be judged by magistrates of one's own estate and class was one of the most envied conditions among the king's subjects. Nobles, scholars, wealthy merchants, miners, and military officers, they all enjoyed this vestige of medieval jurisprudence."[44]

Although a common set of prerogatives seemingly placed nobles of blood and nobles of privilege on an equal social plane, corporate membership certainly complicated any attempt to define neatly what it meant to be noble in the latter category. In the university, students sought to relate to the concept of erudite nobility that emerged in Spain during the sixteenth century.[45] "Nobility," however, was a very ambiguous label in this institution because different determinations of calidad supported different nobility claims. Forty percent of graduates in the eighteenth century went to great lengths to demonstrate their "nobility" through genealogical certifications (such as the one from the Hurtado de Mendoza family addressed above), which was the most common type of document used to prove such status. The other 60 percent did not provide documentation detailing distinctive deeds, services, or lineage as merits of this condition. Proofs of limpieza and references to the occupation of the father were the main bases of nobility claims in this sector of the student population, and students addressed these in their letters as proper attributes of "noble" people.[46] The outlining of these attributes usually preceded any formal declaration of nobility, and perhaps this is why these individuals presented themselves (and their parents) unproblematically as *personas nobles*. For them, their nobility could be inferred from the nature of their parents' occupation, and not the other way around. Scholars have pointed out that the growth in university graduation rates during the eighteenth century relates precisely to the social status that individuals claimed through their appointments in public and religious institutions.[47] In this sense, university students were members of an academic milieu that sought to ennoble their institution, for which they identified the university with the very social attributes that they claimed. This is perhaps the reason that limpieza became the basis of the quest for status, honor, and nobility among those Spaniards pursuing academic degrees.[48]

The cathedral of Mexico provides a case study relevant to this phenomenon: it shows how erudition, as an attribute of "noble minds," was the focus of musicians who followed an institutional path of professional growth from childhood with several stages of development, in which limpieza was a main requisite. The degree of bachiller and priesthood were the culmination of this journey, which made individuals eligible for the post of chaplain, an appointment given to the "most noble" individuals in light of calidades accumulated after a lifetime of service. The study shows that while the institutional trajectory of chaplains articulated calidad in similar ways to Spaniards affiliated with the university, music was the main strategy that chaplains used to engage in this process. Chapter 4 extends this discussion by showing that ways of thinking about music were also steeped in these racialized identity constructs.

Music: Strategy for an Ecclesiastical Career

The church was an institution dominated by American Spaniards not in small part because Iberians were usually preferred for office appointments in the royal administration. As the spiritual leader of New Spain, the church offered social prestige and good stipends, as well as a much desired political standing in society.[49] For individuals coming from families of means the clergy provided an avenue to attain a prominent social position. There were middle-class Spaniards who could afford the cost of registration in the university and the final examinations for the degree of bachiller. Some families even had enough money to endow a chaplaincy in perpetuity for their son, and if a sponsor appeared in the family's circle of acquaintances the youth could very well continue to pursue a doctorate.[50] The path, however, was not so promising for those without appropriate resources and political connections. These individuals culminated their academic preparation with the first degree, which enabled them to become presbyters (full priests). Overall, the church aimed to ordain people with proven means of sustenance—be it a chaplaincy or personal sufficiency, like wealth or employment. Without these types of resources the professional prospects of a cleric were rather limited. But there was a loophole: the ability to speak an indigenous language also enabled people to become priests, even if they did not have other assets. Clerics ordained under this provision (*a título de idioma* or "under language title") had hardly any education and rarely completed academic degrees. Authorities discouraged ordination under these circumstances not only because of the proliferation of poorly educated clerics but also because they hoped to provide livings for candidates with more merit.[51]

Without a chaplaincy, personal means, or appropriate connections, a bachiller degree could only bring people to some of the less prestigious parishes in small towns. At best, individuals could be appointed priests in one of these churches, although it was more common for them to be employed as vicars in exchange for food, lodging, and some extra money. For a lot of presbyters this was in itself a reward for their efforts, especially considering that a good number of presbyters in the largest dioceses (such as Mexico City) were forced to beg in the streets. Financial need was the main motivation for poor Spaniards to join the clergy. If some of them studied in their local towns (where the prospects of employment were less than enticing) it was because they could not afford to move into the city for some years to attend the university and the seminary. The possibility of making a living in Mexico City was even less promising due to the high competition for benefices among a large crowd of clerics with better education than those in smaller towns. Only presbyters with doctoral degrees were considered for appointment in any of the parishes close to the city. Although some of these were rather attractive in terms of the remuneration that they offered, the urban-minded holding doctorates preferred to keep a house in the city while an employed vicar would do the parish work for them outside of town. Presbyters with bachiller degrees in the city vigorously competed for such vicar posts or for available chaplaincies, and their record of service and accomplishments played a critical role in the competition. Those unable to secure these alternatives lived out of alms that people gave them for officiating at Mass in one of the city convents, or at worst, begged for charity.[52] For Spaniards of little means who lived in Mexico City it was clear that some sort of employment and affiliation was necessary to become presbyters and that an excellent record of service would be important to develop a network of relationships, in itself key for professional advancement. This path, so people hoped, would enable them to develop a profile in which social background, education, professional achievement, and rank would inform perceptions of their status, which, associated with their limpieza, would reflect their social condition ("decent," or otherwise "noble") as Spaniards.

This is why many Spanish families sought to place their male children in the Colegio de Infantes of the cathedral of Mexico. Following the Spanish tradition of teaching music to the *seises* or *mozos de coro*, the cathedral chapter established this college for choirboys in 1725. The practice of teaching music to boys in the cathedral had a long tradition; its antecedents can be traced back to medieval Spain. Humanist trends pushed for the opening of opportunities for education in urban ecclesiastical institutions during the twelfth century, especially because of a growing concern for the academic growth of future clerics who came from poor families.[53] It was not until the fifteenth century, however, that Spain secured papal bulls to establish officially a position for an instructor of choirboys in cathedrals.[54] By the sixteenth century the tradition was well established, and records show that plainchant and counterpoint comprised the core of music education in America.[55] In the case of the cathedral of Mexico, the teaching of plainchant and counterpoint persisted at least until the mid-eighteenth century, although the education of boys comprised more than music.[56] The first provincial council of Mexico (1555) explicitly stated that boys also had to learn the basics of Latin so that they could read and conjugate verbs.[57] Education was central to the professional development of Spanish boys, for it guaranteed not only advancement within the institution but also social honor.[58] Members of the chapter, therefore, voiced strong concerns about the future of youths well into the eighteenth century. It was because of these social concerns that the canons deployed initiatives to reinforce the curriculum of the Colegio, so that the cathedral could prepare children for everything pertaining to music and ritual practices, as well as for a clerical career.

Today there is still no precise knowledge about the type of literature that the chapter introduced in the Colegio. Sources from the cathedral of Valladolid in Michoacan, however, provide some glimpses. An inventory from 1796 shows that choirboys in Michoacan read Saint Jerome, Cicero's epistles, the work of Ovid, and the documents of the Council of Trent, among other things.[59] Along with Latin grammar, this literature exposed children to a series of classic and medieval texts that formed the basis of their education and of their institutional and professional development. Specifically, the chapter's efforts to promote education derived from an interest in preventing children from falling through the social cracks: according to some canons, once out of the cathedral children could "fall into perdition" (*se perdían*) because of their young age and all of the free time they had.[60] In 1725 the chapter thus established the Collegio de la Asunción de Nuestra Señora y Patriarcha S.S. Joseph para los Ymphantes de el Choro de la Santa Iglesia Metropolitana de México (College of Our Lady of the Assumption and Patriarch Saint Joseph for Choirboys of the Holy Metropolitan Church of Mexico).

Enlightened currents further influenced not only curriculum planning but also the overall educational and social mission of the Colegio. Their classes in Latin grammar prepared them to take philosophy in the seminary later on.[61] These basics in the liberal arts prepared children to enter the university to study in one of the major areas, namely, law, canon law, and theology. Although the university treated arts (*artes*) as an individual discipline, it was considered "minor" because its core courses (logic and philosophy) were required to study in any of the other major areas.[62] In this way, the mission of the Colegio was not music instruction per se. Rather, its mission was to use music as a springboard to produce the future priests and chaplains of the cathedral, so that, in the end, individuals would become "ideal and useful ministers to the church."[63] The main purpose of the Colegio was to recruit children from among the poorest Spanish families in the city, giving them scholarships.[64] The Colegio provided clothing, room, board, education, access to the university (to pursue a bachiller degree), and an annual stipend that usually went to the parents. For families of scarce means this meant extra income and the possibility that the child could develop a career in the church, in addition to the relief from having one less mouth to feed. These were reasons why the chapter was flooded with applications every year from parents eager to place their child in the cathedral. In 1559, the number of admitted children was fixed at twelve. However, the chapter revised this number in 1664 due to the overwhelming number of applicants, and increased vacancies to twenty-four. By 1725, the guidelines of the Colegio specified a minimum of sixteen positions available, and if finances allowed these could be extended to twenty-four.[65]

There were several requirements for admission to the Colegio and these had to be presented following the verification of limpieza de sangre. According to the bylaws, aspiring choirboys had to be between eleven and twelve years old, although records show that the canons sometimes admitted boys as young as eight. Children also had to know how to read and write and have a good voice.[66] These, however, were the most basic requirements (calidades); the full list of attributes was meant to establish the child's limpieza. Accordingly, children had to be "Spanish, from legitimate birth and legitimate matrimony, for which they will show their record of baptism, as well as information about the fact that their parents are poor and of honest trade ... and these qualities (*calidades*) shall not be exempted ... for the objective [of the Colegio] is that these children be raised and taught to become clerics."[67] Note that while a good voice was certainly a requirement, letters from parents emphasized more the apparent love for the clerical path and blood of their children rather than their aptitude for music. The letter from Pedro Rodríguez Calvo, for instance, read thus:

> [I,] Don Pedro Rodríguez Calvo ... legitimate husband of Doña María Ignacia Díaz Tirado, with all humility and veneration say to you, my dear sirs: among the legitimate children that we have had in our matrimony, José Ignacio Mariano de los Santos of nine years of age is one of them, who by his own inclination and love for the clerical path wishes with all eagerness to enter the Colegio de Infantes of this holy metropolitan church, for which he has made the necessary arrangements to appear before you today as one of the nominated boys for the award of four available scholarships, which your lordships will bestow on those with most merit. And regarding the voice, or music, which is the main

reason why children are chosen, I do not think my child to be the worst, as he does not sing bad at all at his young age, and because of his ability, capacity, and inclination he is equal to the best of the contenders, as he is equal as well because of the illustrious and distinguished blood that assists him (see appendix 3.3).[68]

Letters like this one were not rare, but by themselves they did not constitute proofs of legitimacy or limpieza. These claims had to be corroborated publicly by witnesses, that is, by "public voice and fame." Testimonials of this sort were oral in nature and were usually recorded by the chapter's secretary. They not only established the child's legitimacy and limpieza, but also his Christian upbringing, as well as his virtuous and decent customs. The testimony of witnesses was meant to assert the social reputation of the family, so that the chapter would know that the child had the desired qualities. Such documents were appropriately labeled *Información de legitimidad y limpieza, vida y costumbres de . . .* ("Information about the legitimacy, purity, life, and customs of"—the child's name followed), and the chapter required these from all aspiring choirboys. The application of Ciprian de Aguilera provides a good example:

Ciprian de Aguilera presented bachiller Don Antonio de Puga, presbyter and chaplain of the Hospital del Amor de Dios, as witness, who after swearing *in verbo sacerdotis tacto pectore*, pledged to say the truth and acknowledged knowing José Aguilera and Doña Gregoria Pérez de Alsivia, parents of Ciprian, and also acknowledged their qualities (*calidades*), background, life, customs, and purity, and is said to know the parents from a long time, knowing that they are Spaniards, clean of any bad race of Jews, Moors, or other casta, and that he never heard that either they or their ancestors were ever punished by the Holy Inquisition or any other secular tribunal . . . also, that he knows they were married according to the order of our holy mother church, and thus procreated as their legitimate child the afore mentioned Ciprian . . . raising him by the good [norms of] Christian education and keeping him from any vices and in the application of good customs, for which he knows that the aforementioned Ciprian is a virtuous and honest person, and with no canonic impediment to his intentions. And that what he (Antonio de Puga) has said is public and noticeable, and it is the truth.[69]

This document is similar in content to other records from children admitted to the Colegio. Its emphasis on (Spanish) blood, legitimacy, and customs aimed to present the child in terms of the attributes that informed perceptions of "Spanishness" in New Spain. From this vantage point it is easy to understand why Juan Sumaya was so concerned about the misplacement of his son's baptismal record. It was a document that attested to Manuel Sumaya's social place, not in the sense that he deserved privilege by being Spaniard, but as a person who, as a member of the Spanish community, had a chance to negotiate his social position through the years and in relation to an increasing series of merits that would elevate his status. Each promotion or appointment was in itself an opportunity for one to negotiate his status, and given that perceptions of Spanish blood (that is, limpieza) were virtually identified with the attributes that a person claimed, one could say that stages of professional advancement presented opportunities to renovate and heighten limpieza as part of one's enhancement of his position in society.

For Manuel Sumaya, the first step within this process was his baptism; his acceptance into the cathedral as a choirboy was the second one. The chapter considered choirboy positions to be entry points through which an individual could pursue a career in the church, and thus, a means of mobility. Recall that a presbyter with a bachiller degree in the city had limited social prospects, and the alternative of finding a job seemed even less promising. That is why choirboys who chose to pursue clerical careers tried their best to stay in the cathedral as chaplains, which seemed by far a more prestigious appointment than working as vicars at parishes outside the city. The cathedral chapter, therefore, made its best efforts to retain choirboys, especially those who were musically talented. That was the case of Manuel Sumaya, who likely entered the cathedral in 1690.[70] The Asociación de Historiadores Mexicanos (Association of Mexican Historians) recently announced the discovery of Sumaya's baptism record, dated January 14, 1680, which makes it probable that he was born in that same year, and that he was ten years old when he entered the cathedral.[71] Primary sources document the encouragement that Sumaya received during his early years due to his musical ability. It was because of his talent that the canons helped him financially when his father fell ill (and eventually died), so that he would not leave the cathedral to help his family by following another occupation.[72] This piece of information is important because it points to an interest by the cathedral chapter in guiding the clerical future of boys.

Documents relevant to the upbringing of Martín Bernárdez de Rivera (who like Sumaya was a Spanish choirboy born in New Spain, and who reached the post of cathedral chapelmaster) are similar regarding this point. Rivera auditioned for a vacancy in the Colegio on January 19, 1742, and was finally admitted in 1743.[73] Rivera also captured the attention of the chapter with his musical ability, which prompted the canons to extend his stay in the Colegio after he completed his six years of study (the amount of time that children were allowed to stay in the Colegio). Seemingly, Rivera had entered the Colegio too young, in part because of his musical talent, but also due to the influence of relatives who were members of the chapter. After six years the canons felt that it was still too early for him to be part of the chapel, not the least because of the tensions that had begun to brew within the group by that time (this was around 1751, after Ignacio Jerusalem had become chapelmaster, something that spurred political tensions in the music chapel; see Chapter 4). For these reasons, the chapter decided to allow Rivera to stay in the Colegio two more years, lest he run the risk of "losing his way" due to his young age, which would have been a shame in someone so talented, the canons thought. The cases of both Sumaya and Rivera show that appointments to a choirboy position were made with considerations about the social future of these children. With this in mind, the chapter enforced "the most diligence to procure that the Colegio could raise children for everything [pertaining to music and ritual], as to avoid that they end up begging in the streets."[74]

If the canons felt that boys had a chance for a better future in the cathedral it was because they could develop a career in this institution. As mentioned before, the concept of institutional career in New Spain referred to a lifelong project of professional growth with several stages of development. Through these stages individuals acquired and refined knowledge necessary for promotion, which in turn elevated their calidad and social position in terms of their knowledge and rank. For cathedral choirboys this project encompassed everything from their early liberal arts studies at the Colegio to their ultimate appointments within the cathedral. As part of this journey, music ministries (such as being a choirboy, choirbook carrier, acolyte, instrumentalist in the chapel, choir assistant, succentor, and chaplain) were levels of development in which individuals acquired knowledge in plainchant, counterpoint, liturgy, Latin, and playing instruments to increase their merit for higher positions. This trajectory comprised the core of an individual's record of service, which the chapter took very much into account to assess their professional growth. After all, the aim of the Colegio was to produce "ideal and useful ministers to the church," for although some musicians chose not to attend either the university or the seminary they were still considered church ministers, and an extension of the cathedral's clergy for that matter.[75] For poor Spaniards, therefore, music was a strategy to follow this institutional road in order to establish their status claims. The activity of Sumaya and Rivera—along with that of other musicians who shared the same professional path, but for whom information is more fragmentary—illustrates how this process unfolded.

Rivera entered the Colegio in 1743, and the cathedral chapter took care of guiding the development of his music skills. At the Colegio, Rivera—like Sumaya and others—learned grammar and counterpoint, as well as how to play an instrument so that he could remain employed in the chapel after his voice changed.[76] Landing a job in the chapel was indeed necessary if youths wanted to remain affiliated with the cathedral after leaving the Colegio, and therefore continue advancing through the ranks. In Rivera's case, organ was his instrument of choice, and information about others like José González and Diego de Reina (1722), Pedro Pablo Velásquez (1733), and Juan Thadeo Priego (1744) shows that boys had to learn the harpsichord first if they wanted to become assistant organists.[77] As assistants to one of the organists, children learned how to play the instrument but they also learned the liturgical sequence of services as well as chant tones and modes, and they continued honing their knowledge of counterpoint. Not all boys had an affinity for the organ, and the chapter also sought to develop performers in every instrument needed in the music chapel. This is illustrated by the cases of Antonio Ximerón, who started to learn bajón (bassoon) in 1712; José Curiel, bajoncillo (tenor bassoon) in 1722; Joaquín Xardón and Gregorio Cansio, violin in 1734; Nicolás Vásquez and Baltazar Monroy the same in 1742, Pedro Brizuela and Antonio Torres, horn in 1750; Manuel Rivera and Hermenegildo Bala, violin, also in 1750; and Manuel Cervantes, bajón during the same year.

For the cathedral chapter, instrumental instruction was a very important component of the Colegio's curriculum, and every year the canons tested the progress of choirboys in their instruments along with their knowledge of music theory and Latin.[78] For some boys instrumental instruction was a means to join the music chapel after leaving the Colegio and thus remain affiliated with the cathedral as either singers or instrumentalists. Not all boys had an interest in becoming clerics, and evidence shows that some remained in the chapel after leaving the Colegio without pursuing further study. There were important advantages to being a cathedral musician and it is quite possible that for these youths a position in the chapel was a desired goal in itself. In contrast, those with a clerical vocation saw the cathedral choir as an incentive to register in the university and to be ordained.[79] As members of the cathedral choir, individuals held prerogatives that set them apart from lay musicians in the chapel. Not only were they entitled to the *fuero eclesiástico* (which exempted clerics from being tried by a secular tribunal) but they also had the right to claim the privilege of noble treatment due to their education, rank, and record of service in the church. In order to get into the choir, boys followed a chain of ministries through which they accumulated merits for promotion throughout their lives. Sumaya is an example of this trajectory, which he shared with Rivera and others who also devoted their lives to the cathedral. While Sumaya and Rivera are exceptional in that they became chapelmasters, they do represent the typical institutional model of promotion to reach a position in the choir that others also followed.

The Choir Chaplains

In a letter to the chapter, Francisco Álvarez de la Cadena mentioned that since an early age he had perfected himself in the singing of plainchant, and that after twenty-three years of service he had earned substantial experience in the performance of psalms and overall liturgy pertinent to the choir, in addition to having developed a well-trained tenor voice. As the choir did not have vacant chaplaincies at that moment, Álvarez wrote, he asked to be considered for a post as choir assistant and that he be allowed to keep his position as tenor singer in the chapel. This favor, he mentioned, had been previously granted to Timoteo Torres y Cuevas, and he now requested the same consideration.[80] Álvarez's letter provides important information: first, it shows that those who aspired to join the choir had spent years devoted to training and service. Moreover, the letter mentions the type of training and skills that those in the choir needed to have, namely, plainchant, structure of the liturgy (which required knowledge of Latin), and a good voice. Finally, it mentions the post of choir assistant as a sort of "steppingstone" before being appointed chaplain. Although not too much information is available about Álvarez de la Cadena's activity, there is, nonetheless, documentation relevant to the trajectory of Timoteo Torres y Cuevas, who just like Sumaya, Rivera, and others used music as a strategy to develop a career in the cathedral throughout his life.

On January 19, 1742, Timoteo Torres y Cuevas—a Spaniard and legitimate son of Don Juan de Torres and Doña Francisca de la Cueva Guerrero—auditioned with two other children for admission to the one vacancy available at the Colegio. For this, Torres presented the required documentation to prove his limpieza and calidades,[81] and although he was already thirteen years old the canons thought that his unique voice merited an exception. The recruitment and retention of choirboys was not only a means of providing children with possibilities for social advancement. It was also an investment by the chapter, as raising competent singers in Mexico would alleviate the cathedral from the financial burden of looking for succentors and chaplains in Spain. Finding good voices in New Spain was difficult, so the canons put special care into preparing choirboys to serve in these capacities.[82] With "good voices," however, the canons did not merely refer to the singing qualities of individuals. There were occasions when the cathedral was "in extreme need of chaplains," but this was likely because the requirements for such appointments reduced the number of potential candidates.[83] In addition to a good voice, candidates had to possess profiles with attributes that were the result of a lifetime of ecclesiastical service. A case from 1781, a year when the cathedral was in need of a succentor, shows the extent to which the evaluation of calidades played an important role. During the chapter meeting of September 26, one of the ministers, Blas José de Vela y Aragón, mentioned that he knew of a person possessing a good voice and knowledge of plainchant who could serve in the choir. The only concern, he said, was that this person was the husband of an actress who played first lady in the comedies of the Coliseo, where he also performed, in addition to performing comedies in improvised public stages (*corrales*) in the city. The canons answered that it would be "improper to have an individual of such qualities (*calidades*) mingling with the chapter in the choir," adding that a good voice and plainchant knowledge were not attributes particular to a succentor.[84]

If for succentors the evaluation of their calidad was important for chaplains the assessment was certainly more rigorous. Admission to the Colegio placed choirboys on a professional path toward that position, which from the beginning was filled with scrutiny of their skills and development. Primary sources do not indicate whether there was a sense of anxiety among boys to attain and keep certain positions. In Torres y Cuevas's case, there was only one vacancy available at the Colegio when he applied; additionally, right after the audition, the canons examined other choirboys to see if any of them could be replaced with one of the other two auditioning children. This raises the possibility that some level of competition might have existed. Interestingly, the chapter was hoping to dismiss someone so that the young Martín Bernárdez de Rivera (who auditioned along with Torres) could be admitted.[85]

Choirbook carrier and acolyte where the first two ministries that children occupied in the Colegio, and one had to be a carrier before he could become an acolyte. As choirbook carriers, children were in charge of taking the full-sized volumes (close to ninety pounds in average weight) from the shelves to the lectern for religious services or whenever the boys received musical instruction. As a boy had to serve in this position to become an acolyte, the chapter received several petitions whenever a vacancy opened up. On October 1750, for example, the canons considered five applications when Juan de Dios Hidalgo relinquished the post. To be eligible for appointment, applicants had to show progress in their studies at the Colegio, particularly in music theory and performance.[86] Torres y Cuevas had gone through the same process when he became choirbook carrier four years earlier.[87] Given the size and weight of the volumes, this position was not an easy task, and boys usually spent more time with the books than the rest of the children. In fact, most choirbook carriers left personal evidence of their appointment to this ministry. Throughout the collection of chantbooks it is common to find (either penciled in or scratched) the last names of boys who served in this capacity (see Figure 3.6). Moreover, scribbles on the music staff also show the use that these books had in musical instruction. As shown in Figures 3.7 and 3.8, writing marks referring to solfège syllables are consistent with primary sources mentioning the pedagogical role that these volumes had in the musical education of boys.[88]

The position of choirbook carrier was usually reserved for the oldest students of the Colegio not only because of the physical demands that carrying such a load imposed but also because this was a position that youths took before their university examinations.[89] Upon receiving this appointment, individuals usually

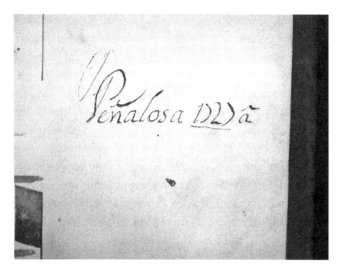

Figure 3.6   Photograph of a chantbook showing the inscribed last name of José Lázaro de Peñalosa, photographed by the author. Archivo del Cabildo, Catedral Metropolitana de México, Colección Libros de Coro, 72 (on the spine).

Figure 3.7   Photograph of a chantbook showing written solfège syllables. Archivo del Cabildo, Catedral Metropolitana de México, Colección Libros de Coro, 72 (on the spine).

asked the chapter for financial assistance to help with the cost of examinations for the degree of bachiller (necessary to become a priest), for which the canons usually gave 30 pesos.[90] While sometimes the canons made appointments after they had removed from the position someone who failed to fulfill his duties, most of the times choirbook carriers filled in vacancies left by those who, after

Figure 3.8 Detail of one of the solfège syllables written in one of the chantbooks. Archivo del Cabildo, Catedral Metropolitana de México, Colección Libros de Coro, 72 (on the spine).

receiving the tonsure, became acolytes or worked to become choir assistants. On June 1734, for example, Ángel Moral and Alejandro Neri—both choirbook carriers—asked to be appointed to a vacant acolyte post that the chapter gave to Moral. In turn, Vicente Santos, Gerardo de Castañeda, and Miguel Ángel Pavón petitioned for the choirbook carrying post that Moral had left open, which ultimately went to Pavón.[91] Although clerical rank was not a requirement to become an acolyte, records show that some individuals had already become either a subdeacon or deacon; at the very least, the chapter expected boys to have passed an examination in Latin grammar.[92] After all, the canons hoped that acolytes would continue in the clerical path until reaching the rank of presbyter, in itself a requirement to be eligible for a choir chaplaincy.

In reality, the position of choirbook carrier was as transitory as the middle clerical stages that youths went through, as the ultimate goal was to have enough credentials to be appointed to the choir, and the rank of presbyter was the last step in that direction. Nevertheless, some form of income (either from employment or personal wealth) was required for a person to be fully ordained.[93] As possessing wealth was not an option for most youths, they sought a vacancy in the chapel and/or an interim position as choir assistant. Records show that some acolytes were quick to petition a place in the chapel—either as singers or instrumentalists—once a vacancy opened up. This not only gave them an income so that they could finish receiving clerical orders, but having the position also added an extra credential to their record of service. José Salvatierra, for example, asked to be considered for a violin position.[94] Francisco Javier de

Aguilar petitioned for a similar assignment in 1746, while Torres y Cuevas asked for a singing post in December 1750.[95] This was the same path that Sumaya and Rivera followed, with the only difference of having chosen the organ as their instrument.

Being an organist was perhaps a more demanding position because individuals had to show keyboard proficiency, theoretical skills in counterpoint and chant tones, and knowledge about the order and structure of the liturgy. These skills were important for understanding music from a practical and theoretical basis, which was crucial if one aspired to become chapelmaster (see Chapter 4). Like other choirboys, Sumaya and Rivera had proven to be competent in grammar and instrumental performance; they had advanced through the ladder of music-related ministries to attend the university and the seminary, and had worked toward getting a position in the choir. Sumaya was an organist by the age of eighteen and records show that he was appointed choir assistant the following year (1699).[96] Records about Rivera are less exact about his age. Nevertheless, it is possible to surmise at least that he became assistant organist at around the age of seventeen, and that he probably became an assistant in the choir the following year.[97] Good and robust voices for plainchant were always in demand in the cathedral and assistants were important for that reason. They helped the succentors and the rest of the canons with the intonation of chants during the divine office, and in doing so they learned skills necessary to be appointed to a chaplaincy later on.

Overall, there were two types of chaplaincies in the cathedral. One of these consisted in singing a set number of Masses every year for the soul of a deceased person. Before his or her death, a patron usually endowed a chaplaincy with an amount of money, which, invested in real estate property, yielded a 5 percent interest return every year; this money was to pay a priest to officiate at the Masses. These chaplaincies were quite important to individuals who needed to show that they had some income before they became presbyters. On July 1712, for example, Salvador Morales, a former choirboy who was serving as acolyte at that moment, wrote to the chapter saying that after twenty years of service in the cathedral he hoped to be appointed to a chaplaincy that happened to be vacant (because of the death of bachiller Pedro de Vega y Bique, who was in charge of it). Morales mentioned that with this chaplaincy he could be ordained as a presbyter, stating that the requirements for ordination mentioned a chaplaincy as an acceptable proof of solvency.[98] Considering that competition for chaplaincies could be intense, the mention of one's years of service was a noteworthy attribute (calidad) that candidates stressed to stand out above others. Some individuals could not become presbyters because of their lack of money; it was with the remuneration that they could perceive from the chaplaincy that they hoped to attain this rank.

Chaplaincies, however, were given to the individuals with the most merit, and candidates did their best to show that their achievements made them worthy of such an appointment. The case of José Lázaro de Peñalosa is a good example. In addition to his years of education in voice, plainchant, counterpoint, and Latin grammar at the Colegio, Peñalosa was also knowledgeable of liturgy, as attested by his writing of items for the plainchant choirbooks throughout the 1730s and 1740s.[99] This type of knowledge, he hoped, could give him an edge over other candidates when he applied for a vacant chaplaincy on March 8, 1735. His experience at the scriptorium and his occupation as acolyte, however, could not put him above the chosen candidate, who was already a deacon.[100] Clerical rank played a very important part in the process of selection, and this is the reason Peñalosa lost another opportunity on June 19, 1736.[101] However, three months later the chapter finally appointed Peñalosa to a chaplaincy with the condition that he had to be ordained presbyter within one year. Otherwise, Peñalosa's chaplaincy would be rescinded, as well as his acolyte post, and he would be dismissed from the church.[102]

While this type of chaplaincy certainly provided youths with financial incentives for clerical promotion, there is evidence to suggest that the second type was perhaps more socially enticing. Positions to sing plainchant in the choir during the divine office, known as *capellanías de coro* (choir chaplaincies), called for an aggregate of qualifications that enhanced perceptions of the calidad and overall social status of chaplains. If granted, this chaplaincy made an individual a member of the cathedral choir in perpetuity; this choir was made up of members of the chapter (canons with doctoral degrees who, because of their appointments as university authorities or episcopal officials, had a prominent political standing) and was the most prestigious clerical group of the most important religious institution in New Spain. According to the cathedral's act of foundation, there were six choir chaplaincies that were paid from the annual collection of tithes (these were known as *capellanías de erección*). During the seventeenth century, however, captain Álvaro de Lorenzana set an endowment to finance eight additional chaplaincies that became known as *capellanías de Lorenzana*, which increased the number of chaplains to fourteen.[103]

If not in itself rigorous, the examination to be appointed to a choir chaplaincy covered years of study in music (stressing vocal ability, the understanding of tones, modes and chant repertoire, and even liturgy),[104] Latin and liturgy (at the Colegio and later at the seminary), and liberal arts and theology (also at the Colegio, the university, and the seminary). After approximately twenty-eight years of service, Sumaya met all requirements, and on June 21, 1708, he applied for a vacant post. Competition was steep, as five other individuals aspired to the same position. Part of the examination required each cleric to demonstrate his proficiency in plainchant and Latin using one of the choirbooks and a breviary.

To be tested in the first category, candidates had to perform a proper intonation of either an antiphon or a psalm; for the second they had to read a lection from the breviary. When Sumaya's turn came, the canons asked him to intone the psalm *Miserere mei Deus* and to read the lection for the feast of Saint Stephen Pope.[105] Sumaya's examples, along with that of other choirboys who also became chaplains, like José González (1733), José Lázaro de Peñalosa (1736), Timoteo Torres y Cuevas, and Martín Bernárdez de Rivera (1760)—as well as others not mentioned, like Vicente Santos and Miguel Ángel Pavón (1736), and Martín Vásquez de Mendoza (1750)—show that the positions of choirboy, choirbook carrier, acolyte, musician in the chapel, and assistant in the choir formed a hierarchical line of promotion in music ministries through which individuals acquired these calidades. These examples show that competence in music and Latin grammar was important to the chapter in the youths who were appointed as choirbook carriers and as acolytes. The examples further indicate that these were transitory positions through which boys could move up in the hierarchy of ministries devoted to music and ritual. The different cases of choirboys mentioned above are similar to the trajectory of Sumaya, something that makes him less extraordinary from the vantage point of his clerical career than musicologists might have previously thought. Much historical study has been devoted to the music works of Sumaya, studies that have placed his name in the pantheon of New Spanish composers. On the one hand, it would be fair to say that the amount of music that he produced and his position as chapelmaster have largely fueled our interest in this historical figure. On the other, the study of Sumaya's clerical career sheds light on an aspect of his profile thus far unexplored, and that puts his musical activity in a wider historical perspective.

Surviving primary sources leave little doubt that Sumaya's musical capacities were above average among his peers, and scholars have expanded this information with further commentary about his compositional abilities.[106] The extent of Sumaya's musical knowledge and proficiency certainly gave him an advantage over other cathedral musicians, probably explaining why he came to occupy the most important post in the music chapel after the death of Antonio de Salazar in 1715. Yet, it is also quite possible that Sumaya's clerical profile served better his efforts to define a place in society. The chapelmastership surely placed him in a privileged hierarchical position within the line of cathedral music ministries. Within the ecclesiastical hierarchy, however, the situation was quite different: being a chapelmaster did not require a clerical rank and the appointment had no bearing in the promotion of an individual in the church. It could be argued that Hernando Franco and Francisco López Capillas (chapelmasters from 1575 to 1585, and from 1654 to 1673, respectively) became actual members of the cathedral chapter. These appointments, however, had more to do with an ecclesiastical benefice that, as clerics, they received from the king than solely with their work in the music chapel. More specifically, Franco and López Capillas were given a *ración* (a "portion") by the king, which was the name for one of the high ecclesiastical benefices that paid a stipend to a person appointed to a cathedral chapter.[107] Like all benefices, a ración was a way of recognizing the ecclesiastical career and credentials of these clerics, and not necessarily their musical talent or accomplishments.

In contrast, the chapelmastership was not an ecclesiastical benefice of any sort and was not necessarily assigned to any one individual in perpetuity.[108] Indeed, the post of chapelmaster did not compare to one of the ecclesiastical appointments at the cathedral of Mexico. The salary of a chapelmaster was set at 500 pesos per year, which was well below the minimum salary earned by what historians have called the "clerical proletariat" of the eighteenth century.[109] It is true that a chaplaincy only paid 200 pesos a year (and after 1735 only 175 pesos due to the financial stress that the cathedral experienced),[110] but these were positions that clerics usually complemented with their salaries as musicians in the chapel, which ranged between 200 and 400 pesos.[111] In addition, musicians received income from obvenciones and from endowed cathedral rituals. Patrons sometimes decided to establish an endowment to celebrate certain festivities, such as the office of matins for Saint Peter or the Masses of Renovation for the Holy Sacrament. The chapter usually invested the money of the endowment so it would earn interest every year, and patrons were very specific as to how they wanted this money to be distributed. In this way, musicians, chaplains, acolytes, and sometimes even the canons received payment for their performance in these rituals.

Surely there was a financial incentive in pursuing a chaplaincy, and records show that chaplains shifted from a capellanía de erección to a capellanía de Lorenzana and vice versa, depending on which one seemed more financially stable at any given moment. A choir chaplaincy, nonetheless, bestowed important privileges and distinctions, attributes that Sumaya and others probably coveted. The chapelmastership was without a doubt a position of corporate leadership in the chapel, which for a cleric was an important credential in his record of ecclesiastical service. After all, music was a strategy for institutional advancement in the cathedral, and being a musician for some was a way to find the place in the church "to which [they] had always aspired."[112] Once ordained, some clerics were "desirous of rising in the profession,"[113] and the examples of Franco, López Capillas, Sumaya, and Rivera suggest that, for some people, the chapelmastership might not have been so much a destination as a stage of professional development in the church.[114] A choir chaplaincy represented a further step in that direction because it enabled individuals to articulate a discourse of status among Spaniards. This was in part because of the many attributes (calidades) that chaplaincies required, knowledge of music and the rank of presbyter among them. And although sometimes deacons could be appointed to a chaplaincy, this occurred only if the candidate was "adorned with all of the other calidades," and with the expectation that he would become a presbyter within a year.[115] Above all, these positions were the culmination of a life of service for individuals from humble backgrounds; unlike Franco and López Capillas, there is no record of a cathedral musician in the eighteenth century who climbed to a position among the canons. Rivera did have relatives in the chapter, but he never moved beyond a choir chaplaincy, and he even shared the chapelmastership with Matheo Tollis de la Rocca and Antonio Juanas. For poor Spaniards, therefore, a chaplaincy represented the highest point of their institutional career, which the rank of presbyter enabled.

Those who aspired to a choir chaplaincy wrote in their petition a list of merits that made them eligible for the appointment. These petitions comprised "life résumés" because each merit represented a level of accomplishment that had required its own accomplishments and time of service. When José Salvatierra applied for a violin position, for example, he mentioned that his "eight years as choirboy and nine years as acolyte represented his short merits" to a vacancy in the chapel, a position that would enable him to be ordained.[116] Being a musician represented a merit in itself given that musicians' knowledge of music and time of service differentiated cathedral musicians from amateurs (see Chapter 4). This is why, in addition to their rank as presbyters, candidates mentioned their positions in the chapel as "calidades" that made them worthy of a chaplaincy.[117] Others with lesser ranks (i.e., subdeacon, deacon) were not shy about setting forth their accomplishments either, especially because, with a chaplaincy, they could claim the income that was necessary to their being fully ordained. On March 8, 1735, for example, José Lázaro de Peñalosa stressed having served the cathedral since childhood and his current position as acolyte. The same document mentions Andrés Arnorin's time of service since he was a choirboy and his rank as deacon. Moreover, Ángel del Moral also emphasized his rank as subdeacon and his position as acolyte.[118]

All in all, these merits represented a trajectory of service and promotion in music ministries that projected a set of attributes telling of the social quality of the chaplains. The requirements to hold a chaplaincy were quite clear on this point and they outlined every single attribute desired in candidates. Chaplains had to be

> cleric presbyters that know plainchant well and that are good students, at least experts in Latin, precisely from New Spain, virtuous and of good social example; legitimate Spanish children . . . always preferring the most erudite and noble (*doctos y nobles*) from this city, and from among these the poorest of them. And for these appointments especial

care shall be given in choosing the priests with the most seniority in this church who work in ministries inferior to that of chaplain . . . so that this position can be an incentive for others to serve this church starting in lower ministries . . . and these chaplains shall enjoy all of the honors, graces, exemptions, and pre-eminences that all of those who form part of the choir enjoy . . . and they shall be treated in an equal manner, as they shall be equal in everything [to the other choir members] and without any difference (see appendix 3.4).[119]

If being fit for letters and the professions was an attribute of noble minds among Spaniards, a chaplaincy in the cathedral choir represented the recognition of such a condition ("always preferring the most erudite and noble"). This attribute was buttressed by the social value that education had among Spaniards (chaplains had to be "erudite") and that allowed individuals to develop careers after years of service and promotion. Even more significant was that chaplains acquired such status using music as a strategy to navigate the cathedral's hierarchy.

This aggregate of attributes (*calidades*), therefore, was a representation of the social appearance (that is, his *calidad* and overall status) that an individual articulated over the years and that he used as a means of social mobility. On occasion, chaplains requested written testimony of such representation—a certification of merit, as it was called—in order to find a better position elsewhere. In 1743, for example, Miguel Ángel Pavón requested a certification indicating that he had served the cathedral for twenty-eight years: fourteen years as choirboy, three as choirbook carrier, three as assistant in the choir, and eight as chaplain. Pavón mentioned that he would use this document in a trip to Madrid for whatever purposes he might find to his benefit.[120] Rivera requested the same in 1761. Records show that by that time Rivera had served as choirbook carrier, organist, assistant in the choir, singer in the chapel, and choir chaplain.[121] Just like Pavón, Rivera's intention was to send this testimony to Madrid, so he asked the secretary to specify in the document "the time and mode of his services to the church since he was a child, as well as his conduct and that of his relatives, who had served in the chapter, choir, and Colegio."[122]

Certification of merits given by *bachiller* Don Juan Roldán de Aránguiz, secretary of the illustrious and venerable dean and chapter of the holy metropolitan cathedral church of Mexico in favor of Don Martín Bernárdez de Rivera, presbyter, choir chaplain of said holy church, upon decree from said illustrious dean and chapter.

[I,] *bachiller* Don Juan Roldán de Aránguiz, presbyter and secretary of the dean and chapter of the holy metropolitan church of Mexico, certify by all possible means that Don Martín Bernárdez de Rivera, cleric presbyter of this archbishopric, is currently choir chaplain of this holy church and musician of its chapel, who was a student of the Colegio of Our Lady of the Assumption and Saint Joseph for choirboys for nine years with all around approval for behaving judiciously and with diligence, always fulfilling his obligations, for which he merited the attention of his instructors, whose report indicates that he went straight into the music chapel and without lingering in positions such as choirbook carrier or acolyte because of his music ability and development. And after more than ten years of having left the Colegio he continues in the ministries mentioned above with the same approval of all of the members of the chapter due to his demeanor, actions, and good example as a cleric, and without eliciting a complaint from anyone in more than twenty years. I also certify that his brother, Don Pedro Bernárdez de Rivera, was a choirboy of said Colegio, and also minister of the choir of this holy church, where doctor Don Juan Bernárdez de Rivera was half prebendary, prebendary, and treasury judge, and bachiller Antonio Bernárdez de Rivera was secretary of its venerable chapter. And therefore, I give the present document for all purposes that might be convenient upon request from Don Martín Bernárdez de Rivera, and upon decree from the illustrious and venerable dean and chapter (see appendix 3.6).[123]

If it is true that the concept of limpieza de sangre played a critical role in the efforts of American Spaniards to secure a place in the religious and political hierarchies of New Spain, certifications of merits were important instruments in the construction of a broader sense of "Spanishness." As career testimonials, certifications were meant to prove the educational preparation and time of service in the church of an individual, achievements that legitimized claims for economic rewards, social privileges, and status. Going back to the *encomienda* system of the sixteenth century, certifications of merit established the worthiness of claims of purity of blood among Spaniards. Together with proofs of purity, certifications of merit allowed individuals to hold religious and public offices and granted them almost immediate noble status.[124] In the same way that university students claimed nobility due to the occupation of their parents, the noble status of chaplains derived from the attributes and calidad that a chaplaincy recognized in the individual, and proofs of purity and certifications of merit worked together to corroborate a person's worthiness for this condition. In this respect, whereas the rampant claims for nobility made this a socially elusive category, its connection with proofs of limpieza and certifications of merit made it an intrinsic component of a historical and genealogical consciousness among Spaniards in New Spain, a consciousness that they used to define their social place through the discursive worthiness of their bloodline.[125]

There is no record that Sumaya was ever appointed to a choir chaplaincy (in the examination process that occurred in 1708, the position finally went to José de Loe Escandón). Sumaya's tenure of the highest position in the music chapel from 1715 to 1738 should not be interpreted as a failure or contentment on his part, especially considering how his story unfolded later. In 1738, after twenty-three years of service, mysteriously and without a warning, Sumaya left the cathedral of Mexico. Up until that year, his peer at the seminary and the university (so records show), Tomás Montaño, had served as arch dean of the cathedral and had been appointed bishop of Oaxaca, taking Sumaya with him as his personal chaplain to that city from which Sumaya did not return. Although informally, much has been speculated about Sumaya's sudden departure from Mexico City. In comparison, the cathedral of Oaxaca (where he eventually became chapelmaster) was a more humble church, whereas the position at the metropolitan cathedral was perhaps the most prestigious chapelmastership in New Spain, and possibly in Spanish America. Sumaya's motives are nothing short of intriguing, especially because there is no record that he held a higher ecclesiastical position in Oaxaca right after his arrival. Beyond any speculation, what is certain is that Sumaya left a precedent in terms of the profile that the chapter would come to expect from a chapelmaster after he left. The following chapter explores the tensions that arose with the candidacy of the Italian Ignacio Jerusalem to the chapelmastership at the cathedral of Mexico. The chapter suggests that such tensions possibly derived from the fact that Jerusalem's profile was quite different from Sumaya's. Given that for Sumaya and others, music was a strategy to articulate a discourse of status through the acquisition of knowledge, the chapter addresses how notions of erudition influenced notions of musicianship. Ultimately, this will show that epistemological understandings of music were influenced by the importance that academic education had in New Spain, and that such understandings also created differences in the perceptions of profiles among musicians.

4

Ignacio Jerusalem and Changes in Music Thought

Introduction

This chapter explores the tensions that surrounded the examination and appointment of Ignacio Jerusalem to the post of chapelmaster in 1750. The chapter shows that musicians and canons had reservations about Jerusalem mainly for two reasons. On the one hand, he did not have an institutional profile similar to that of former chapelmasters. On the other, his lack of "musical knowledge" according to cathedral standards made people doubt his fitness to be an authority figure in the chapel. The chapter highlights the institutional underpinnings that informed notions of musical knowledge in the cathedral. Such notions, the chapter argues, aligned music study with understandings of academic knowledge that had social value among Spaniards. The chapter shows that this understanding was important for musicians who developed careers in the church to construct discourses of status. The chapter concludes by showing that while Jerusalem's appointment brought about a change in cathedral music practices, it also triggered political frictions among musicians.

Politics in Music Thought

On the heels of a heated controversy, on August 3, 1750, Ignacio Jerusalem became the first Italian to hold the position of chapelmaster at the cathedral of Mexico. For musicians and the chapter this represented a turning point in the cathedral's musical life, as Jerusalem's views of music poetics were at odds with notions of musicianship that, until then, had formed the basis of music pedagogy, composition, and performance.[1] Originally from the region of Lecce in the Italian south, Jerusalem arrived in New Spain in 1743 under contract to work in Mexico City's Teatro Coliseo. In 1746, the cathedral chapter hired him

to help with the composition of *villancicos* (a poetic and musical genre of composition in Spanish language that was sung in some religious services, like the
matins service). This appointment gave him the opportunity to apply for the
vacant chapelmastership three years later. For this position, however, Jerusalem
was examined with the rigor of two centuries of musical tradition, according to
which he had to know counterpoint, a key component in a theoretical grammar
that informed notions of musicianship in Spanish ecclesiastical institutions.[2]
The results of the examination were painstakingly reviewed, for not only were
musicians in the chapel concerned about Jerusalem's "lack of cathedral experience" (*por no tener costumbre de catedral*) but also about the extent of his musical knowledge, despite the fact that some of the canons had originally regarded
him as "intelligent in all music and composition" (*inteligente en toda música y
composición*).[3]

Previously, scholars have thought that such reservations were a sign of the
weight that hyper-religious and orthodox attitudes had on music practices at
the cathedral of Mexico upon Jerusalem's arrival.[4] To some extent, this interpretation resonates with one of the most frequently cited critiques against the
incursion of Italian music trends in the Spanish church, that of Benito Jerónimo
Feijóo y Montenegro, who considered the Italianate style of theater music inferior to the "majesty" of Spanish sacred compositions.[5] Surviving works showing
Italian influence by Jerusalem's predecessor, Manuel Sumaya, and the eventual
appointment of Jerusalem himself as cathedral chapelmaster complicate this
interpretation, nonetheless. Sumaya's music shows that Italianate trends were
part of cathedral music practices by the second decade of the eighteenth century, which suggests that stylistic differences between the theater and the church
were not totally rigid.[6] This possibility makes reactions by Spanish musicians
and ecclesiastical authorities rather puzzling (if not politically suspicious), and
it is not surprising that some scholars have decided to dismiss them altogether.
In addition, the fact that previous studies promoted historical narratives of
"national music" based on these reactions also moved scholars to consider such
comments as a "historiographic cliché" that could only cloud our understanding
of Spanish musical life during this period.[7]

While this line of studies has made new inroads in our view of stylistic devel-
opments in early-modern Spanish sacred music, more recent scholarship has
sought to provide a more holistic account of music culture, encouraging a reas-
sessment of these tensions. Some of these new studies suggest that an exces-
sive focus on the church as an isolated center of European musical activity has
ignored how individuals interacted with this institution as they participated in
local musical life.[8] This research focuses on the interaction of individuals with
institutions to demonstrate the complex landscape of musical activity through
which people pursued different social agendas, and that enabled them to

define their place in society.[9] Ecclesiastical musicians could not be impervious to stylistic music changes because such changes had come to form part of the institution through which they claimed a social place. This suggests that while assessing the reactions of Spanish musicians to the incursion of Italian trends is important, the analysis ought to go beyond the realm of musical style. As mentioned in Chapter 3, for Spanish cathedral musicians, their institutional affiliation represented a pathway to enhanced social status in which notions of knowledge (of music) and purity of blood (Spanish blood), among other things, were important. People like Sumaya and others were part of this paradigm where counterpoint played a central role. But this does not mean that cathedral musicians were indifferent to Italianate trends, and some of Sumaya's music shows that. Nevertheless, there can be little doubt that, through his musical activity, Jerusalem moved beyond the polyphonic approaches that had been the model of music education at the cathedral. For musicians and the chapter, the problem was not that Jerusalem disregarded previous compositional practices but that he ignored theoretical principles that had institutional, and therefore, social value.

To consider reactions against Jerusalem as anachronisms dismisses the impact that aesthetic changes had on an institutional paradigm of social mobility that hinged on a specific understanding of musicianship. From a historical vantage point, Jerusalem's way of thinking about music spurred debates in the cathedral about what musicianship was (i.e., what it meant to "know" music, and what it meant to be a musician) mainly because of the sociopolitical interests that musicians pursued relying on musicianship as an important institutional component of their social quality and position. At the cathedral of Mexico, musicianship was a concept relying on notions of academic knowledge mainly because, as an activity, music enabled individuals to pursue an enhanced status in which erudition was important. This was especially true for Spanish musicians, who, coming from poor families, used their lineage as currency to enter the cathedral during childhood so they could take advantage of the opportunities for professional development that this institution offered. For these people, musicianship related to institutional standards of musical knowledge that were the basis of an individual's erudition, and mastery of these standards was necessary to advance in the cathedral's ranks. The post of chapelmaster acquired special significance in this context because it was a position of leadership and authority over a group of people who built their social profiles through this institutional model. For this reason, in the music chapel, views of leadership related not only to an individual's understanding of cathedral approaches to music pedagogy, composition, and performance (in which counterpoint was an important basis). Leadership also related to perceptions of a person's social quality (calidad) in relation to his hierarchical position in this system. Musicianship therefore represented more than a view of music poetics: it was a knowledge base that, due to its institutional underpinnings, enabled musicians to claim a higher social place. Against this backdrop, the tenure of the cathedral chapelmastership by Ignacio Jerusalem poses a fascinating case study about how changes in music aesthetics produced tensions among cathedral musicians due to the competing views of musical knowledge that this shift produced.

Archival records show that attitudes toward Jerusalem were influenced by mixed reactions about his musicianship and background, views that, interestingly, also inform appraisals of his profile in extant scholarship today. In contrast to Robert Stevenson's earliest description of Jerusalem as a parvenu, later scholars have emphasized that Jerusalem's compositional skill might have been overlooked in Stevenson's appraisal. In their assessment of his music they suggest that he was likely well esteemed during his time, as he was referred to as *el milagro musical* (the musical miracle).[10] These contrasting assessments provide an interesting historical parallel to the social and political tensions that surrounded Jerusalem's life in New Spain. If it is true that Stevenson's "parvenu" remark might not account for Jerusalem's compositional craft, it does point to his sudden rise to a position of leadership that, in the opinion of cathedral authorities and musicians, he was unfit to hold.[11] This chapter suggests that while cathedral standards of music erudition enabled Spanish musicians to claim status, Jerusalem also considered his compositional skills in Italianate trends an asset in aspiring to the privileges associated with this institutional affiliation. After all, members of the chapter had supported his admission to the music chapel due to his being "intelligent in all music and composition."[12] But while some thought that the "advanced and exquisite state of the art of music"[13] required individuals of such intelligence, others doubted that Jerusalem was fit to lead the chapel given his lack of "music erudition." This apparent lack of knowledge weighed heavy in the canons' minds. On the one hand, it put in question his ability to be the authority figure of an ecclesiastical corporation (i.e., the music chapel). On the other, it accentuated their reservations about his theatrical background. In contrast, records show that Jerusalem relied on his compositional abilities to qualify his expertise in current aesthetic trends and to legitimize his institutional position and the benefits due to him as "*maestro* by decree." This chapter, therefore, takes the case of Ignacio Jerusalem as a point of departure to explore the political tensions permeating shifts in music thought at the cathedral of Mexico during the eighteenth century. This assessment considers the competing views of musical knowledge that derived from this shift and the social interests that these views supported. Ultimately, the chapter illustrates how Jerusalem's appointment altered an institutional paradigm of status construction in which notions of musical knowledge were important, and how this led to political tensions in the music chapel. These tensions are the focus of Chapter 5.

Profiling a Chapelmaster

In 1743, an agent sent to Spain by José Cárdenas Guzmán y Flores (manager of the Teatro Coliseo) signed Ignacio Jerusalem along with seventeen other individuals to come to work in Mexico City.[14] According to Robert Stevenson, the contract specified that performances at the theater were to begin on March 1744, suggesting that Jerusalem arrived in the city the previous year. It is well known that he approached the cathedral looking for work in 1746, something not unusual among Coliseo musicians who tried to supplement their income by playing in a church. After all, work in the theater was seasonal and there was no exclusivity clause in his contract with Cárdenas Guzmán y Flores.[15] At that moment, the cathedral needed someone to compose villancicos, and seemingly there was no other composer in the city, so one could say that Jerusalem's arrival was timely. This would not be the first time that the cathedral chapter hired someone to help with the composition of new music. In 1710, for example, Sumaya had been appointed to assist chapelmaster Antonio de Salazar with this task.[16] Similar cases had occurred with previous chapelmasters, like Francisco López Capillas, for whom the chapter appointed Guillermo Carvajal as assistant composer in 1669; or Fabián Ximeno, who was assisted by Juan Coronado in 1658.[17] Upon Jerusalem's arrival, however, some canons voiced concerns about his theatrical background (possibly because previous assistants had been primarily ecclesiastical musicians) while others wondered whether he was even married.[18] Travel records showed that Jerusalem was indeed married, and in the end the majority of chapter members did not see his involvement in the theater unfavorably (*no le perjudicaba*).[19] Thus, Jerusalem came to share responsibilities with Domingo Dutra y Andrade, a presbyter and singer in the chapel who was put in charge of musical activities after Sumaya left the cathedral in 1738. It is important to note that by hiring Jerusalem the chapter was not considering him for the post of chapelmaster. The cathedral was in need of a composer, so the canons thought that Jerusalem could be useful, and as he was reputed to be intelligent in all music and types of composition, they employed him only for his compositional skills.[20]

Jerusalem's appointment was very possibly a way of complementing Dutra y Andrade's duties, as he was probably not a composer and served mostly in an administrative capacity, according to primary sources. For the most part, making inventories of music materials and administering obvenciones (earnings from paid performances outside of the cathedral) comprised the bulk of Dutra y Andrade's activity.[21] Moreover, in treasury records his name was registered as musician and not as composer, the reason he did not get paid for villancicos performed during major feasts (e.g., Saint Peter), when private endowments paid for newly composed pieces every year.[22] Other information suggests that

Dutra y Andrade was possibly self-conscious about the extent of his music skills, which supports the idea that he did not hold a position of leadership in the chapel. The minutes from a chapter meeting held on July 29, 1735, for example, indicate that some musicians thought he should not have been in charge of teaching the choirboys (a duty usually carried out by the chapelmaster) because he did not have adequate knowledge of music. The minutes also show that Dutra y Andrade gave in to these comments without contest and asked to be removed from the task so that a better person could be appointed.[23] But Jerusalem's arrival probably dealt a harder blow to his confidence, as he fell into a state of depression right after this. Seemingly, Dutra y Andrade interpreted Jerusalem's hiring as a sign that the chapter had lost esteem for him because of his limited skills.[24] Given his long-standing service to the cathedral the chapter felt sorry for him, and in order to lift his spirits the canons agreed to appoint him nominally as chapelmaster, although without assigning any extra salary and only until a suitable candidate for the post appeared.[25] His image among musicians did not improve with this appointment, however, and it only aggravated his depression. After a while it became obvious that "due to his condition, he cannot take care of anything, for which the chapel lacks governance."[26] Therefore, the chapter asked Dutra y Andrade to retire in 1749, right after which the canons issued an *edicto* (call for applications) to fill the chapelmaster vacancy.

Dutra y Andrade's case suggests that in appointing him nominally, the chapter was well aware that he did not meet the requirements of a chapelmaster, not the least because his musical knowledge was questionable. The fact that the canons agreed to his "nominal" appointment only until a suitable candidate could be found only adds weight to this conclusion. If perceptions of knowledge appear particularly linked to views of leadership in relation to the position of chapelmaster it is because of the value that knowledge had among Spaniards. As mentioned in Chapter 3, having an aptitude for letters and the professions was a particularly important attribute for Spaniards wishing to move up in the social ladder. Knowledge was central to proofs of calidad, given that erudition reflected years of study and preparation in developing a career, something that enabled individuals to claim social status. In this regard, scholars consider that the growth in university graduation rates during the eighteenth century relates specifically to the value that academic study added to an individual's status. The enhancement in status did not relate to one's field of study but to the positions that one could obtain in public and religious institutions.[27]

The designation of status and privilege through this institutional paradigm was not arbitrary; it stemmed from a racialized corporate mentality that was integral to the cultural baggage that Spain brought to America and that was in full operation in New Spain during the eighteenth century.[28] Chapter 3 showed that for Spaniards from poor families, music was an avenue through which to pursue this institutional model of social mobility in the cathedral, and the canons recruited choirboys with this purpose in mind. As cathedral musicians acquired a heightened political identity after a lifetime of institutional service, it is reasonable to think that the position of chapelmaster held special significance and weight in this context. For this reason, appointing a chapelmaster was a delicate matter, involving a rigorous process of evaluation that went beyond the compositional abilities of an individual. Ultimately, the chosen person acted not merely as composer but also as administrator, pedagogue, performer, choir director, conductor, and business manager of the music chapel.[29] A chapelmaster needed to possess an aggregate of attributes that placed him as authority, and thus, as liaison of a Spanish corporate group in society. Dutra y Andrade was far from possessing this profile, and canons and musicians were aware of this. As a composer Jerusalem possessed skills that quite possibly made him more versatile than other musicians. After all, the canons knew that music was "very advanced and different from past times,"[30] and Jerusalem's proficiency in these trends was indeed an asset. Given the importance of such aesthetic changes— and that there was no other composer in the city at that moment—this position with the cathedral probably represented an opportunity for higher corporate employment for Jerusalem. The problem was that, aesthetic changes notwithstanding, these abilities did not necessarily legitimize someone's place as cathedral chapelmaster, especially considering that the institutional profile of the last leader—Manuel Sumaya—in all probability still loomed in the memory of cathedral musicians.

In contrast to Jerusalem (who was a theater musician recently arrived in New Spain), Sumaya was an example of someone for whom music was a means of institutional advancement and a strategy for the construction of his social profile. He not only rose through the ranks to become an organist but also pursued academic study to become a priest. Records show that Sumaya most probably got his bachiller degree and the tonsure in 1700, one year after he was appointed choir assistant.[31] After this, he continued his upward trajectory through the ranks of subdeacon (1702), deacon (1704), and presbyter (1705).[32] As mentioned in Chapter 3, this path was necessary if one wished to become choir chaplain, which Sumaya attempted in 1708. The fact that he did not attain a chaplaincy at that time, however, does not mean that he held a less prominent position in the music chapel.

Academic preparation was important, and notions of musical knowledge were influenced by this view, with theoretical study acquiring an academic tone as a type of "erudition." Only by proving that they had this knowledge could youths like Sumaya advance to higher positions in a hierarchy of music-related ministries. In the case of Sumaya, he became assistant organist and choir assistant in 1698 and 1699, respectively. Eventually he received appointments as assistant composer (1710) and chapelmaster (1715). Sumaya's institutional profile and rank in the chapel related not only to his knowledge of Latin grammar and liturgical and instrumental performance but also to his knowledge of counterpoint as the basis of his erudition as a musician. The chapter required its musicians to learn counterpoint—especially those reared in the Colegio de Infantes—but the fact of the matter was that not all were very proficient in it. In an assessment that Antonio de Salazar made of cathedral musicians in 1709 he was careful to separate the names of those who showed progress in their music studies from those who did not and outlined the main deficiencies of people in the latter group. For Sumaya, however, Salazar dedicated a separate paragraph to highlight his merits:

> In the same form, and under the same oath, I mention to your lordship, to rest my conscience, that bachiller Don Manuel Sumaya is such an eminent composer of counterpoint that he could be chapelmaster in the royal chapel of his majesty. He has just finished a Mass for the day of the Conception of Our Lady, which I could not have accomplished with all of my duties (see appendix 4.1).[33]

It was because of his skills that the canons appointed Sumaya to assist Salazar with the composition of all the music needed for ritual purposes as well as with the teaching of counterpoint in 1710.[34] The appointment was probably encouraged by Salazar himself, who was unable to fulfill these tasks because of his deteriorating sight and health.

Although these allusions to Sumaya's contrapuntal knowledge make reference to his compositional abilities, there was an important theoretical component behind it. Primary sources show that, as a theoretical principle in music education, counterpoint had probably the deepest institutional meaning and value in terms of how it related to views of musical knowledge, a central element in establishing status claims among cathedral musicians.[35] At the cathedral of Mexico, "knowledge of music" alluded to musicianship (i.e., what it meant to know music and to be a musician), an attribute that reflected the experience of an institutional model of education that departed from the rhetoric of Spanish music treatises. This model gave musicianship an academic character as a type of erudition, and counterpoint was an important component of this notion. This is not to say that cathedral music practices were limited to the performance of contrapuntal music. Surviving pieces by Sumaya show that newer stylistic trends in composition were part of cathedral music practices by the second decade of the eighteenth century.[36] Pieces such as "Hoy Sube Arrebatada" (1719) and "Ya La Gloria Accidental" (dated 1715 by Alice Ray Catalyne) are good examples of this. In "Ya La Gloria Accidental," shown in Example 4.1, the harmonic movement

Ya La Gloria Accidental

Manuel Sumaya
ca. 1680 - 1755

Example 4.1 Continued

Ya La Gloria Accidental, continued

and rushing vocal and instrumental melodic lines are stylistically aligned with the Italianate trends of what people called *música moderna* or music in the *estilo moderno*.[37] Moreover, primary sources show that arias and cantadas had become common by 1750, and the cathedral chapter and musicians considered such music an indicator of the "advanced and exquisite state of the art of music" at that time.[38]

Despite these innovations, counterpoint continued to be a central component of music pedagogy for the cathedral chapter, and thus, of good musicianship. This is something that the canons were very clear about, and they reiterated this understanding when they considered accepting Jerusalem's application for the position of chapelmaster. Specifically, the chapter stated: "counterpoint is necessary in order to know how to compose and make music."[39] Robert Stevenson has mentioned that such focus on counterpoint derived from Sevillian custom—which the cathedral of Mexico observed as the sister church of Seville's cathedral—and was likely informed by Spanish music treatises that circulated in New Spain.[40] Extant scholarship mentions that Pedro Cerone (*El melopeo y maestro*), Andrés Lorente (*El porqué de la música*), and Pablo Nassarre

(*Escuela música según la práctica moderna*) were the authors most widely known in the New World throughout the seventeenth and eighteenth centuries.[41] Considering that Cerone influenced Lorente and Nassarre substantially, it is not surprising that some historical studies have devoted more attention to the Italian theorist.[42]

Cerone's *melopeo* (and by consequence Lorente's and Nassarre's treatises) not only considers counterpoint as the foundational element of music-making, but also makes a sharp distinction between *música especulativa* (or *teórica*) and *música práctica* as categories of musical knowledge. While the latter referred to an ability to compose and perform, the first term denoted an acquired capacity to understand music from a theoretical basis, as well as being able to communicate such understanding.[43] This is the notion that other Spanish theorists took from Cerone, which became a trope in narratives about what characterized "true musicians." For example, Nassarre observed that there were composers who called themselves "wise *maestros*" whose lack of knowledge was "an attack on reason itself." A composer, he wrote, "ought to understand everything through speculation (i.e., música especulativa) so that the practical aspect of music is done with propriety."[44] Moreover, when referring to instrumentalists and singers in the theater who dared to call themselves musicians, Cerone declared that because of their lack of knowledge, it was inconceivable that "these ignorant people place themselves in community with virtuous maestros and excellent musicians."[45]

Archival records show that cathedral pedagogical approaches strongly agreed with these tenets, and that the chapter made a clear distinction between theory and practice when gauging an individual's musicianship. For example, when chapelmaster Matheo Tollis de la Rocca examined a choirboy in 1781, he said that he was "more or less well taught in theoretical [music] and in practical [music]."[46] Primary sources also show that the word "music" was used only and exclusively to refer to theoretical aspects, especially when the canons examined someone who auditioned for the music chapel. For instance, José Salvatierra, violin player, was examined in "violin performance and in music" before joining the ensemble.[47] On September 15, 1751, the singer Juan Baptista Sánchez was also "examined in music and made a demonstration of his voice."[48] Of José Pissoni the chapter said that he was "very intelligent in music and has proficiency in violin and trumpet."[49] Moreover, when choirboy Francisco Cerezo was ready to audition for a post as instrumentalist in the chapel the canons asked the chapelmaster to examine him "in music and in his instrument."[50] After examining Juan Rodríguez, the chapter was told that "as far as instrumental proficiency in violin goes, he is capable, and as a musician he needs more study."[51] The extent to which knowledge of music was valued and required to join the chapel is also addressed in sources showing that musicians were dismissed from the ensemble for lacking musical knowledge. Such was the case of Sebastián de Hereida who after taking a leave of absence was not readmitted because he did not know music.[52]

Sources show that cathedral music education largely emphasized plainchant, counterpoint, and *canto de órgano* (roughly translated as "organ chant." This is a term that today seems to be generally understood as applicable to polyphonic music.)[53] However, in these sources, counterpoint and canto de órgano appear as interchangeable terms, and music treatises do little to explain this. In *El melopeo*, Cerone mentions that counterpoint is a concerted mode of singing with voices that are almost juxtaposed.[54] Cerone further observes that canto de órgano is "metric music" (*música métrica*), understood as a diversity of unequal figures, the duration of which is augmented or diminished according to the mode, time (*tiempo*), and prolation.[55] The author suggests a relationship between both terms (counterpoint and canto de órgano) through an understanding of *música rítmica*, which he relates to composition without further explanation; the basis of both, he says (música rítmica and composition), is counterpoint.[56] If for Cerone música rítmica had a direct relation to the ways in which "metric music" (canto de órgano) organized sound in time, it is possible that canto de órgano was understood as the compositional realization of counterpoint. Lorente adds more weight to this possibility. In *El porqué de la música* he cites Cerone's definition of counterpoint almost verbatim. However, Lorente adds that counterpoint is a number made up of different consonances, and that this number acquires definition in the art of canto de órgano, the latter being made up of a multiplicity of units arranged in binary or ternary patterns.[57] Nassarre also follows Cerone in his definition of counterpoint, which he explains as a harmonious concordance of juxtaposed voices. Nassarre echoes Cerone's and Lorente's definition of canto de órgano as well.[58] Regarding the relationship of both terms, Nassarre further repeats Cerone's words about música rítmica being the art of composition (*compostura*) and its origin being counterpoint.[59]

More recently, scholars have pointed out that, while canto de órgano possibly alluded to the practical realization of counterpoint, counterpoint could have also referred to an improvisatory skill and not just to a conceptual compositional procedure.[60] In his book *From Serra to Sancho*, Craig H. Russell emphasizes this possibility. Russell suggests that, on etymological terms, canto de órgano was linked as much to the idea of counterpoint as to the organ as a musical instrument.[61] For this reason, he adds, the two ideas (counterpoint and canto de órgano, texture and instrument, concept and practice) were intertwined and not easily separated, either compositionally or in performance.[62] Archival records from the cathedral of Mexico show this to be the case. For example, in a letter to the chapter from 1710, Antonio de Salazar asked to be excused from teaching counterpoint to musicians due to his old age and poor health. In this letter,

Salazar stressed that, after all, this was something that only could benefit those interested in composition or in becoming succentors.

> A letter from Antonio de Salazar was read today . . . in which he asks to be excused from attending the escoleta to teach counterpoint to all of the musicians and choirboys, as well as to one or two individuals to prepare them to be succentors, for the cited reasons: his frail health, not being necessary that all singers [in the chapel] know counterpoint to be proficient [in singing], being sixty years old, and almost blind (see appendix 4.2).[63]

Moreover, in a different letter complaining about Manuel de Cárdenas—an individual whom the chapter expected to become succentor—Salazar commented how he had failed to learn canto de órgano, something that he considered necessary for this position.

> Bachiller Don Manuel de Cárdenas, who earns 200 pesos, which his lordship assigned to him as salary so that he could improve in canto de órgano to become succentor, from the day in which he received such money until today, he has not taken one single lesson (see appendix 4.3).[64]

Despite Salazar's suggestions, records show that the cathedral chapter continued to enforce the learning of counterpoint among all musicians, regardless of instrument, and these documents also show the mixed use of both terms. For example, when singer Francisco Gabriel de Aguilar petitioned to be hired in the music chapel he stressed the qualities of his voice, as well as his "intelligence" in counterpoint.[65] The cases of Juan Thadeo Priego and Juan de Montesdeoca y Amaya are also consistent on this point. Instead of counterpoint, however, documents mention that both individuals were examined in canto de órgano before joining the chapel.[66] Records related to the teaching of choirboys show that counterpoint and canto de órgano were interchangeable terms. When asking for the choirbooks to teach the boys, Diego López de Lois (who was helping Antonio de Salazar with this task) referred to "the books of canto de órgano," the term that Juan Pérez used twenty-one years later for the same purposes.[67] This information suggests that for cathedral authorities, "intelligence in music," referred to an aspect of music learning in which counterpoint had theoretical and performance dimensions. It is not known which type of study the cathedral chapter required from musicians in order for them to be considered "knowledgeable." We know that choirboys were instructed in plainchant and counterpoint but there are no records that outline specifically how the latter was taught. Moreover, we do not know whether the same was required of instrumentalists;

most of the sources that mention counterpoint are from singers. What is definitely sure is that the chapter made a distinction between practical ability (either singing or playing an instrument) and knowledge of music. Just as music treatises differentiated between música especulativa and música práctica, the canons used the word "music" exclusively to refer to a theoretical and intellectual basis. As not all musicians became clerics (and therefore neither succentors nor choir assistants), it is possible that counterpoint functioned as a line of demarcation to define musicianship, if not practically (not all music performed was contrapuntal), at least conceptually. Seemingly, this type of knowledge was the theoretical apparatus that legitimized music study from an academic vantage point, and that distinguished cathedral musicians by their erudition.

Knowledge of music was indeed important if one wanted to climb through the cathedral ranks, and primary sources indicate this with considerable detail. Chapter 3 showed how children willing to develop an institutional career advanced in a line of ministries that included being a choirboy, choirbook carrier, acolyte, musician in the chapel, and assistant to either the organists or in the choir. Cathedral authorities closely monitored the development of children through each of these positions and every year tested them on *gramática, música y propiedades* (grammar, music, and properties). More specifically, these labels alluded to knowledge of Latin, music principles, and a child's proficiency in either singing or playing an instrument.[68] Of these, however, "music" was the element that the canons stressed the most, to the extent that children were not allowed to learn either grammar or an instrument during their first year at the Colegio, so that they could focus only on "music."[69]

Miguel Ángel Pavón provides a good illustration of this, as he was required to show his knowledge of music before surrendering his post as choirbook carrier to become acolyte in 1734.[70] In turn, vacated choirbook carrying posts were given to children who also showed progress in their studies (such as Joaquín Pacheco and Timoteo Torres y Cuevas in 1746).[71] After six years, boys were ready to leave the Colegio, and in their letters they emphasized that their years of service as choirboy, choirbook carrier, and acolyte were accomplishments that reflected their growth and development and that made them suitable for a vacancy in the chapel. The case of singer Francisco Gabriel de Aguilar shows that counterpoint, however, was the first thing that the canons checked before making an appointment. Like other choirboys, Aguilar was well aware of this, and in his petition he emphasized that his vocal proficiency and his "intelligence in counterpoint" were qualities (calidades) that made him worthy of a position in the music chapel.[72] Due to the limited number of vacancies, Aguilar had to wait four years before joining the ensemble, and records indicate that the canons tested him again even then.[73] This shows that counterpoint, as indicative of musical knowledge, enabled youths to climb a hierarchical ladder of positions devoted to music and ritual. Moreover, if the word "calidades" appears consistently in archival records it is because the aggregate of these appointments represented important attributes that established an individual's merit for future advancement.[74] Moreover, surviving information and music sources suggest that contrapuntal music by Spanish composers such as Cristobal de Morales, Tomás Luis de Victoria, Francisco Guerrero, and Alonso Lobo likely served as the pedagogical model of this understanding, at least throughout the first half of the eighteenth century, and that it was possibly still in use until the 1780s.[75] It is true that aesthetic changes also introduced pedagogical needs to teach students how to perform music in the estilo moderno. However, there is no evidence that there was a treatise or method in New Spain that addressed these needs, which partially explains why cathedral authorities continued to endorse traditional theoretical approaches throughout the eighteenth century: it was the only pedagogical tool available to teach music from an academic standpoint in New Spain.[76]

If notions of leadership and authority in the music chapel relied on perceptions of erudition it was because knowledge was at the center of a paradigm of promotion and career development in Spanish institutions. When it came to music, counterpoint was a central component of musical knowledge. Possessing this attribute enabled musicians to follow an institutional trajectory that created social differences between them and amateurs or unaffiliated musicians, mainly because of the calidad that the institutional membership and knowledge of the first reflected. Considering that Sumaya had spent all of his life working, studying, learning, and advancing through the ranks under this paradigm, it is reasonable to think that his profile as a knowledgeable musician, university graduate, and presbyter still weighed heavy in the minds of his peers as a model of what a chapelmaster ought to be. Moreover, Salazar's way of thinking about music was possibly a sort of ontology that chapel musicians of this generation shared in common, of which Sumaya was regarded as the most accomplished example. Furthermore, the cathedral chapter had decided to follow the guidelines used for Sumaya's appointment in 1715 as a model for the examination in 1750. Therefore, it is quite probable that Jerusalem was compared to the previous chapelmaster in all matters related to this position. This was very likely the mentality that Jerusalem encountered in 1746—despite music's advanced state—which possibly inspired reservations among canons and musicians about his ability to be a leader in the chapel.

Música Práctica versus Música Especulativa

For Jerusalem, the first three years of employment (1746–1749) passed without noteworthy events. Primary sources mostly document payments due to him from the composition of misereres and for repairing and renumbering the collection of chant books.[77] It was as soon as he applied for the vacant chapel-mastership that problems started. On November 28, 1749, Jerusalem formally submitted his candidacy for the post.[78] The moment seemed ideal: the canons had asked Dutra y Andrade to retire and there was no other composer in the city. Sixty days passed without an answer from the chapter, however. Seemingly, Jerusalem's was the only application that the canons had received, and so they decided to extend the deadline, this time sending copies of the call to Puebla, Guadalajara, Valladolid (now Morelia), and Oaxaca in hopes of attracting more candidates.[79] Despite these efforts Jerusalem still remained the only applicant by April 7, 1750, when he inquired once again about the status of his request, but the chapter remained silent.[80] The canons' hesitation could be indicative of an interest to enlarge the pool of applicants, but other information suggests that perceptions of Jerusalem's profile were possibly a factor too. This was because some members of the chapter doubted that he could lead the chapel. For one, some canons had observed that musicians "did not respect him, and never would, because of the roughhouse rapport that he has with them."[81] Not only did he lack experience in composing music for the church, but he also seemed to neglect his duties, something that people associated with the atmosphere of informality and lack of discipline of the theater. As a former musician and conductor of the Teatro Coliseo, Jerusalem knew this environment only too well.[82] Considering that cathedral musicians were regarded as church ministers, perhaps Jerusalem's informality tinged views of his social profile given his theater background. After all, church musicians claimed being *gente decente* (see Chapter 5), and theater musicians and actors were quite removed from such status. It is true that, upon hiring him in 1746, members of the chapter had said that Jerusalem's theatrical activity was not detrimental (*no le perjudicaba*) to his being a musician and composer in the music chapel. However, it was one thing to join the music chapel and quite another to become its chapelmaster.

As no other candidate responded to the call for applications, the canons agreed to examine Jerusalem on June 30, 1750, but not without hesitation.[83] A series of concerns spurred the examination, especially among the canons, as some realized that political tensions were likely to arise from the reservations addressed above. It is possibly for this reason that the canons thought the examination was necessary to legitimize the appointment—even if Jerusalem was the only candidate—lest musicians would not respect and obey him.[84] Although perceptions of his background and demeanor certainly raised eyebrows, doubts about his musical knowledge were of special concern. Specifically, primary sources point toward contradictory considerations of music poetics, in which vexing opinions about Jerusalem's knowledge formed the basis of a heated debate. The canons had decided to look back at the call for applications used in

1715—when Sumaya competed for the chapelmastership against Franciso de Atienza—so that it could serve as a model to issue a new call for this examination. The 1715 document read thus:

> To all musicians and instructors . . . we make known that the chapel-mastership of this holy church is vacant due to the passing of Antonio de Salazar, last possessor. And given that it is necessary to appoint a capable person to this post, who can write and will write all of the compositions needed in the choir according to how it has been done by previous maestros who have been in this holy church, we issue our letter and call for applications, through which we summon all musician composers who would like to make opposition (*oposición*) to the chapel-mastership of this holy church, to come to us fifteen days after the day of the posting of this notice to demonstrate their sufficiency and skill in such art, and after this we will do them justice by appointing the one who has such skill as chapelmaster with the salary of 500 pesos, in addition to obvenciones (see appendix 4.4).[85]

All in all, the tenor of the document seems to be straightforward: it summons, specifically, musicians who can demonstrate their skills in the art of composition. The canons alluded to such art not only with the mention of "musician composers," but also by stating that the cathedral needed someone to write all music for the choir. However, there seems to be something that for musicians and the chapter was implied in this document, specifically in relation to their views of composition and the profile of composers.

If Cerone—who was apparently a theoretical cornerstone for Spanish writers like Lorente and Nassarre—gives any clues to this, it is in consideration of how counterpoint was possibly associated with these two terms (i.e., composition and composers). As mentioned above, for Cerone counterpoint was the basis of the art of composition. While singers and instrumentalists were probably not required to know counterpoint in such depth (theoretically and compositionally), the case was different for a chapelmaster. Cerone considered counterpoint to be a key component of the theoretical knowledge base that a composer needed to have, and it is possible that this understanding permeated the drafting of the call for applications from 1715. Moreover, a composer needed to have such a broad theoretical understanding of music, according to him (i.e., música especulativa), so that the practical aspect of music (composition and performance) could be done with propriety. Given that Salazar—for whom counterpoint was a necessary component in the education of those interested in composition—had influenced a whole generation of individuals in the music chapel, this is an issue worth considering. For Salazar, Cerone's *El melopeo y maestro* was a scholarly measure to legitimize counterpoint as an important component of cathedral music practices, as we discuss below. If Salazar shaped ways of thinking about music at the cathedral during his tenure—which he probably did—then, it should not be surprising that Cerone was at the center of his efforts. Records relevant to his evaluation of candidates for the chapelmastership at the cathedral of Oaxaca add weight to this possibility.

In 1707, the chapter of the cathedral of Oaxaca examined four individuals for the post of chapelmaster. The pieces written by each person were sent to Mexico City cathedral for evaluation, where Salazar served as juror. In his essay "Carrasco or Mathías? Plagiarism and Corruption in an Eighteenth-Century *Examen de Oposición* from the Oaxaca Cathedral," Mark Brill addresses Salazar's evaluation process. Brill shows that the chapelmaster's critique of the candidates' compositions departed from Cerone as a basis to gauge their knowledge of music.[86] Although the title of the article suggests that the case of plagiarism by one of the candidates (Juan Tovar de Carrasco, who allegedly used parts of a piece by Juan Mathías in his own composition) is the center of discussion, Salazar's reaction to the music of Francisco de Herrera y Mota is no less intriguing.

As part of the examination, candidates were asked to compose a motet in imitation on a given plainchant, as well as to write a villancico based on a text provided in advance. While the writing of villancicos required a specific process to set music according to the images evoked in the text, the writing of the motet is what usually showed a composer's music erudition. For this, Herrera y Mota was asked to write a four-part counterpoint based on the Mass introit for the day of Saint Peter. In addition, he had to write a four-part counterpoint on the hymn "Decora lux" sung at vespers during the same feast.[87] According to Brill, Salazar's assessment of Herrera y Mota's music is largely scathing. Seemingly, Salazar wanted to show that Herrera y Mota's mistakes derived from his lack of musical knowledge according to "classical authors in the field." Salazar shows that such knowledge could be inferred if the candidate had demonstrated an appropriate handling of chant melodies, chant tones, clefs, as well as an adequate lowering of B flats, which, judging from the first piece, he did not. Because of these errors, it seemed apparent that Herrera y Mota "must not have been aware of Don Pedro Cerone."[88] The composer's ignorance was further corroborated, according to Salazar, by the way he wrote the hymn, in which he took many liberties with the chant.

Brill agrees with Salazar's assessment in that Herrera y Mota approached the plainchant melody rather whimsically, something that indeed defeated the purpose of the examination. Brill also agrees with the improper handling of B flats in the first piece, and with the improper writing of clefs, although, in the final analysis, he considers Salazar's comments "unfair, given the quality of the piece."[89]

There is a very good possibility that Salazar was biased (as Brill suggests) toward one of the candidates, Juan Pérez de Guzmán, who grew up as a choirboy at the cathedral of Mexico and was his student. The chapelmaster's praise of Pérez de Guzmán's composition and the derisive tone with which he critiqued the others shows a tone of partiality, at least. Nevertheless, it is hard to entirely dismiss Salazar's criticism as pure bias given Herrera y Mota's mistakes. Although a personal appraisal by Brill of Herrera y Mota's piece would have provided more clarity about the quality of his music, in all probability this analysis would show that Herrera y Mota was breaking away from the paradigm of musical knowledge that Salazar and the canons at the cathedral of Mexico observed. As a matter of fact, Brill gives a further hint that this might be the case.

After reading Salazar's evaluation, the Oaxaca chapter opted not to appoint a chapelmaster. Instead, they asked the chapelmaster from the cathedral of Puebla, Miguel de la Riva y Paz, to examine Herrera y Mota individually. This examination involved a questionnaire about theoretical elements according to traditional Spanish treatises (Brill mentions Cerone, Lorente, and Francisco de Montanos),[90] as well as an evaluation of a new motet and a new villancico written for this occasion. This time, so it seems, Herrera y Mota was careful to do his homework: Riva y Paz not only found Herrera y Mota knowledgeable in music according to these writers, but his compositions also leaned more to the traditional side. Riva y Paz wrote that, although in Puebla and Spain music was written in a "newer style," this should not be a reason to disregard the pieces written by Herrera y Mota in this second examination. With proper training, Riva y Paz said, the composer could "easily execute what is practiced today."[91] Riva y Paz's letter does not provide an analysis of Herrera y Mota's music and Brill's final comments help little to know how different these pieces were from the ones evaluated by Salazar. Nevertheless, Brill's essay points to important conclusions. The incursion of modern trends in composition and performance were already inspiring some individuals to move beyond the limits of an established tradition in Spanish sacred music writing. Herrera y Mota possibly was an example of that, for even though he seemingly knew the tenets of such tradition (as the assessment by Riva de Paz suggests), his creative and more personal approaches toward contrapuntal music (first evaluated by Salazar) were at odds with the parameters that defined musical knowledge at the cathedral of Mexico.

Regarding the centrality of Cerone in the understanding of this tradition there are antecedents that point to him well before Salazar. Recent scholarship has shown the wide diffusion that *El melopeo y maestro* had in the New World.[92] This treatise was a common item in the personal libraries of chapelmasters, indicating its influence in early modern Spanish music thought.[93] More specifically, Cerone was central to a tradition that was contrapuntally understood. Counterpoint was a foundation of music thought and also a central trait of a "school" of music-making that musicians considered to be distinctively "Spanish."[94] In the case of the cathedral of Mexico, there is evidence showing that Francisco López Capillas (chapelmaster from 1654 to 1673) was heavily influenced by Cerone, and that Cerone was possibly a mainstay in cathedral music education during the seventeenth century.[95] One of the cathedral choir-books (labeled MEX-Mc: MéxC 6 by Javier Marín López) contains two masses composed by López Capillas, and in an included preface (labeled *Declaracion de la Missa* or Explanation of the Mass) the chapelmaster mentions the influence that Cerone had in his compositional approach to these works.[96] Also well documented is the extent to which Sor Juana Inés de la Cruz's music thought was influenced by Cerone; she not only had her own heavily annotated copy of *El melopeo y maestro*, but scholars have also speculated that it was through her collaborations with López Capillas that the Geronimite nun probably became acquainted with this treatise.[97]

Some scholars suggest that Cerone's intention was to write for "practical musicians," as the treatise seems "free of mathematical and philosophical pedantry to an astonishing degree, essentially human . . . scholarly, clear, and sincere."[98] To this reading one must juxtapose two points. The first point is that Cerone's aim was to help individuals become "perfect musicians" (*músico perfecto*). The second point is that late seventeenth- and eighteenth-century New Spanish musicians related to this treatise without dismissing the philosophical overtones that possibly permeated music study. As an academically educated nun, Sor Juana considered that such was the basis of genuine music understanding, which was in itself a "steppingstone of the human arts and sciences" and necessary to climb to the "pinnacle of sacred theology."[99] Sor Juana approached music through this intellectual mindset, and it is not surprising that for her the mathematical component of music rested at the core of a Pythagorean speculative tradition that considered music a science: "the intellectual discipline of reflecting on music and its place in the universe, its mathematical structures, its philosophical and psychological implications."[100]

Recent scholarship has suggested that, in all possibility, it was not Cerone but Athanasius Kircher who was the basis of this intellectual paradigm. Specifically, scholars have proposed that, due to the presence of contemporaries of Kircher in New Spain, the ideas of this theorist most likely permeated music thought. What seems interesting about this argument is its unproblematic assumption about Kircher's influence, specifically in regard to Sor Juana's and Juan Gutierrez de Padilla's musical thinking (the latter was chapelmaster at the cathedral of Puebla from 1629 to 1664). "Although there is no proof or documentation about what [Gutierrez de Padilla] read or about his social circle, that is no impediment to imagine that his compositions used concepts expressed by [Kircher]."[101] A less imaginative reading of Cerone shows that he attributed the "immortal rules" of music to Kircher, but also to Zarlino, Tarini, and others.[102] Moreover, Kircher's theories (as well as Cerone's) are permeated with Boethian undertones that go unacknowledged in this assumption, which at that point had had more longevity than the ideas of the German Jesuit theorist himself. Furthermore, given that Sor Juana herself had her own heavily annotated copy of Cerone's *melopeo*, it is puzzling that Kircher's name appears associated with ways of thinking about music among those in the New Spanish intellectual milieu.[103]

The mathematical understanding that informed the study of tones, intervals, consonances, and their contrapuntal realization most likely was buttressed by Cerone's writings, and actual evidence only supports that. For the Italian theorist, composers like Morales, Guerrero, Victoria, and Lobo (as well as others like Palestrina, Porta, and Pietro Vinci) were among the best examples of this conceptual framework, which Salazar made sure to enforce in the cathedral.[104] In 1700, Salazar mentioned to the canons that when he was hired in 1688, all he had found in the music archive was "some books torn up and thrown into a corner." All of the music performed at that point was new, composed by Salazar, but it also incorporated some music that he had brought with him, written "by the most eminent maestros from Europe."[105] When the chapter asked Salazar to make an inventory of all the music that he had brought, the chapelmaster produced a list of twenty-five choirbooks featuring motets and masses by Lobo, Victoria, and Guerrero, but also by Sebastián de Vivanco, Francisco López Capillas, and Hernando Franco. Franco was cathedral chapelmaster from 1575 to 1585, and records show that he had also promoted this repertoire in the sixteenth century.[106] Such was the music thinking that probably transpired at the cathedral of Mexico for a century (or at the very least, after Salazar became chapelmaster in 1688), which could explain why the call for applications for the chapelmastership in 1750, even if supposedly based on the one from 1715, was substantially different:

> Given that, because of the retirement of Don Domingo Dutra y Andrade, the chapelmastership of this holy metropolitan church is vacant, and given that it is necessary to appoint an individual to such position, by this means we summon all persons intelligent in plain and figured chant (*canto figurado*), and especially in the science and art of music, and in the composition of villancicos, verses and other pieces, who would like to apply (*oponer*) for such position, to appear with the secretary of this chapter after sixty days, for which employment the appointed person shall receive a salary of 500 pesos every year, as well as the corresponding obvenciones. And so that this call gets to be known by all intelligent individuals in the said art (*facultad*) of music and composition we send the present convocation, which will be affixed [to the walls of] our

holy metropolitan church and in the ones of the surrogate bishoprics of Puebla, Valladolid, Oaxaca, and Guadalajara (see appendix 4.5).[107]

Unlike the previous call for applications of 1715, which summoned musician composers skilled in the "art of composition," this document was quite specific. It seemed that cathedral authorities needed to clarify the type of person and the skills that they desired. This was not a generic call to "composers," whose creative impulses now seemed to diverge from traditional musical thought. Rather, this call was intended for all of those intelligent in the *science and art* of music. The word "science" was not just an obscure allusion to the mathematical underpinnings that made music a quadrivial *scientia*. More specifically, it was a reference to a body of scholarship by authors considered "classic in the field"—Cerone, to be precise—who promoted principles that departed from an orthodox understanding of musical knowledge. Perhaps it would be problematic to rely on Sor Juana to defend the notion that music, as a science, represented such an intellectual field of inquiry. Sor Juana's example is indeed extraordinary, but it would be ludicrous to use this as an excuse to dismiss the whole case when evidence is all around.

If Sor Juana considered music a step in the human arts and sciences it was probably because of the academic value that the arts (*artes*) had in higher education. Artes was considered one of the minor disciplines (*facultades menores*) at the university, and a degree in artes was required to pursue one of the major areas of study, namely, theology and canon law.[108] In New Spain, music was conceptualized as being part of artes, and therefore, was thought to have a place in academic study.[109] But while this does not prove whether anyone shared Sor Juana's view, it does point to the academic character with which music was probably perceived at the cathedral. Such character departed from the notion that knowledge of music should be informed by the rhetoric of Spanish treatises, which in turn made one a true musician (*músico perfecto*, in Cerone's words).

For more modern musicological minds this paradigm might possibly seem stranded given the aesthetic changes that had already permeated New Spanish music practices in the eighteenth century. I would argue that the relevance of this paradigm lies not on whether it was in sync or at odds with approaches to music performance and composition in the estilo moderno. Its importance had less to do with sound preferences than with the academic legitimacy that it gave to the careers of institutionalized musicians, mainly because of the value that academic erudition had in New Spain. It is here where we encounter one of the most tangible influences that the phenomenon of limpieza de sangre (i.e., claiming Spanish blood) had on an intimate realm of experience. Being fit for letters and the professions was an important component of one's profile; dedicating one's life to study and pursuit of a profession in a Spanish institution enhanced one's calidad.

By endorsing academia, Spaniards subscribed to a notion of "nobility" that went back to the sixteenth century, which made their limpieza all the more important.[110] As an activity linked to a Spanish institution, music was highly susceptible to this paradigm. Approaches to music education departed from a Spanish musical tradition—with Cerone as a scholarly basis—that informed efforts to construct racialized status discourses. In light of this context, the cathedral chapter possibly tried to clarify in the second call for applications the type of profile that candidates for the position of chapelmaster ought to have. What is almost certain is that the canons chose individuals sensitive to this paradigm to oversee the examination, who unsurprisingly were influenced by Salazar.

First, the chapter elected two of its members—Dr. Luis Fernando de Hoyos Mier (precentor) and Dr. Francisco Jiménez Caro (penitentiary)—as deputies to organize the selection process. In turn, the deputies established a committee to conduct the examination. This committee was formed by Martín Vásquez de Mendoza (succentor), José González (choir chaplain), and Miguel de Herrera (musician). José González is an example of someone raised in the cathedral for whom music was a means of advancement. Records show that by 1722 he was already a choirboy and that he showed interest in learning to play the harpsichord. This instrument would enable him to learn the organ later, for which training in counterpoint was essential.[111] He happened to grow up during the tenure of Sumaya, who, like Salazar, used the music of Spanish renaissance composers as a contrapuntal model. Cathedral records show that González was a member of the chapel by 1732, and that two years later Sumaya recommended him for a salary increase due to his musical proficiency.[112] By 1733 González had already been ordained and had graduated with a university degree, necessary requirements to be appointed choir chaplain that year.[113] The years of music study and practice at the cathedral likely equipped González with knowledge representative of the type of musicianship desired by the chapter; after all, the canons appointed him to examine choirboys, musicians, choir assistants, and aspiring succentors.[114]

Although not a cleric, the appointment of Miguel de Herrera was important because he was one of the most veteran musicians in the chapel, and seemingly one of the best trained. Just like González, Herrera was part of an older generation: he was a member of the chapel as early as 1699, and by 1709 Salazar considered him to be among the most advanced musicians (*más aprovechados*) in counterpoint.[115] Moreover, when the chapter discussed in 1747 the need to dismiss some of the oldest musicians (either because of their inability to serve or because of their musical ineptitude) Herrera's name was among those spared, and given that he also had been a member of the examination committee when Sumaya became chapelmaster in 1715 he was an obvious choice to the deputies.[116]

In contrast to González and Herrera, Vásquez de Mendoza was part of a younger generation. However, records show that his musical background was still in tune with that of the other two committee members. Vásquez de Mendoza was admitted to the Colegio in 1735 at the age of eight, and just like other choirboys he was examined every year to measure his progress in music and voice, separately.[117] Extant information shows that by 1750 he was already choir chaplain and was put in charge of examining choir assistants along with José González. Moreover, in 1774 he was in charge of examining musicians seeking employment in the chapel.[118] Accounting for the profiles of González, Herrera, and Vásquez de Mendoza is important in order to assess the unfolding of events during the examination process. If knowledge of counterpoint was an important measure of a chapelmaster's musicianship, the fact that these committee members served the cathedral during the tenures of Salazar and Sumaya sheds light on the conceptual framework that informed their assessment of Jerusalem's music, of his musicianship, and ultimately, of his fitness to lead the chapel.

The examination proceeded first with a questionnaire about theoretical issues to test Jerusalem's musical knowledge. After that, the committee gave him twenty-four hours to compose a piece in counterpoint on the antiphon "O Emmanuel Rex," and a villancico on a text provided in advance.[119] A week later, when the committee met in the choir to listen to the pieces, it was the antiphon that inflamed the controversy with further doubts and concerns, because the committee could not tell whether what they heard was actual counterpoint.[120] In this piece, shown in Example 4.2, Jerusalem tried to abide by tradition placing the cantus firmus in the soprano line. However, his imitative figures (between the alto and tenor) lack any sense of independent contrapuntal character according to the renaissance stylistic parameters that were familiar to cathedral musicians.[121] The harmonic structure seems to be the main focus of the piece; its functional progressions point to a concern for tonality. The use of suspensions (e.g., the G major in measure 5) shows an interest in color, although harmonic explorations remain overall conservative, going from F major (mm. 1–4) to C major (mm. 5–17) to D minor (mm. 18–35). All throughout, the relentless figurations of the alto and tenor voices are bound to harmonic functions and provide textural contrast to the soprano and bass lines. It seems that the committee was baffled by these approaches; the piece was far from the modal contrapuntal inventiveness that they knew from works by Guerrero, Morales, or Lobo. For this reason, they asked Jerusalem to compose another piece on the antiphon "Iste sanctus protege Dei sui," only this time specifying that he had to show the use of "fugues and canons."[122] The first antiphon ("O Emmanuel Rex") remained the main point of focus, however, as the committee kept referring to it during the evaluation.

Example 4.2 "O Emmanuel Rex" (excerpt), by Ignacio Jerusalem. ACCMM, Canonjías, book 1, no. 65, fols. 114r—116v.

O Emmanuel Rex

Ignacio Jerusalem
1707 - 1769

* The bass appears untexted in the manuscript, possibly because it was played by an instrument.

The committee submitted its assessment to the deputies, who in turn gave their own opinion about the whole process to the chapter for final deliberation. Regarding Jerusalem's compositional ability the committee showed varied opinions. While for the younger Vásquez de Mendoza, Jerusalem's skill was evident, González and Herrera were not so convinced. González pointed out that, judging by the antiphon ("O Emmanuel Rex") and from compositions written for the chapel

Example 4.2 Continued

O Emmanuel Rex, continued

up until that point, he wrote mostly short things, and not the types of works that the cathedral needed.[123] Herrera voiced concerns that were somewhat similar to those of González. Referring to the antiphon, Herrera said that Jerusalem had composed this piece "in his own way, and not how it should be."[124] The canons agreed with the committee and remarked that Jerusalem lacked practice in writing music for a "religious choir," and in that he was mostly experienced in music for the theater.[125]

In addition to the three committee members, the deputies also solicited the assistance of friar Miguel Gallegos, organist of the Convento de la Merced, and Juan José Durán y León, a local merchant considered by the deputies as a music connoisseur. In contrast with the cathedral committee, these individuals gave a quite positive assessment regarding Jerusalem's contrapuntal music.

After examining "O Emmanuel Rex," Gallegos mentioned that the committee had not specified which contrapuntal techniques to use, and for this reason, Gallegos thought, Jerusalem had opted for using "general counterpoint," which in Gallegos's opinion was well executed.[126] Durán y León reiterated Gallegos' appraisal mentioning that although "there are different types of counterpoint, such as fugues and canons, the candidate fulfilled this requirement [of the examination] appropriately."[127]

Such contrasting appraisals (inside and outside the cathedral) are rather puzzling, and one can only speculate whether there were other reasons informing the committee's assessment. After all, Gallegos and Durán y León were only looking at the score of "O Emmanuel Rex," whereas the committee went beyond the music text to assess Jerusalem's musicianship. The records of the examination suggest that the extent of Jerusalem's knowledge of música especulativa became a decisive factor: for although Gallegos considered that the antiphon score was enough to say that Jerusalem did not lack this type of knowledge, for the cathedral committee—as well as for the chapter—musicianship did not rely on a practical ability to write or perform music, but rather on an academic—if not intellectual—capacity to understand it theoretically, as well as to communicate such understanding. The committee was unanimously concordant on this point, and their final (and negative) observations were influenced by the results of the theoretical examination, which to the committee said more about Jerusalem's erudition than his compositions could show.

González wrote to the chapter that, regarding knowledge of music, Jerusalem was able to answer some questions while unable to answer others satisfactorily.[128] Herrera corroborated González's words adding that this lack of knowledge was because of Jerusalem's "lack of cathedral experience."[129] Vásquez de Mendoza's opinion echoed González's and Herrera's in concluding that Jerusalem was not fit for the post because "a chapelmaster ought to be a compendium of the abilities of all of the other musicians, so that what someone does not know the chapelmaster knows, and what others know the chapelmaster does not ignore, and this is not evident in Jerusalem."[130] As witnesses of the examination process, the deputies gave their own rendition of the events, also emphasizing this as the main point of tension. Both deputies agreed with the committee in that it was hard to say whether Jerusalem had the musical knowledge expected from a chapelmaster. De Hoyos Mier and Jiménez Caro stressed that language might have been an issue, because, allegedly, sometimes either Jerusalem would not understand the questions or the committee would not understand his answers, for which the deputies needed to act as translators between both parties.[131] But although this might suggest that the committee remained unaware of Jerusalem's knowledge due to a language barrier, the composer's final remarks likely sealed the conceptual divide between him and the committee.

The deputies observed that, in a final instance, Jerusalem was asked to explain in his own way what he understood music to be. And using broken Spanish, Jerusalem explained, according to the deputies report, some issues related to *música armónica* (plainchant), *música cromática* (canto figurado), and composition, concluding that "such was the way in which music was taught and learnt in his native Italy and all other foreign nations, and there was no need of further arguments or old books to understand, teach, or learn music well, except what he had said, *for only the arranged execution of music was its true science*."[132] With this answer Jerusalem took a clear stance regarding knowledge of music and positioned himself in an opposite conceptual camp.

While for the committee and deputies música especulativa was an important element of musicianship, for Jerusalem música práctica (its "arranged execution," hence, composition and performance) was seemingly a far more important basis. After Jerusalem's final remarks, the deputies mentioned, there were not more disputes or arguments but it was clear that the examination did not erase any prior concerns about the sufficiency of the Italian composer in the minds of the committee members and the deputies. Aware of this situation, De Hoyos Mier and Jiménez Caro did not make any direct recommendation. If anything, they washed their hands saying that it was up to the chapter to justify the final appointment.[133] In a meeting on August 3, 1750, the canons ultimately decided to name Jerusalem chapelmaster, although only because the chapelmastership was not a *colación* (and therefore, neither exclusive to any one individual nor assigned in perpetuity), for which the chapter could appoint a more suitable person if someone appeared later.[134] In this way, the chapter took the same route as when Domingo Dutra y Andrade was appointed, also in consideration that the individual lacked the desired musical knowledge and profile.

The Limits of Música Práctica: Caveats for a Parvenu

The appointment passed unnoticed—or probably ignored—among some musicians in the chapel because they continued to operate as if they did not have to answer to the new director. Two years later it had become apparent that Jerusalem did not have control over the chapel and that musicians did not see him as their leader, much less as an authority figure. Musicians started to be absent from cathedral services frequently, and *zangonautlas* (contracting performance events independently, without the chapter's or the chapelmaster's consent) became pervasive. At their first meeting of the year in 1752, the canons tried to find a solution to this situation. They wanted to put an end to the lack of discipline of musicians who by then were openly disregarding their cathedral duties and had made a habit of capitalizing from opportunities outside the chapel. The canons even contemplated the possibility of bringing musicians from Spain (perhaps with better skills and knowledge) who could reinforce the corporate strength of the chapel, and thus, force the others to align with the group again.[135] Although records do not show whether the canons talked about expenses at that meeting, the proposition was costly. It would involve sending someone to Spain to find competent musicians willing to travel to New Spain to work in the cathedral. The salaries and benefits (obvenciones, specifically) would have to be attractive enough for people to make the three-month journey to Mexico City, and the treasury was still recovering from the mishandlings of Manuel Roman in 1745 (see Chapter 2).[136] Moreover, the canons had a problem trying to regulate obvenciones because of the ongoing zangonautlas, and therefore, they could not guarantee that benefit.

The chapter chose to approach the situation from a different angle. Above all, the music chapel was an ecclesiastical corporation in which musicians occupied hierarchical positions, from the newest to the oldest musicians, and the chapelmaster was supposed to be at the top. Such seniority assigned priority in the performance of obvenciones and in the percentage that a musician got from these events.[137] The chapter was aware that such structure had begun to falter; everything seemed to point at Jerusalem's lack of political presence, which the canons had foreseen. It may very well be that musicians saw him as an equal: after all, his "erudition" was questionable and his performance skills were not necessarily better than those of other proficient performers in the group; at least primary sources do not give a contrary account. His compositional craft was not in itself a credential either, because there was a previous record of individuals who worked as composers who did not become chapelmasters. Musicians also had access already to the cathedral music archive to use music for their own particular needs, something that Jerusalem himself allowed. He gave musicians open access to scores and even gave the keys to those who asked for them. This is something that the canons lamented and considered it the main reason the music archive was in such an unorganized state.[138] It was clear to the canons that Jerusalem was a peer among musicians and not a leader, and that as chapelmaster he did not put himself in a position to command respect and obedience.

In part, this was a reason for the lack of discipline experienced in the chapel, which began to cause political frictions among musicians. Obvenciones were the occasions when this became particularly acute; some musicians disregarded the position of Jerusalem as head of the chapel and instead tried to contract performances by themselves, engagements that were supposed to be the responsibility of the chapelmaster. Moreover, musicians failed to join the chapel in obvenciones contracted by Jerusalem, and some would show up just to mock the chapelmaster and those who agreed to play under his direction.[139]

While the canons considered that this was Jerusalem's fault, the chapel-master pointed out that the attitudes of some musicians were to blame as well. Particularly, he denounced how "musicians were set against him, treated him with provocative and demeaning words, and disrespected and disobeyed him as chapelmaster." When he summoned musicians to play somewhere, he added, "some attend just to ridicule the ones who come to play, thus making the service look bad."[140] The tension was clear and musicians were not shy about showing their dissent. Jerusalem was in a difficult situation and this context suggests that Robert Stevenson was probably right in considering that the Italian musician had prematurely risen to an institutional position he was not fit to hold. He had no authority, his position as chapelmaster was openly disregarded, and as a con-sequence his corporate benefits were also at stake. Jerusalem complained to the canons about all of this and demanded their support so that he would be treated respectfully.

> I, Ignacio Jerusalem, chapelmaster of this holy church according to its
> bylaws (*por erección*), with the utmost respect and veneration, say: that
> for a long time the music chapel has been robbing me of the privileges
> that I should enjoy. And I beg to your lordship to advise the administra-
> tor of the music chapel to include my name in all functions, big or small,
> in which the music chapel plays, whether the chapelmaster attends or
> not, for this is a privilege of all chapelmasters everywhere because of
> the music scores that they provide, even knowing your lordship that
> other musicians take with them more scores, for it is the responsibility
> of the chapelmaster to take with him the scores that he has worked on
> for these functions. It is necessary for your lordship to modify this by
> asking the administrator to include the chapelmaster in these perfor-
> mances and prohibiting others to take scores with them, for this is the
> privilege of the chapelmaster (see appendix 4.6).[141]

For Jerusalem it was clear that he had earned the chapelmastership "right-fully," and his compositional skill was the basis of his claims to corporate privi-leges (obvenciones, in this case). He makes specific mention to his position as chapelmaster according to cathedral bylaws (*por erección*), and above all, of his privilege to provide music for every performance. It is quite possible—indeed, probable—that he considered that his proficiency in modern stylistic trends gave him an advantage, especially given that, allegedly, he had been the only composer in the city. Musicians and cathedral authorities were aware that music was in an advanced state and different from past times, so Jerusalem possibly thought that this shift was an opportunity to place himself in a prominent music position within an important Spanish institution.

Composition in the estilo moderno was his main asset and he used it to legitimize his appointment every time it became necessary. Such was the case when Matheo Tollis de la Rocca arrived in the city, becoming in 1757 the second chapelmaster of the cathedral at the behest of Doña Luisa María del Rosario de Ahumada y Vera, marquesa de las Amarillas and the wife of viceroy Don Agustín de Ahumada y Villalón. In 1758 Rocca was named *maestro de polifonía* (master of polyphony), although Jerusalem remained as first chapelmaster. As expected, the pairing of the men did not go well and Jerusalem jealously guarded his duties and privileges. Above all, he demanded that only he could act as head of the chapel (only he could "govern the chapel," were his actual words, although the context above brings into question his ability to govern). To uphold his claims, Jerusalem asked the chapter to name an erudite person (*un facultado*) in composition to declare if both Jerusalem and Rocca were experts in such art, and to determine which one of them was actually better fit to hold the chapelmastership. For this, he asked that both men be locked in a room without instruments and with nothing but ink to write a setting of a plainchant antiphon—which is what Rocca was used to, according to Jerusalem—so that afterward the capacities of each could be determined.[142]

Seemingly, Jerusalem took his compositional craft quite seriously, writing ever-longer pieces to assert his authoritative presence in the chapel. An example of this is his matins service for the Virgin of Guadalupe, which he reworked on two occasions.[143] According to Craig H. Russell, the Nocturns in this service are roughly equal in length and compositional scale to full acts in an opera or an oratorio.[144] Another opportunity arose in 1760, when Jerusalem wrote a cantata for soloists, chorus, and orchestra, a work considered today to be the most extensive composition from eighteenth-century New Spain known to survive.[145] This piece was written as part of a celebration that took place at the university to commemorate the coronation of Charles III. The cathedral also held a special religious service to honor the coronation, for which Jerusalem wrote the music as well.

The chapter started to resent Jerusalem's compositional spirit, nonetheless, specifically because of the length of his pieces. Whether Jerusalem began to write longer works as a reaction to Rocca's arrival is a matter of speculation. What seems true is that the canons recognized that "from only a few years ago until now [1760] the services of this holy church have become quite long because the music compositions need a lot of time, as there are glorias that last half an hour, and credos that last three quarters of an hour. And it would be convenient to shorten these pieces to not deviate attention or devotion [from services], for it is true that these last ones have become intolerable."[146] For the canons, the aesthetic changes introduced by music practices in the estilo moderno had seemingly excluded music that, because of its length, "does not fit in [the spirit of] these times, when there is an abundance of modern compositions of delicate taste, brief, and proportionate to the solemnity of [religious] services."[147] The question here would be whether Jerusalem's compositional efforts were a response to political pressure, either because of the way musicians treated him or because he felt threatened by the appointment of a second chapelmaster. The question is especially pertinent if we consider that canons and musicians initially thought that he did not have cathedral experience. After all, they had said originally that Jerusalem was mostly experienced in writing short things and not the types of works needed by the cathedral, as tradition previously had it.

While there are grounds to say that Stevenson's "parvenu" remark about Jerusalem has some validity, it is not possible to ignore that the composer was also caught in a period of transition. Clearly, his uncertain position had more to do with the way in which he engaged with an institutional paradigm of musical activity than with any possible conceptual ambiguity in relation to theoretical matters. For cathedral musicians, Spanish treatises (more specifically, that of Cerone) provided an important basis for engaging with music as an institutionalized academic activity. It was the fact that Jerusalem was alien to this system of study and understanding that made his position in the chapel questionable (more than stylistic issues in his compositional approaches), which ultimately undermined his hierarchical role within the ensemble.

Yet it is not possible to say that this paradigm unilaterally structured music practices or the structure of the chapel, even before 1750. Political tensions regarding obvenciones between the ensemble and the chapelmaster had begun to arise during Sumaya's tenure. Ongoing socioeconomic conditions and aesthetic changes had an effect on the political structure of the chapel, and it is possible that the problems caused by Jerusalem's appointment were directly related to these. As shown in Chapter 5, these two factors altered hierarchical relations among musicians, inside and outside of the cathedral. The relationship between the chapelmaster and the ensemble became more democratic, and the position of the chapel in the city with respect to other musicians was compromised as well. The situation became especially acute when musicians of mixed race openly competed for performance privileges with cathedral musicians, which shows that eighteenth-century urban musical activity was sensitive to the unstable state of the *casta* system. Chapter 5 explores the way in which the music chapel adapted to these transformations to ensure the survival of the corporation. The chapter further considers how cathedral musicians resorted to an invocation of "decency" as a zealous measure to safeguard their racialized claims to status and privilege during this time of turmoil.

5

Decency in the Music Chapel

Introduction

The last chapter began to address the tensions that arose in the music chapel after the appointment of Ignacio Jerusalem to the chapelmastership. In part, such tensions are telling of how knowledge of contrapuntal theory had buttressed notions of leadership within the ensemble, and how aesthetic changes had begun to question these notions. Nevertheless, events occurred during the tenure of Manuel Sumaya suggest that a more complicated set of precedents gave rise to these political frictions. Specifically, these events point to a conflation of aesthetic and economic conditions that began to undermine the hierarchical structure of the ensemble, and that eventually compromised its position in society. Aesthetic shifts prompted the hire of individuals who, while proficient in new music trends, did not necessarily endorse notions of musical knowledge that at the cathedral were the basis of merit and promotion. And there lay the problem: on the one hand, older cathedral musicians debated the financial benefits that these newcomers received without merit. On the other, newly appointed individuals challenged the authority of the chapelmaster—and with this, traditional notions of musical knowledge as a basis of legitimate merit—in the midst of financial pressures.

Following Sumaya's departure, the music chapel operated independently for more than ten years. This proved to be a vulnerable time for the group, and it was connected to a period of economic hardship in New Spain. Financial stress and the lack of oversight fostered the growth of zangonautlas. The chapel's internal structure decayed as musicians partnered with others from outside (regardless of race) to play at events that, by law, were exclusive to cathedral musicians. This activity ultimately compromised the social position of the chapel as well as its corporate claims to performance privileges. Evidence, therefore, suggests that the tensions that transpired in the cathedral after 1750 derived from a complex situation, and Jerusalem's lack of "erudition" cannot account for it alone. Chapter 5 explores this context in an effort to explain the reasons the music chapel lost its internal organization and its corporate benefits. In order to do this, the chapter is divided in two parts. Part one outlines the aesthetic, ideological, and financial factors that created a precedent for this situation. Part two, then, continues with a narrative of how these issues affected cathedral musical activity. This second part shows that the music chapel became vulnerable to competition from musicians of mixed race and others expelled from the church within the context laid out in part one. Part two also explains how this context influenced the efforts of cathedral musicians to regroup. Finally, the chapter closes by showing that the invocation of "decency," as a racialized discourse of status, was central to these efforts: it was an attempt by the corporation to regain its social position during a time when musicians of different races and perceived social quality competed for Spanish corporate privileges.

Part One—Antecedents

The Chapelmastership under Challenge

> From this your lordship will infer that the reason [that the administrator] caused this commotion with the musicians about the feast of the Holy Sacrament is to make me look bad in front of your lordship, tying up my hands with defamations, so that these slanderers, without respect for this illustrious chapter, can set their laws. And some of them are driven by avarice, for although they have just started working in this church, they already have salaries of 300 pesos, thus starting where their instructors ended, because this holy church has never paid anyone 300 pesos without presenting merits of many years of service (see appendix 5.1).[1]

Sumaya was being accused of embezzling money from *obvenciones*, and so he sent this letter to the dean and chapter to set the record straight. The chapelmaster had offered to perform for no payment at a ceremony in which the daughter of a close friend (Don Manuel Rodríguez de la Rosa) was to take her vows as a nun. Rodríguez de la Rosa was in dire straits and Sumaya was doing this in the spirit of friendship. The chapelmaster knew that not all musicians would agree to play without being paid, and therefore, he called only those who he thought would agree to do this as a favor. One of the other musicians, however, had told the administrator (Juan de Salibe) that the patron was in fact quite affluent and that he had paid 25 pesos for the music. Rumors started to heat up among musicians that afternoon and Sumaya did his best to reassure the entire chapel that the patron was in no position to pay; for this reason he felt that he should not ask the whole ensemble to participate. Some musicians, however, claimed that the chapelmaster had handpicked people to play at this event and took it as an excuse to do the same when he was not around. During a time when Sumaya fell ill (June 5, 1727), canon José Navarijo arranged an obvención, a burial service at which only half of the chapel was supposed to play. (The chapel divided itself in three turns or *tandas* to play in obvenciones. These events usually required a few musicians and not the entire chapel, and tandas rotated to give all musicians an equal chance to earn money.) Once Navarijo arrived to the event with the corresponding tanda the administrator arrived with his own group of musicians saying that "if the chapelmaster took *his* musicians wherever he wanted, then the administrator would also take *his*."[2]

The whole case apparently hinged on a dispute about rights for compensation, but the events pointed to a more complex situation that had begun to unfold in the music chapel. The administrator had instigated musicians to work separately, perhaps thinking that the chapelmaster was ridding them of obvenciones. Salibe and others formed a group to contract performances "against the honor and title of chapelmaster conferred to me by your lordship, which after a public opposition and examination, and based on the bylaws of this holy church, entitles me to the obedience of these musicians on everything pertaining my station," argued Sumaya.[3] With this letter, the chapelmaster was not only refuting the accusations of embezzlement but also asserting his position as authority and leader of the chapel. He was in charge of the ensemble and invariably summoned the whole group whenever an event paid 20 pesos or more. If events paid from 10 to 20 pesos, he then called half of the ensemble (on a rotational basis). The problem was when Sumaya refused an offer because patrons could only pay 4 or 6 pesos. These occasions incited a few musicians to perform on their own, although these individuals were not the troublemakers. Young and of limited experience, they were content with a small bounty that they could divide in three or four parts. Their activity was in fact a reflection of the dissent perpetrated by the administrator who, with better and more accomplished performers (who had salaries of 300 pesos), had started to contract high-paying events separate from the chapel.

The corporate role of the chapelmaster was at stake and Sumaya's allusion to "merit" was important because it related to changes that were affecting the hierarchical structure of the chapel. Unlike others in the ensemble, some of the performers who teamed with Salibe did not have a record of cathedral service, which in itself was considered the basis of merit for promotion and benefits. Knowledge of music was particularly linked to this notion of merit because it enabled individuals to advance in a hierarchy of ministries devoted to music and ritual (see Chapters 3 and 4), and Sumaya was careful to inform the chapter whenever a musician—who auditioned for a job in the chapel—had a "music" deficiency. As mentioned in Chapter 4, all graduates from the Colegio de Infantes had to prove that they had proper knowledge of music before they joined the ensemble, and the situation was not different with musicians who came from other places. For example, when Benito Martino auditioned for a violin position in 1721, Sumaya mentioned that he was "proficient in Italian music, but in the music that we esteem in Spain he is not."[4] Given that knowledge of music allowed musicians to develop a career in the cathedral (and thus, enhance their status), it is not unreasonable to think that the "music that *we* (i.e., we Spaniards) esteem in Spain" was a reference to stylistic and theoretical principles valued in this Spanish institution. In 1736, José de Torres alluded to such principles as "the rigorous style of Spain,"[5] which stood in contrast with current Italian trends in composition and performance.

For cathedral musicians, this knowledge was the cornerstone of their long-standing careers, and of their corporate and political identity, calidades that enabled them to claim specific privileges. This is possibly the reason that in 1730 Sumaya submitted a rather perfunctory assessment of José Laneri's audition: "the individual plays the violin dexterously and understands music from toccatas and other Italian compositions. This is what I am being asked about this person, and your lordship will decide the best."[6] It well could be that the tone of these remarks was influenced by the events of 1727. After all, the chapter hired Laneri as well as Martino although they did not have the proper knowledge; the canons expected them to improve by attending the escoleta. Laneri's starting salary was 300 pesos a year, and his percentage from obvenciones derived from this pay rate.[7] It is true that the canons pushed for musical study, but aesthetic trends were changing and the cathedral needed musicians proficient in music of the estilo moderno. This shift produced tensions in the music chapel because its internal structure was based on a hierarchical line of professional development that musicians climbed through years of work and musical study. The assignment of high salaries to individuals with neither proper musical knowledge nor seniority undermined this structure, and for insubordinate performers—without merit—to challenge Sumaya's authority only corroborated that.

This episode foreshadowed the collapse of the chapel's internal structure in the next twenty years, not the least because the position of the chapelmaster was undermined. The incident above stemmed out of financial concerns, but the challenge to Sumaya's authority points to other aesthetic issues that have to be considered as well and that are relevant to Jerusalem's case.

The Issue of Erudition

There can be little doubt that, by the early eighteenth century, approaches to music composition and performance were not based on solely traditional contrapuntal practices. Aesthetic shifts altered cathedral musical activity in two ways. The first change happened in the escoleta. Plainchant and counterpoint had been traditionally taught as part of the same class. With the arrival of Jerusalem, however, the escoleta was divided into two different groups: *estilo* (style) and *armonía* (harmony). In armonía, individuals continued to study polyphony while in estilo they learned new trends in music performance. The latter was especially attractive for singers because they were taught falsetto techniques and ornamentation from people like Nicolás Delmonte (also spelled Del Motte in some sources) and the castrato Francisco Bozzi.[8]

The second change had a direct effect in the internal organization of the music chapel. The incursion of music in the estilo moderno emphasized the importance of practical aspects of performance. Notions of music proficiency and musician-ship, therefore, derived from performance proficiency in new stylistic trends and not necessarily from theoretical understandings. This meant that performers could be equally knowledgeable in music depending on their instrumental abil-ity, which equalized hierarchical relationships among musicians in the chapel. Although the chapter continued to enforce the teaching of counterpoint until at least 1780 (see Chapter 4), the activity of musicians like Sumaya and others addressed below makes one wonder what was the place that counterpoint had in actual music practices. After Jerusalem there is no record of another examination occurring in the cathedral to gauge the knowledge of a chapelmaster. The hire of Matheo Tollis de la Rocca in 1757 was more by imposition of the archbishop (no doubt pressured by the viceroy) than by institutional interest or need, thus fore-going any formal examination. The chapter later appointed Martín Bernárdez de Rivera after Rocca's passing in 1781, because he had "intelligence for it, and good image (*porte*), and conduct." His was an interim appointment, however, as the official process required a proper call for applications and exam, accord-ing to the canons.[9] Records have yet to be found about the selection of Antonio Juanas for this position in 1791. Cathedral records only show that he was one of four musicians that the chapter hired directly from Spain, who were expected to begin duties on October 11 of that year.[10]

Cathedral musicians continued to claim status based on calidades (insti-tutional affiliation, erudition) that informed perceptions of "Spanishness" in eighteenth-century Mexico City. But while erudition was still important, the ideas that buttressed this attribute changed. The proliferation of modern music was part of new customs, tastes, and ideologies that entered New Spain with the Bourbon succession to the Spanish throne in 1700. Knowledge and erudition remained important attributes among Spaniards seeking status and privilege through their institutional careers, and research shows that uni-versity degrees only increased by the end of the eighteenth century for this reason.[11] However, the university needed to adapt to incoming ideological changes brought by the Enlightenment, and notions of erudition were caught in this transformation.

Seemingly, medieval scholasticism lingered in the university, and students kept being tested according to the Aristotelian method of inquiry.[12] Meanwhile, new intellectual currents had begun to enter Mexico City by that time. There is information about the impetus that certain subjects (which were previously in the background) acquired after the Bourbon succession. The scientific importance of subjects like physics, geology, and mathematics increased among a nascent class of literati, while empiricism brought a new interest in medicine, which before was considered "the profession of poor people."[13] Personalities like José Ignacio Bartolache (1739–1790) became known for their activity promoting scientific study during the eighteenth century, which is telling of the influence that secular empiricism had in New Spanish society. Bartolache was a student of the Colegio de San Ildefonso (surrogate to the Royal and Pontifical University of Mexico) and of the Seminario Tridentino. His first studies were in sacred theology, although he was later persuaded to focus on medicine and mathematics. In 1769 he published his *Lecciones matemáticas*, and from 1772 to 1774 he coordinated the publication of *Mercurio Volante* ("Flying Mercury"), the first journal to showcase news relevant to physics and medicine in New Spain.[14]

The libraries in the houses of notable individuals also featured literature that reflected these interests. The shelves of Miguel de Berrio y Zaldívar (marqués de Jaral de Berrio and conde de San Mateo de Valparaíso), for example, had books on medicine, geology, and philosophy.[15] Among other titles, he owned *Teatro moral de la vida de los filósofos antiguos y modernos* (Antwerp 1601), Juan Riquelme's *Para qué tiene el hombre razón* (Seville, 1687), Descartes' *Meditationes de prima philosophia* (Amsterdam, 1698), eight copies of Juan Bautista Berni's *Filosofía racional, natural* (Valencia, 1736), and two copies of Pedro Rodríguez Morro's *Oráculo de los nuevos filósofos* (Madrid, 1776).[16] Like other individuals who were receptive to new literary currents, Berrio y Zaldívar had these books next to titles on sacred theology, the life of saints, sermons, Spanish and universal history, treatises on medicine and particular ailments, as well as books on geography, geology, astronomy, and mathematics.

Amid this topical variety, it is important to highlight that the marqués also had room for Spanish literature, to which he devoted considerable attention. The inventory of his library shows three copies of Sor Juana Inés de la Cruz's *Obras poéticas* (Barcelona, 1701), one copy of the nun's *Obras espirituales* (Seville, 1703), six copies of Pedro Calderón de la Barca's *Autos sacramentales* (Madrid, 1717), two copies of Miguel de Cervantes Saavedra's *Historia de Don Quijote* (Antwerp, 1719), four later editions of the same title (Haya, 1746), and four further copies of said *Historia*, printed in Madrid in 1771. In addition, he owned two copies of *Obras ejemplares* by the same author (Antwerp, 1743). The presence of this type of literary works was not necessarily overwhelming in the library of the marqués, but it would be also a mistake to say that volumes on medicine, physics, or mathematics comprised the bulk of his collection. The holdings of Berrio y Zaldívar suggest that the marqués, like other nobles, culti-vated a diversity of interests, in which secular thinking and sensibility featured quite prominently.[17]

Therefore, it is possible to say that rationalist empiricism mingled with Aristotelian scholasticism as much as counterpoint and polyphonic music inter-acted with the trends of the estilo moderno. Such mingling was telling of ongo-ing aesthetic and intellectual shifts in New Spain, and music was susceptible to these changes. Enlightened emphases on reasoned thought and natural empiri-cism made música práctica an important basis of musical understanding. This is especially important if we consider that new approaches to composition and performance posed pedagogical demands for which Spanish treatises offered little help.[18] The notion of musical knowledge, thus, became subject to interpre-tation and sensitive to new ways of understanding and relating to music. Among the treatises that circulated in eighteenth-century New Spain, the writings of Antonio Eximeno were the first to emphatically address these changes, as well as to set the bases for new understandings of musical knowledge.

> In short, I became convinced from experience that the theory of math-ematics is useless to the practice of music; and that if I would retain the first lessons of counterpoint that I received according to the rules that father Kirker [*sic*] attempts to derive from numbers, I would have the most decisive document . . . to make the most stupid men cover their ears or laugh. And although by then I already suspected that music had nothing to do with mathematics, I discarded such thought as vain, considering that at least music theory was a part of them, like many other similar things that such [mathematical] sciences encompass, so useless to the practice of the arts like the subtleties of Aristotelian thought (see appendix 5.2).[19]

For Eximeno, physicist and mathematician, prevailing theoretical principles were incompatible with modern trends in music practices, and being able to realize this inconsistency was a reflection of the intellectual capacity of a person. Even "the most stupid of men" could understand this by relying on practice and experience, and this empiricism made him disavow the mathematical under-pinnings of traditional music theory, which according to him had hindered the progress of Spanish music.[20] Eximeno's reaction to the lingering presence of out-moded theoretical views—which he linked to the writings of Pedro Cerone and Pablo Nassarre—appeared most eloquently in his novel *Don Lazarillo Vizcardi* (possibly written in Rome, and published posthumously in two volumes in 1872 and 1873). In this novel, one of the characters, Agapito Quitóles, becomes demented from studying *El melopeo y maestro*.[21] Eximeno's critique of Cerone's outmoded longevity was kindled by the enlightened hermeneutics of a system he proposes to understand music from "nature and experience, which [dictate] the true principles and rules of harmony."[22] This meant that musicians—in Jerusalem's words—were not looking back at "old books" to understand music; only the arranged execution of music (i.e., composition and performance, see Chapter 4) now encompassed its true science.

New music trends were just as important to the nobility as their literary interests, and this made modern music more socially visible than counterpoint. Berrio y Zaldívar had a keen appreciation for instrumental performance in this new music style. He owned twenty-six violins (three by Stradivarius), four violas, one organ, two guitars, and a music collection of 115 entries on different genres and titles (some with more than one copy) that featured Italian composers such as Pugnani, Locateli, Albinoni, Vivaldi, Torelli, and Boccherini.[23] Due to the favor that modern music received, elements of elite taste and sensibility (e.g., dance, literature) likely influenced views of it. Social gatherings (which featured music in this new style) were especially conducive to the exchange of ideas that were in tune with the enlightened sensibility of the Bourbon monarchy. These events—sometimes *saraos*, but also *tertulias* as they were called when they happened in the evening—took place in the houses of the nobility, most often in the *gran salón* (great hall) or *salón del dosel* (canopy hall). In these rooms, arias, concertos, and dance music were the backdrop of discussions about Descartes or Newton, always witnessed by the gaze of the monarch's portrait placed in the hall under the canopy.[24] Along with the music, poetry and general literature were erudite components important to the nobility.[25] Poetry had a special place in this circle; it was not only a manifestation of good taste but also a public display of intellectual aptitude and cultivation.[26] Although there is no direct evidence, there is a possibility that, due to its literary connection, as well as its association with the erudite character of elite forms of socialization (i.e., saraos and tertulias), musical dexterity in the estilo moderno was perceived as an indicator of the knowledge and intellectual breadth of musicians.[27]

> Regarding singing I think [Manuel Andreu] did it quite well, not only because of how he did it but also because what he sang was in a very modern style. He reiterated this with more certainty and experience when at the house of Don Francisco Reyna, in front of various distinguished people, as well as amateurs and professors, he played from five in the afternoon until eleven in the evening in different instruments, either solo or in concert, which he executed freely and with taste and dexterity (see appendix 5.3).[28]

The estilo moderno was making strides in the ways people thought about music but it was through vocal music that musicians forged a new intellectual field. Exasperated after trying to make sense (reasoned sense) of how traditional contrapuntal principles related to music practices, Eximeno came to a realization while listening to a solo setting of the sequence "Veni sancte spiritus" by Niccolo Jommelli (1714–1774), that music was no more than prosody to give language grace and expression.[29] In a way, this connection between music and language showed the same affinity for which Italian humanists had found an expression in the madrigal centuries before. Nevertheless, Eximeno's realization did not depart from the numerical consistencies that Renaissance theorists saw between poetry, music, and mathematics (although he made only brief allusion to this relationship).[30] For Eximeno, the connection between music and language related to a preference for secular taste, grace, and expression in music rather than for mathematical ordering. Such attributes were considered to be "poetic" in nature, which made music one of the *artes del ingenio* (ingenious arts, like painting and poetry), separate from the more "vulgar" mechanical arts meant to satisfy quotidian needs.[31]

These ingenious arts, Eximeno mentioned, were guided by human instinct and good taste, without which intellectual reflection could bear little fruit.[32] That meant that the erudite character of music could be perceived according to secular values such as grace and taste, which maintained an important distance between intellectual (and now socially refined) endeavors and mechanical trades. In reality, this vision was not entirely new. The redefinition of music as a subject to be studied not according to mathematics but according to poetry and taste has been addressed as one of the main achievements of Renaissance theorists.[33] What was novel was the way in which this shift gave erudition new meaning, and how this "new knowledge" made it possible for others to be seen as competent musicians, and thus compete for status and privilege with the cathedral's chapel.

Although there is extant information to confirm that Eximeno's writings circulated in Mexico City during the eighteenth century,[34] it is not possible to know with certainty to what extent they were read. Yet, research shows that the city's artistic environment was receptive to the ideologies and aesthetic trends that he promoted. In addition to Berrio y Zaldívar, José Ignacio Bartolache was another prolific personality of New Spain's enlightened society who paid attention to music. He did own a copy of Cerone's *El melopeo* and Nassarre's *Tratado de música*, but he also owned an array of sonatas and arias that were "understood by those intelligent [in music]."[35] The word "intelligence" denotes a cultivated connoisseur, and the Enlightenment movement experienced in Mexico City makes one wonder if such cultivation had more to do with literature and poetry than with Cerone and Nassarre. In addition to *El melopeo* and Nassarre's *Tratado*, Bartolache owned an array of theory treatises on religious music.[36] His collection of music scores, however—along with his copy of Tomás de Iriarte's *La música, poema* (1779)—brings into question the possible connection that those cultivated in the "ingenious arts" might have made between "intelligence in music" and traditional music scholarship in the second half of the eighteenth century. It is interesting that, for Iriarte, treatises were in themselves "didactic poems" written to explain in artful verses the doctrine of ingenious arts.

> But [the motive] that moved me to publish this [metric composition] was the consideration that various ancient and modern ingenious writers have treated in didactic poems the sciences and arts, leaving music strangely and unjustly relegated, given that its sister, poetry, has merited that its doctrine be explained in verse by Horace, Vida, Boileau, and other poets (see appendix 5.4).[37]

The engraving by Manuel Salvador Carmona (1734–1820) featuring an allegory of Music and Poetry playing from the same lyre in Iriarte's treatise (shown on Figure 5.1) suggests a possible connection between both arts in the Spanish imagination, as well as the importance that poetry had in other ingenious arts as well. Studies show that in eighteenth-century Mexico City painters and engravers stressed the relationship between poetry and art in order to ennoble their profession, and thus, define their social place in the city's highly racialized corporate environment. In contrast with guilds (which mostly organized the learning and execution of manual trades), painters promoted an image of their profession that emphasized its intellectual foundations and its affinities with other liberal arts that had an academic basis. This measure enabled them to associate art with imagined notions of "Spanishness" (in which erudition was an important attribute), and to claim a notion of status that dissociated painters from individuals in mechanical trades (e.g., carpenters, carvers, viol makers, and other craftsmen).[38]

Painters aimed to establish an academy in which they could use limpieza de sangre as a requisite for membership so that they could claim status according to the Spanish corporate identity that the academy would bestow. Just as with cathedral musicians, this claim departed from the erudite basis of their profession, and painters alluded to the connection between painting and poetry to emphasize the intellectual and theoretical dimensions of their activity. *Ut pictoria poesis* (as is painting so is poetry) was the premise behind this notion, which made painters "professors of the very noble arts of painting and sculpture."[39] Ut pictoria poesis also became a trope among writers discussing the work of New Spanish painters, and references to artists in the *Gaceta de México* (the first newspaper printed in New Spain, published with interruptions in 1722, 1728–1739, and 1784–1810) aimed to reinforce their social quality and status as cultured

Dibuxada por G. Ferro.   Grabada por M. S. Carmona.

Música y Poësía
En una misma lira tocarémos.

CANTO V.

Figure 5.1 "Música y Poesía, en una misma lira tocaremos," engraving by Manuel Salvador Carmona (1734–1820). In *La música, poema* by Tomás de Iriarte (1779).

professionals due to their collaboration with poets and writers.[40] These made painters "noble artists" whose profession was distinctively "Spanish" and with similar exclusionary rules as those used by the Royal and Pontifical University of Mexico, the institution that painters took as their corporate model.[41]

It is interesting that in the midst of the intellectual and aesthetic changes occurring in New Spain, the university loomed as the institutional hinge of these transformations. Regarded as the "Imperial, Pontifical, and ever August Mexican Athens,"[42] the university became an important site for the re-inscription of "erudition" in music. Current research shows that the university was a place where a new erudite culture reinvigorated an interest for poetry, which in New Spain continued to draw from seventeenth-century literary stylistic conventions. There was a history of poetic competitions at this institution, and authors were awarded for the originality of their literary submissions. Prizes encompassed vases, salvers, and platters of engraved silver; jeweled snuffboxes, lengths of silk, satin, and velvet.[43] These competitions were an homage that the university paid to Euterpe, the Greek muse of lyric verse, the giver of delight, and later also known as the muse of music.[44] The marriage of both arts was symbolically important, especially because during the eighteenth century, New Spanish poetry continued to use older forms of lyric inspiration. However, this art was meant to express a new interest in refinement, grace, and secular taste, which is why music of the *estilo moderno* became the enlightened voice of older literary forms.[45] But most important was the new and privileged position that poetry and literature had among a cultured elite, which clothed the colonial imaginary of "music erudition" with an altogether different character.

The music chapel of the cathedral of Mexico participated in one of the most prestigious literary contests of the eighteenth century: a poetry competition to celebrate the coronation of King Charles III in which the winning entry would be set to music by the cathedral chapelmaster, Ignacio Jerusalem. This event (held in 1760) was a symbolic representation in which the now "Mexican Minerva" (an allusion in the poem to the university as the guardian of wisdom) commemorated the coronation of the new monarch, which legitimized new notions of academic erudition with royal signifiers.[46] The event also reiterated the important position of the university as the site of erudition, where music served as the modern aural realization of this concept.

The notion of music erudition, therefore, was being negotiated between the realms of science and art, mathematics and literature. As its new basis, poetry inspired readings of erudition that were sensitive to academic understandings, through which a Spanish elite cultivated an appreciation for rhetorical and literary strategies. Music in the *estilo moderno* was the enlightened dress of such a notion, as it now relied more on affective attributes (grace, refinement) than on scientific aptitudes. Performance skills—an affective realization of this new understanding—acquired central importance, and this explains why the growth of zangonautlas with musicians not affiliated to the cathedral became a concern.

If acculturation with Spanish customs and demeanors informed perceptions of one's social appearance, the ability to appeal musically to enlightened Spanish sensibilities, then, could be an important attribute to those seeking social mobility. There is the possibility that for individuals of mixed race musical proficiency was a strategy to become gente de razón (that is, people of different castes who learned Spanish mannerisms, attitudes, and behaviors), a label that partially filtered readings of race through the purifying eyeglass of Spanish socialization.[47] According to scholars, Europeans (non-Spanish) were labeled de facto as gente de razón because of their previous experience of Catholicism in Europe,[48] but it is not clear whether such labeling persisted after perceptions of "Spanishness" shifted from religious concerns to an interest in social appearance. Although no definite answer can be found to this query at the moment, the question is no less pertinent, especially considering that criollos, Mestizos, and Mulattoes in the middle classes comprised the bulk of gente de razón, where privilege and sometimes "Spanishness" were highly contested. The main difference for people in these groups was the possession or lack of wealth, which relates to the constant striving for benefits among musicians in this social class.[49]

Financial Concerns

Aesthetic changes positioned performance proficiency at the center of new understandings of what competent musicianship was supposed to be. Therefore, it is possible that notions of authority within the music chapel changed as well. This was partly the reason why musicians did not recognize Jerusalem as a leader and continued to operate independently. After all, he did not have adequate knowledge (as he was supposed to have, according to institutional guidelines) and his performance skills were not necessarily better than those of other musicians. Sumaya's precedent, however, suggests that financial factors were also a strong motivation for this behavior, which together with ongoing aesthetic changes, affected the chapel during a vulnerable period.

Prior to Jerusalem's appointment the chapel had functioned unsupervised for more than ten years, and it is possible that the corporate role of the chapelmaster became undermined then. Zangonautlas were the activity that started it all as a direct reaction to New Spain's socioeconomic difficulties. Chapter 2 addressed the economic crisis experienced in New Spain during the first half of the eighteenth century and how it affected the cathedral. The local economy depended primarily on resources from three activities: mining, manufacture, and agriculture. Of these three, the last one largely affected the others, as well as commercial activity. Every agricultural crisis triggered a domino effect in society: hunger, disease outbreaks, fewer marriages and births, migrations to the city, a shutdown of manufacturing industries (like textiles), and political tensions.[50] These problems unfolded parallel to the steady rise of prices during the eighteenth century—disproportionate to salaries—which created periods of scarcity; also, the hoarding of coin by merchants and the export of metal to Spain hampered the local circulation of currency.[51] Scarcity was the motor of credit, the main functioning mechanism of the economy and the activity that solidified an alliance among miners, merchants, and the church.[52]

In the city, the church, and more specifically, the cathedral, was a lending institution sought after by local merchants. The chapter also responded to requests from musicians in the chapel, who used portions of their salary as collateral.[53] In dire economic conditions, petitions for salary increases and loans by musicians were quite pervasive. Even chaplains asked frequently to change from a capellanía de erección to a capellanía de Lorenzana—and vice versa—depending on which one seemed more financially stable at a given moment. But, as mentioned in Chapter 2, the mismanagement of finances by accountants put the cathedral in trouble at least twice. The canons stopped providing loans to musicians during the early eighteenth century. They also considered dismissing ministers on more than one occasion (1709, 1711, and 1712) to make payroll cuts, cancelled two chaplaincies in 1735, and even some rituals ten years later.[54] By 1745, the situation had deteriorated and the canons were aware that musicians and chaplains were the most affected.

> Mr. Castillo said that the reason to summon the chapter was to say that ministers, chaplains, and musicians had asked for their salaries, and that it was a pity to see them so frail because of illness and because of their lack of means, and that he wanted to ask how would salaries be paid, because even the allocations for the canons were due as well and the treasury was without any funds (see appendix 5.5).[55]

Money was certainly a preoccupation and one can see how under these circumstances the lack of leadership in the chapel from 1738 (when Sumaya left) to 1750 could have fostered free enterprise among musicians. By the time Jerusalem arrived at the cathedral, zangonautlas were a common modus operandi that had affected the internal structure of the chapel and compromised its corporate claims to performance privileges. The tensions that arose in the group with Jerusalem's appointment derived from this background, and making him entirely responsible for not being able to control and lead the ensemble would be to disregard these historical antecedents. It is true that his lack of musical knowledge according to traditional cathedral standards is a factor that has to be considered. But to say that the corporate transformations that occurred in the music chapel—that is, in terms of its musical activity, internal structure, and corporate integrity—related primarily to intellectual and aesthetic changes would be an oversimplification. Aesthetic shifts are important to consider, especially if we are to understand how cathedral music practices (in terms of composition and performance) changed in this period. However, it is necessary to contextualize those shifts (when and how they occurred) to account for how musicians changed their way of engaging with music as an activity. This contextualization can provide a better description of the changes that altered the corporate environment through which musicians constructed their social status. The situation, therefore, derived from a conflation of factors—aesthetic and economic—that affected the chapel's hierarchical structure during a vulnerable period. Jerusalem's purported lack of musical knowledge pointed to only one of them.

Part Two—Transforming the Music Chapel
The Loss of Corporate Structure

Chapter 4 showed that the examination for the post of chapelmaster was set to gauge a candidate's knowledge of theoretical music principles (música especulativa). This erudition in the "science of music" was important for cathedral musicians and authorities because it legitimized the authority of a chapelmaster within the music chapel and placed him at the top of its internal hierarchy. Jerusalem lacked such knowledge, however, and this made his candidacy for the position questionable. It is true that some of his compositions show ambitious polyphonic designs and large-scale structures,[56] but these works do not compare well with pieces by Tomás Luis de Victoria, Cristobal de Morales, or Alonso Lobo, which for cathedral authorities represented the realization of contrapuntal knowledge.

It was clear that, as far as cathedral notions of erudition were concerned, Jerusalem did not have the desired skills, but who did? Members of the examining committee were familiar with the type of repertoire that demonstrated skill in counterpoint, promoted by Salazar and Sumaya. Of the three, however, José González and Miguel de Herrera were the only two likely to know counterpoint well. Both individuals had outstanding credentials in regard to their musical knowledge, which earned them the endorsement of Salazar and Sumaya. In contrast, there is not enough information to give us a firm idea about Martín Vásquez de Mendoza, the third committee member. From one of his examinations when he was a choirboy we know that he studied "the minimum" and that he knew the basics of music.[57] Aside from this, and from his appointments to examine choir assistants and musicians, we only know that he was impressed by Jerusalem's compositional skills. His exact words were: "regarding composition, I confess that [his talent] abounds," which makes one wonder if Vásquez de Mendoza himself had the coveted erudition that the committee was supposed to assess.[58]

It is quite possible that by the mid-eighteenth century only a few individuals stood out in the chapel in terms of their knowledge of counterpoint. Records show that Sumaya had problems trying to enforce attendance in the escoleta for the teaching of counterpoint already in 1734. Reluctance was especially acute among adult musicians hired by the chapter who still needed to improve in "music." At one point, the canons even decided to stop paying Sumaya the 200 pesos allocated for teaching counterpoint. Sumaya protested, arguing that, if lessons were canceled, it was because musicians failed to show up. The chapter ultimately agreed to repay Sumaya the 200 pesos and asked him to report the names of those absent in the future.[59] It is not known whether Sumaya continued having problems enforcing attendance, but surviving records suggest that right after this incident the situation began to deteriorate.

By the end of that year the canons had assigned the teaching of choirboys to Domingo Dutra y Andrade, but musicians said a year later he was unfit for the task due to his lack of musical knowledge (see Chapter 4).[60] In 1735 Sumaya asked for a two-month leave of absence (patitur) to recover from an unspecified accident.[61] The next information available shows that Sumaya remained absent until April 1736, and that during this period the canons would not hire musicians until Sumaya had examined them first.[62] Dutra y Andrade acted as second chapelmaster in the meantime and continued in charge of teaching and examining choirboys.[63] One can only wonder if he carried out these duties satisfactorily, as upon Sumaya's return, some children appeared to have "good principles and theoretical aptitude, but not enough to make a [musician]."[64] Sumaya took up his duties again in late 1736 and remained active until his sudden departure in 1738, when Dutra y Andrade was left in charge.[65]

This information suggests that instruction and the assessment of musical knowledge had begun to falter somewhat by 1734, and it is very possible that it continued to wane after Dutra y Andrade took over. Therefore, it would not be surprising if competent knowledge of counterpoint was quite elusive by 1750, and comments by the canons point to that possibility. During the meeting when the chapter agreed to examine Jerusalem for the post of chapelmaster, some wondered if there were individuals who could undertake the process because, seemingly, there was no one in the chapel who knew counterpoint well.[66] González and Herrera were part of a previous generation—Sumaya's generation—and they were better prepared than musicians taught by Dutra y Andrade to make an evaluation. It is likely that Dutra y Andrade grew up seeing a lack of interest in counterpoint from adult musicians, which in addition to his deficiencies as a counterpoint teacher, influenced their musical education. In this respect, if Sumaya had trouble encouraging musicians to learn counterpoint it would not be unreasonable to think that for Dutra y Andrade the challenge was even bigger, given that musicians thought he lacked the skills to teach the subject. The incursion of modern music trends was a probable cause for this neglect, although one must also consider the financial needs of musicians during times of economic depression.

As mentioned above, New Spain's economy was far from stable during the first half of the eighteenth century. Prices rose disproportionately in relation to salaries (the salary for the chapelmaster, for example, remained at 500 pesos from 1688 until 1761) and the reliance on credit was widespread. These were proper conditions for the growth of zangonautlas, and we begin to see hints of this toward the end of Sumaya's tenure. The letter from Sumaya addressed at the beginning of the chapter suggests that zangonautlas were occurring well before 1738. The first mentions of musicians neglecting "music" study because of these activities, however, come from a little after this letter. When the chapter met to discuss Sumaya's payment for teaching counterpoint in 1734 the canons mentioned that one of the reasons musicians did not attend the escoleta was that they were usually playing somewhere else. This was something that had started to affect cathedral ceremonies because, instead of fulfilling their duties, musicians were performing outside to earn money.

After Sumaya's departure, zangonautlas only increased, in part for financial reasons, but also because the music chapel did not have a leader and musicians were free from oversight. The canons tried different strategies to curb this activity, which affected the treasury and cathedral services. First, they assigned one bad point every time a musician was absent from a scheduled service (possibly playing elsewhere). The idea was to look at the record of points accrued every six months and penalize those who disobeyed.[67] Six months was a long time, however, and the strategy did not work. Some musicians started to neglect even some of the most important cathedral services (e.g., Holy Week), and this moved the dean to levy fines—instead of points—to discourage absenteeism.[68] At first, musicians were able to persuade the chapter to pardon penalties due to their poverty, but canons became less lenient as the situation persisted. The chapter also opted for redistributing the money that the chapel as a whole received from performing at important rituals. For the matins service on Christmas Eve, for example, payments were distributed only among those who performed at the service, leaving out others who did not attend.[69]

It would be misleading to surmise from these accounts that the music chapel became divided between those who complied by the rules and those who did not. Most musicians were involved in zangonautlas at one point or another; even Martín Bernárdez de Rivera, whom the chapter held in high esteem because of his demeanor and behavior, had to ask forgiveness for participating in these activities.[70] Zangonautlas were rampant by the time Jerusalem became chapel-master and he complained about them, given that he was supposed to receive a percentage from these performances (one real out of every peso earned by the chapel).[71] One might think that Jerusalem was mostly interested in claiming his fair share, and indeed he was. However, his complaints also pointed to a more pressing concern. He was well aware that cathedral musicians were not the only ones affecting his financial interests. Itinerant ensembles made of musicians from other parishes or convents, and amateurs of different races were involved as well. Chapter 2 showed that instances of this problem appeared as early as 1664. In a letter to the chapter, Antonio Visencio (music instructor at the Colegio de San Juan de Letrán) mentioned that people of lower trades—blacksmiths, stocking tailors, fruit vendors—and of "broken skin color" played music at events that were supposed to be exclusive to the cathedral's chapel and to those permitted to play in them by the chapter.

Two years after his appointment Jerusalem wrote to the canons about this same issue, noting that the presence of these musicians devalued the obvenciones. This was not only because of the dire economic situation affecting New Spain but also because other ensembles offered their services at a much lower fee.

> It is evident the decay of obvenciones because of the problems in commerce as well as because of the widespread poverty of Mexico. Before it was possible to get 100 and 200 pesos repeatedly from the celebration of ordinations and funerals . . . and now there have been only two or three of this size in the last two years, given that now the income from obvenciones has decreased by two thirds because, among other things, musicians and servants from other parishes . . . and a large number of itinerant Mulatto singers officiate the functions of this music chapel, reducing performances to a despicable price. And if this vicious situation has been tolerated is to not give the impression that the musicians of the chapel are ambitious or avaricious. But given that the situation has reached such excess the musicians of the chapel want to remind the chapter of their right to these functions according to ordinances by the high court, the archbishop, and this cathedral chapter (see appendix 5.6).[72]

These unauthorized performances also occurred at nunneries where the chapel supposedly held performance privileges. Here, the same itinerant ensembles played and sang along with musician nuns (*músicas religiosas*) who possibly came from the music school of San Miguel de Bethlen, where cathedral musicians were in charge of music instruction.[73]

This information suggests that the monopoly of the cathedral chapel over a landscape of musical activity—comprised by ecclesiastical centers under the cathedral's jurisdiction—was far from consolidated, and that by the second half of the eighteenth century this became an even more contested territory. Things were quite different after 1750: it was not just amateur musicians of broken skin color who undermined the privileges of the music chapel. Cathedral musicians were now openly involved with others from outside—regardless of race—contracting zangonaultas, and this compromised the corporate claims of the chapel. Musicians from parishes, convents, the Coliseo, and even freelancers, usually joined members of the chapel to play at ecclesiastical centers surrogate to the cathedral's authority, where they could not perform on their own. This landscape of activity developed in relation to the unstable state of the city's caste structure: it was a mixed, unruly, changing, and dynamic society, rather than strictly stratified according to race, in which different castes increasingly competed for the benefits of Spaniards. Music practices largely resonated with this social context in the sense that independent initiatives by cathedral musicians to collaborate with others undermined the internal structure of the chapel, its social position as a Spanish corporation, and thus, its claims to performance privileges.

The challenges that Jerusalem experienced as the new leader of the ensemble occurred in this situation, and the precedents were too complex to attribute such tensions simply to his lack of music erudition. Reservations about his knowledge might seem a bit hypocritical at first, considering that knowledge of counterpoint in the music chapel itself was questionable. The issue, nonetheless, was important to the chapter—which continued to push for the teaching of counterpoint, even if inefficiently, from 1735 to 1750—and to musicians. It was important enough for members of the previous generation (e.g., José González, Miguel de Herrera) to petition the removal of Dutra y Andrade as teacher of choirboys in 1735. It was also important to a new generation of musicians— taught by Dutra y Andrade—who, according to Martín Vásquez de Mendoza, thought that a chapelmaster "ought to be a compendium of the abilities of all of the other musicians, so that what someone does not know the chapelmaster knows, and what others know the chapelmaster does not ignore," even if music was "different from past times."

The fact of the matter was that Jerusalem's appointment happened at a moment when things had been in a state of transition, the organizational structure of the music chapel being one of them. These changes related to aesthetic and financial factors that jointly affected cathedral musical activity from 1738 to 1750. On the one hand, musical practices were passing an aesthetic threshold. The chapter continued to push for music to be taught according to traditional standards, but arias and cantadas in the estilo moderno had also made their way into religious services. Whether musicians refused to learn counterpoint during the first three decades of the eighteenth century is not clear. However, the lack of contrapuntal study after that—for aesthetic reasons or not—did affect the chapel's internal hierarchy. Dutra y Andrade's questionable skills possibly perpetuated the lack of interest among musicians to learn counterpoint that Sumaya experienced. What it surely did was to compromise his position as head of the chapel, and the ensuing self-serving activity of musicians only undermined this hierarchy even more. On the other hand, musicians tried to cope with financial pressures, which the lack of a leader only facilitated. The occurrence of zangonautlas grew from 1738 to 1750 precisely for this reason. Chapel musicians were free to break into small groups, which, joined by other musicians, benefited from performing at venues where only members of the chapel could play. The formation of ad hoc groups precluded the entire chapel from working as a unit and this also undermined the ensemble's internal structure.

The chapelmastership was highly vulnerable during this period of changes, and it could be that views of authority in relation to this position became compromised. Upon Sumaya's departure the chapel was left without a leader. Dutra y Andrade was far from being such a figure, and he was caught embezzling money from obvenciones, so it is highly probable that musicians did not have a good image of him altogether. As it turned out, the accountant had failed to remove Sumaya's name from the entry books that recorded the percentages that he received from obvenciones after he had left. As new—even if nominally—chapelmaster, Dutra y Andrade was claiming his percentage from these performances, but also Sumaya's portion. When Jerusalem arrived in 1746, he noticed the discrepancy and informed the chapter, which immediately ordered Sumaya's name removed from the books.[74] More than an oversight, this was a deliberate silence that allowed Dutra y Andrade to benefit from obvenciones just as musicians benefited from zangonautlas. If his lack of music knowledge made Dutra y Andrade's position questionable, his complicity in defrauding the chapel was a definite blow to the ensemble's hierarchy. The chapter asked for his retirement in 1749, since, due to his condition, he could not take care of anything. His alleged depression was possibly a factor, but it seems more feasible that his profile and image were the reasons the chapel lacked governance and direction under him.[75]

Therefore, the musical activity that ensued from 1738 to 1750 was influenced by aesthetic and financial factors that affected the corporate integrity of the music chapel. In order to reclaim the social position of the corporation (and its privileges), cathedral musicians would need to restore its internal structure of operation, and reconsidering the hierarchical role of the chapelmaster was part of that process. In this regard, while traditional views of musical knowledge continued to have institutional relevance, canons and musicians also realized that "the art of music" was changing.[76] The incursion of trends in music of the estilo moderno put practical aspects of performance at the center of a new understanding of musicianship. This shift led to questions about the relationship between musical knowledge and authority within the chapel, and placed musicians on an equal plane in terms of their skills and proficiencies in this modern style. In order to reclaim its social position the ensemble needed to regroup, and there lay the predicament, as Jerusalem's skills were not necessarily superior to those of other performers. Cathedral musicians would need to resolve this issue if they were to restore the corporation and its claims.

Rescuing the Corporation

The chapter was aware that zangonautlas were the main cause for the chapel's state of disarray, and in 1749 the canons attempted to get to the root of the problem. At their first meeting of that year the chapter read a letter from members of the chapel who complained about the situation. There is a chance that Jerusalem was the one who encouraged others to write this letter because now that Dutra y Andrade was gone, he was the person who earned the highest percentage from obvenciones. The chapter recognized that the situation had reached a crisis point, and although there had been efforts to put a stop to zangonautlas the previous year (1748), they continued to flourish.[77] For the chapter, the bottom line was financial: zangonautlas hurt the treasury, but they also hurt cathedral musicians by preventing them from participating in obvenciones. These earnings derived from a corporate benefit that the music chapel held by decrees from the high court, which gave the ensemble the exclusive right to perform at venues under the jurisdiction of the cathedral. Nevertheless, members of the chapel had undermined this privilege by acting independently with others from outside. Paying patrons and ecclesiastical centers also saw this as an opportunity to hire whichever group offered the best price. In order to restore the structure and social position of the chapel, the canons ordered an investigation to learn who was at the root of zangonautlas.

First, they asked the accountants for a report about these activities, and on April 26, 1749, Francisco Javier Gómez Beltrán and Juan José de Mier submitted an illuminating account. Martín Vásquez de Mendoza (member of the committee in Jerusalem's examination, and the one impressed with his compositional skills) was in charge of bookkeeping obvenciones. Part of his duties consisted in entering in the book every event in which the chapel performed along with the money received. After that, Vásquez de Mendoza was supposed to give the book to the accountants, so that they could tax the portion that belonged to the treasury. But according to the accountants this was not what Vásquez de Mendoza actually did and zangonautlas were rather the norm:

... not only for eight or ten pesos ... but for forty or fifty pesos ... and not a single one of these events was entered in the book. This is the reason why we beg your illustrious lordship to give the most severe deliberation to remedy this situation. Because if musicians continue there will be a time when not a single event will be entered in the book, which will affect the Congregación de Nuestra Señora de la Antigua (the musicians' confraternity), the cathedral's treasury, us (the chapter) and even some musicians who complain about this, as José González can attest. Because not all musicians go to these zangonautlas, but only those who are partial to the ones who arrange them with the help of the chapelmaster, as well as Vásquez, who could and should stop this (see appendix 5.7).[78]

It is interesting to see that, at this point, Vásquez de Mendoza and Jerusalem seemed to have a mutual understanding, and that Jerusalem was also involved in zangonautlas, at least until April 1749. On May 7, the chapter named Jerusalem interim chapelmaster in hopes of restoring a sense of discipline and structure in the chapel. The canons thought that appointing a chapelmaster—hopefully more capable than Dutra y Andrade—would put a stop to the "immoderate liberty with which musicians abuse one another."[79] This called for "the most immediate and serious deliberation to stop the harm caused by the lack of sub-ordination to the person appointed for the governance and organization of the chapel."[80]

The first step of this resolution was to name Jerusalem provisional chapel-master. What followed was an interview of every musician to find out who was instigating zangonautlas. Jerusalem was the first person interviewed, and after accepting the honor of his new position he was quick to denounce Antonio Rafael Portillo y Segura as the main perpetrator.[81] Portillo did not mention Jerusalem in his interview, although he did give away the names of Luis del Castillo, Vicente Ramírez, Juan Rodríguez, Domingo Alacio, and Vicente Santos. When interrogated, Luis del Castillo said that, in fact, all musicians did zangonautlas out of financial need, something that Francisco de la Rueda confirmed by saying that he had been invited to play in zangonautlas by almost every musician. Gabriel de Aguilar, Thadeo Priego, and Juan Pérez de Rivera were of the same opinion, although they did not single out any particular individual. However, it is inter-esting to note that other musicians mentioned some of the names that Portillo gave away too. The reports of Mariano Macías, Nicolás Gil, and Jacinto Zapata all mentioned del Castillo, Ramírez, and Rodríguez. In the reports of others, the names of Santos and Alacio joined these last three, although their appearance is less consistent. When interviewed, Alacio also named his peers del Castillo, Ramírez, and Rodríguez, but he additionally put Portillo and Jerusalem in the mix. Only Balthasar Salvatierra (not mentioned by anyone) singled out Jerusalem as the main person, while Juan de Velasco (also spared by everyone) pointed to Portillo. All these statements point to del Castillo, Ramírez, and Rodríguez as the three main suspects, but other information shows that they were unlikely the organizers. Records suggest that Jerusalem and Portillo were the leaders of the pack, and that this could be the reason political frictions started in the ensemble after Jerusalem became chapelmaster.

If Salvatierra and Alacio mentioned Jerusalem in their interviews it was because, quite probably, he did call on musicians in arranging events on his own, but Portillo was equally guilty. Up until 1750, the chapel had functioned unsupervised and some musicians (like Portillo and Jerusalem) had become very skilled in organizing people independently. Institutional affiliation with the chapel was a profitable credential for them because it gave them access to parishes, convents, and monasteries surrogate to cathedral authority to contract different events. By naming a chapelmaster, the canons were trying to put an end to these operations, which after more than ten years were quite established among musicians.

The appointment was a major boon for Jerusalem not only because of the salary and promotion but also because he was to have corporate monopoly over this territory of musical activity, for which he possibly had had to compete until then. Given that his music knowledge was in question and that musicians probably regarded him as just one of their peers, it is very probable that for some individuals (like Portillo) Jerusalem did not have the profile (better profile than theirs) to claim sole authority over the ensemble, much less a higher percentage from obvenciones. It is for this reason that when Jerusalem called on musicians to perform at an event (after becoming chapelmaster), some refused to show up. This was clearly an act of dissent and also a measure to curtail the competition. If the performance under Jerusalem's supervision would not go well, patrons could likely try a different ensemble led by one of the other musicians. Portillo and Salvatierra had their own group of followers not only in the chapel but also from the Coliseo, and later from other ecclesiastical centers. This is something that some of the oldest musicians like Nicolás Gil lamented because, ultimately, the money from zangonautlas, benefited other musicians and not cathedral ministers.[82] But there was a strategy to this: by working with musicians from outside (regardless of race), Portillo and Salvatierra not only competed with the chapel by charging less; they also got more for themselves by paying these musicians well below the percentage that a cathedral musician would get.

Upon Jerusalem's appointment, the competition became acute, more so if we consider that the aim of the chapter was to restore the hierarchical framework of the chapel, lest the group would be like a "body without a head."[83] But even with the chapter's endorsement, some musicians failed to recognize the authority of the new chapelmaster. Complaints from two different parties discussed at the meeting of February 1, 1752, show how this situation developed. At the meeting the canons read a formal protest by Portillo with the support of Vásquez de Mendoza, Rodríguez, Priego, Aguilar, Alacio, and Ignacio Pedroza. Specifically, the group disputed a fine that cathedral accountants levied on them due to their participation in zangonautlas. The musicians argued that their participation in services held at the parishes of San Lorenzo, Amor de Dios, and San Pedro y San Pablo was merely political (to not offend the hosts) and that they had not charged a fee. Allegedly, the organizers had merely thanked them with a token of appreciation.[84] The accountants were well informed, however, and retorted that these musicians were actually paid quite handsomely for these three performances, thus depriving the entire chapel of these earnings.[85]

At this same meeting the canons read a letter that Jerusalem submitted in support of the fine. In it, the chapelmaster mentioned that these musicians were "set against him, treating him with demeaning and belittling words, and disrespecting and disobeying him as chapelmaster."[86] As proof, Jerusalem pointed out that this group had failed to show up to perform at the matins service for San Pedro Nolasco at the Convento de la Merced, even though he had summoned the whole chapel to play at this service. If anything, the chapelmaster wrote, they showed up "attempting to make such service look bad by making fun of those who did perform."[87] In response, the musicians justified their dissent by saying that if they had failed to show up, it was because they resented the fact that this event paid Jerusalem ten pesos to compose new villancicos for the occasion. This is something that the chapelmaster did not do, as every singer took with him his own arias to perform, and so Jerusalem did not deserve that money.[88] Jerusalem argued that he was in fact entitled to this money just for attending the service as chapelmaster, as well as for bringing his own scores.[89]

The chapter supported Jerusalem's entitlement to his extra ten pesos on the basis of his attendance at events. After all, this had become standard practice after Dutra y Andrade had begun receiving this money when he was interim chapelmaster, and just for attending as well. However, the musicians had a point: for matins services the treasury usually paid chapelmasters ten pesos specifically for the composition of villancicos. Antonio de Salazar had received this money for such task, even when the chapter had attempted to rescind this payment on the grounds that villancicos stopped being published after 1711. Salazar argued that the ten pesos were not for printing these pieces but rather to pay for their composition.[90] Jerusalem, therefore, was receiving this money for no effort, but this was largely the chapter's fault for their lack of oversight when Dutra y Andrade created this precedent. Other than his attendance at obvenciones (probably to conduct the ensemble) Jerusalem did not have any other way to qualify for these earnings. For a while, it seems that he did not compose villancicos or that he even provided any new music. In fact, records suggest that he was quite liberal with the actual holdings of the cathedral's music archive:

> [The canons] discussed at length the issue that the papers of the music archive were fleeting around, even for sale, as some people said that bachiller Vicente Santos had already given an estimate for some of the music [to be sold] . . . and that Alacio as well as Aguilar had in their possession many music papers which belong to this holy church, for which the music archive was without any proper care, and that chapelmaster Ignacio Jerusalem gave the keys of the archive to anyone who wanted them, which caused all this disarray that called for remedy, because Jerusalem does not give himself the estimation proper of his station, and he does not fulfill his obligations as chapelmaster by composing villancicos for matins services (see appendix 5.8).[91]

The case is quite petty but informative about the politics brewing in the chapel. These frictions rose from a complicated situation that Jerusalem had fomented in part, and from which he was now trying to disentangle himself. As new chapelmaster, he wanted to put a stop to zangonautlas, which now affected him professionally and financially. By doing this, however, he was trying to adopt a hierarchical role over the ensemble that, on the one hand, he was seen unfit to take, and on the other, he had already undermined before. In all probability, his sudden rise to a position for which some regarded him unworthy made musicians challenge his merit to benefits, and with it, the very reason behind his appointment as chapelmaster. Up until his appointment he had been one among the musicians with stakes and claims to performance benefits, and the fact that by 1751 he was still congenial enough to share the keys of the music archive only hints at the very strong probability that musicians saw him more as a peer and not as their leader. For a while he had arranged zangonautlas (just like Portillo) and had not composed new music. Rather, he used the archive's scores, just like Santos, Alacio, Aguilar, and probably Portillo did. Therefore, Jerusalem was part of a circle of entrepreneurial activity that had evolved in the music chapel since 1738, in which he was one among equals. Upon his arrival in 1746, it is possible that Jerusalem tried to fit within the ensemble, and one can only speculate whether this involved developing relationships with other musicians, especially if he was interested in making money on the side. When he applied for the vacant chapelmastership he was immersed in this interrelational dynamic and the canons knew that. They saw that for chapel members he was just another musician and that they treated him accordingly.[92] Now, with the appointment being official, Jerusalem wanted to change these dynamics of engagement with chapel members. He wanted to claim his place as *maestro de capilla por erección* (according to bylaws), but he found it hard to justify the title.

The competition ensued and not just from within the chapel but also from other parishes, convents, the Coliseo, and even freelancers. Jerusalem's letter to the chapter from February 22, 1752, shows this (addressed above, appendix 5.2). In addition to mentioning how other ensembles competed for obvenciones with the chapel Jerusalem also pointed out that the nuns at convents surrogate to the cathedral fostered this.

> [We ask this venerable chapter], in the name of the protection that it offers to its ministers, to beg the illustrious archbishop, our prelate, to order in the convents of his jurisdiction that the nuns sing, either alone or with the chapel of this church, or the chapel alone, as it was done before to the satisfaction of these nuns, without allowing, as they do allow (not without protest from us) clerics from other monasteries, as well as other individuals and Mulattoes to sing in their churches. [So we ask the illustrious archbishop] to reinstate the chapel of this church to its privileges of officiating all masses, burials, and music functions in all convents under his jurisdiction (see appendix 5.9).[93]

Jerusalem was trying to amend something in which he had been involved for three years and that now compromised the corporate claims of the music chapel. The problem was also aggravated by the fact that some cathedral musicians kept collaborating with others from outside of the chapel. The dean and chapter hoped that applying more severe fines would set a necessary example to "extinguish itinerant groups of musicians."[94] The chapter also discussed the need to dismiss those perpetuating this activity. The first target was Balthasar Salvatierra, who used his position as cathedral minister to contract zangonautlas. At the meeting of February 22, 1752, some canons said that instead of taking time to go to the hospital to get cured from an alleged illness (for which he requested patitur), Salvatierra was caught in the street wearing his cathedral frock and presenting himself as a minister of the church to arrange performances.[95] The chapter dismissed him promptly from the chapel, but this did not necessarily put a stop to zangonautlas. On August 14, 1753, the chapter once again had to levy fines on Juan Argüello and Thadeo Priego for performing at events independently.[96]

The next measure that the chapter took, then, was to change the person doing the bookkeeping for obvenciones. Vásquez de Mendoza had been in charge of this task until 1752, when the canons found that he was an accomplice in arranging zangonautlas. The chapter asked José González to take care of this duty instead, given that he was not only one of the most senior members of the chapel but also was not involved with any of the delinquent musicians.[97] After this, the canons dismissed Portillo on August 17, 1754. Portillo was caught stealing money from the treasury, although this incident was the last straw in a string of events rather than the sole reason for his expulsion. Before that, Portillo had allegedly committed fraud and had even defamed some of the canons. He earned the reputation of being a swindler, to the extent that, "if it was not because of his cathedral frock and being a minister of this holy church—which is what is most useful to his scams—he would have been apprehended a while ago."[98]

Portillo had been a choirboy, originally admitted in the Colegio de Infantes in 1736.[99] Things seem to have gone awry with him, however; ten years later the canons reprimanded him for not fulfilling his singing duties and asked him "not to set foot in the Colegio" (*que no ponga los pies en el Colegio*).[100] Portillo, probably in his early twenties at that time, asked to be hired in the music chapel promising to change all of his wrongdoings, and to study to become succentor within a year.[101] But Portillo had failed to achieve this six years later. This history, in addition to his constant involvement in zangonautlas, made him fall out of the chapter's sympathy, and by 1754 the canons had had enough. Portillo left, but others remained who continued to collaborate with him. Vicente Santos, the irredeemable presbyter and succentor known for his gambling habits and for procuring loans under false pretentions (see Chapter 2), helped Portillo to recruit cathedral musicians after the latter was expelled. This did not involve the older and most senior members of the chapel. As a matter of fact, everything seemed to be calm among these individuals. It was the younger generation of students coming out of the Colegio—the ones learning music and an instrument to eventually be hired in the chapel—which Santos approached. At the meeting of February 19, 1762, the canons discussed how Santos, along with Portillo, were instigating young choirbook carriers, acolytes, and choir assistants to join them in zangonautlas with others from outside.

> For the last three months the chapel has remained in calm, without attending zangonautlas with musicians from outside. Only choir assistants, acolytes, and choirbook carriers are the ones perturbing the peace, as they have joined those in the streets in detriment of the music chapel not only by doing zangonautlas, but also by procuring private homes to arrange performances [in advance], thus impeding patrons from coming to the cathedral [to arrange such events with the chapel] (see appendix 5.10).[102]

Seemingly, Portillo and Santos used these youngsters as a façade whenever they contracted a performance, supposedly on behalf of the cathedral. It was because these boys entered the event wearing their cathedral frocks that patrons believed that they had hired the music chapel, for which Portillo and

Santos charged the corresponding fee. The canons, therefore, expelled Santos hoping that this would bring peace once and for all, but problems were, in fact, just beginning. Things had changed a lot since Sumaya left. Until that point the internal structure of music chapel had mirrored the structure of the cathedral's clergy. An aggregate of calidades (in which rank was no doubt important) differentiated canons from chaplains, chaplains from deacons, deacons from subdeacons, and subdeacons from other ministers (like musicians). For the canons, the chapel was an extension of this clerical hierarchy and it was bound by the same rules. The chapelmaster was an important link in this hierarchical line; he ranked higher than the other musicians and he was a liaison between the chapel and the canons. That is why his position needed to be buttressed by a set of calidades that set him apart, knowledge of music being perhaps the most important. Nevertheless, the theoretical underpinnings of this knowledge were losing relevance, as technical aspects of performance provided the basis for new notions of music proficiency. The problem was that, in part, the lack of a theoretical academic basis had erased hierarchical boundaries between musicians and the chapelmaster. In this respect, while the "art of composition" (not the science of music) might have been the means that Jerusalem used to validate his position, his efforts seemed more a way to cope with the open disregard for his authority, and not necessarily a way to assert it.

In a letter to the chapter (addressed in Chapter 4, see appendix 4.6), for example, he complained how musicians were snatching part of his payment from obvenciones, to which he was entitled not from attending events (as he claimed before, even if he would not compose new villancicos), but from bringing scores that he had composed himself. For Jerusalem, his compositional skills became an important basis for validating his place as chapelmaster, which he tried to legitimize by composing ever-larger works. The canons indeed recognized that this craft was at the center of his duties when they raised his salary from 500 to 800 pesos with the "precise and inviolable condition that every year he ought to compose something new of what is needed or lacking in this holy church."[103]

Therefore, whereas Jerusalem had failed to produce music before, records show that composition had central importance for him afterward, and it was a means that he used to try to control performance activity within the chapel. When the ensemble performed at obvenciones, Jerusalem would not release music unless he attended the event. Musicians complained about this, especially because younger musicians were not included in the best paying obvenciones, which were attended only by the most senior members and by the chapelmaster. Smaller performances were left to the younger players, and Jerusalem not only failed to attend these but also to give the musicians music to play, even when he claimed a percentage from the event.[104] Even toward the end of his life Jerusalem refused to give to the cathedral the copious amount of music that he had written since 1750. The chapter felt entitled to this body of music since the treasury had spent more than 2,000 pesos just in copying the scores.[105] The chapter had requested Jerusalem to deliver all of his music twice in 1767, the second time under protest from musicians.[106] His reluctance to release music and the ensuing complaints from chapel members suggest that restoring respect and obedience for the figure of the chapelmaster was not as important to him as watching for his benefits from obvenciones, which he tried to protect by restricting the circulation of sheet music.

It seems that, in reality, the authority and leadership of the chapelmastership had been severely undermined, and Jerusalem's compositional skills, even if more accomplished than anyone else's, could not restore its former hierarchical role. With Portillo, Salvatierra, and Santos out, the chapel gained a sense of internal balance, but the ensemble still needed to implement a new organizational structure. Soon Portillo started to organize his own ensemble to compete with the cathedral's chapel not only for performances but also for the social position of his music group. Cathedral musicians, therefore, needed to reintegrate into a functioning corporation if they were to fend off this competition. Considering that obvenciones were initially the reason the chapel became dysfunctional, and that now they had become the main turf of corporate challenge, it is not surprising to learn that the administrator became the main liaison between cathedral musicians and the chapter.[107]

After José González (who replaced Vásquez de Mendoza) the canons named Francisco Gabriel de Aguilar chapel administrator in 1762.[108] In lieu of a corporate authority figure, the administrator was the person appointed to take care of bookkeeping as well as other duties. He became the main representative of the chapel and took care of every aspect of obvenciones, always under the scrutiny of musicians and the chapter. The administrator arranged events and made sure that there were enough musicians for every performance. He also made sure that all musicians rotated so that every member of the chapel could have an equal opportunity to play in high-paying obvenciones. Whether Jerusalem tried to hamper this new system of operation would be a speculation. However, the fact that he was restricting the use of his music is very telling. Earlier in this chapter we addressed how Jerusalem initially qualified his percentage from obvenciones not by composing new music (which he did not write) but by saying that his sole attendance was enough. Now, almost ten years later, Jerusalem claimed that he was entitled to his percentage from obvenciones—whether he attended events or not—because of the music that he wrote and brought with him. Judging from the document cited above (see appendix 5.11) it seems that the administrator was assigning money to Jerusalem based on a previous understanding. It also suggests the possibility that Jerusalem was not in charge of these operations (the arranging of events and management of the chapel), which in part explains why he would not release music for some events. The question that remains unanswered is why he chose not to attend these obvenciones or to give music for them. He was entitled to do so as chapelmaster, and also to receive compensation. There are a number of reasons that could be surmised but the fact of the matter was that the chapelmaster was no longer the center of the chapel's corporate functioning. At that moment the ensemble needed to stake its claims as a Spanish corporation and the administrator alone did not have enough institutional weight. The chapel also needed to make sure that every member was represented equally—in front of the chapter and in society—lest dissent would threaten to divide the group once again.

On May 30, 1768, canon Juan Ignacio de la Rocha (precentor and the one assigned to oversee the chapel) met with the entire ensemble to appease younger musicians, who complained of not benefiting from obvenciones enough, and who were prone to join others outside in zangonautlas. At that meeting the precentor and all musicians established new guidelines of operation, which changed the profile of the chapel to that of an assembly in which every member had an equal vote. The administrator was not appointed by the canons anymore; he was to be elected by unanimous vote among musicians. In addition, obvenciones were not to be regulated by the administrator alone. From that moment on, every four years the chapel elected deputies who would advise the administrator on how to rotate musicians, so that every member of the chapel could have an equal opportunity to earn money from obvenciones. For this, the deputies formed three groups (tandas) that alternated between large and small events. According to a report by the precentor, everybody agreed to these new guidelines, except for Jerusalem who did not attend the meeting.[109] In this way, the music chapel passed from being a hierarchical ecclesiastical group to being a democratic council with elected officers, and records show that this structure remained after Jerusalem had passed away.[110] The chapelmaster did continue to earn a more substantial percentage from obvenciones than the rest of the musicians, but he was not the authority figure of the corporation. With these new constitutions the cathedral chapel regained its corporate integrity at a crucial moment; Portillo was about to make a rather audacious move.

Decency: The Calidad of the Corporation

Prior to Portillo's expulsion, Jerusalem had asked the canons for their support to uphold the chapel's right to perform at venues under the cathedral's jurisdiction. In his letter, Jerusalem stressed that the high court had granted this privilege after several litigation cases tried by previous chapelmasters, such as Juan Coronado (1679), Antonio de Salazar (1697), and himself (1753).[111] This letter shows that cathedral musicians had a long history of disputing this right, which due to their corporate identity (long-standing members of a Spanish institution, and trained in music throughout their lives) they had been able to preserve. Such privilege, nonetheless, was to remain in heated contest—even with the court's ruling—because of Portillo, who gathered musicians from different parishes and convents to play at churches that were part of the cathedral's turf.

Of all ecclesiastical centers, the parish of the Casa Profesa (a Jesuit convent) was especially known as a hub of freelancers who played wherever there was an opportunity. It was known that individuals from different castes (Mestizos, Mulattoes, Chinos)[112] frequented the parish's music chapel, where those dismissed from the cathedral usually ended up as well. Together, these musicians made a makeshift ensemble that played at the Coliseo, in small churches, and even in private homes.[113] For some, however, the parish was possibly a "steppingstone" before they could get a better position. This was the case of Gregorio Panseco, violin player and chapelmaster at the Profesa, who approached the chapter in hopes of employment in 1761. Versatile musicians were always attractive, and given that Panseco played violin, violón, and flute the canons tried to hire him. The problem was that Panseco also wanted to keep his employment at the Profesa, and it was known that the Coliseo hired him regularly to conduct the theater's orchestra as well.[114] The canons hired him, but only with the condition that he had to relinquish his position at the Profesa, which he seemingly did.[115]

It is possible that for Panseco leaving the chapelmastership was not a big loss. By 1761 the Profesa ensemble seemingly had decayed a lot, in part because of the itinerant nature of the group.[116] Up until that point, the Profesa was only one of several points within a network of musical activities (which included churches surrogate to the cathedral's jurisdiction) in which musicians not affiliated with the cathedral moved. Nevertheless, this changed after the chapter dismissed Portillo. He became a highly accomplished contractor, who organized and mobilized musicians efficiently. He became famous—or infamous—for his ability to coordinate a good number of small itinerant ensembles in the city, which included musicians of different castes.[117] In 1762 Portillo (aided by Salvatierra) formed his own music chapel with a steady roster of musicians from the Profesa, and by 1765 he was hired as chapelmaster of this parish.[118] In this way, Portillo affiliated his new ensemble to a religious institution, which enabled him to contend with the cathedral's music chapel for the status of his ensemble.

Portillo aggressively competed for performances using different tactics, for even when he was not able to win a contract he would try to make cathedral musicians look bad. This happened on occasions when the chapel administrator would book two different services that happened at the same time and at different venues. In order for the chapel to fulfill all of its obligations the administrator—Juan Baptista del Águila at that time—would send different tandas to cover different events. But some performances called for large ensembles and in that case the administrator was forced to call on musicians from outside of the chapel to fill in. Such collaboration worked both ways. Sometimes freelancers were able to secure performances in venues outside cathedral jurisdiction, but without having the instrumental forces needed to do the job. These musicians would tell the administrator of the cathedral's chapel to assign the event to one of the tandas, to thus, share the payment. This arrangement became standard after it was made known that Portillo overtaxed his musicians.[119] Some individuals decided not to get involved with him for that reason and preferred to work alone. Juan Campusano and his two sons (the group on which del Águila relied the most, either to fulfill the chapel's obligations or to share performances) were a good example. For del Águila, collaborating with "the Campusanos" was especially important, given that Portillo would make cathedral musicians look bad at all cost. For example, when del Águila hired musicians from the Casa Profesa to help cover performances they would back out at the last minute under Portillo's instructions.[120] In other cases Portillo would forbid musicians in his ensemble to participate in any way with the cathedral chapel. The fact that Portillo became "the most subtle, astute . . . favored, protected, and intrepid" musician in the city led del Águila to call him the "enemy of the post" (*enemigo del puesto*). The period 1765–1768 was probably a challenging period for the chapel; del Águila certainly called this "the most tortuous and critical [time] . . . full of debates, controversies, challenges, and pretentious disdains," seemingly because of Portillo.[121]

Portillo and his chapel were a central cause of concern, especially because his ensemble was hampering the corporate privileges of cathedral musicians. Seemingly, Portillo recruited "all types of musicians available in the city: good and bad, white and black, and none of them affiliated with the cathedral."[122] What seemed even more outrageous was that important personalities of the city's elite actually supported such a motley group. If the *siglo de las luces* emphasized the importance of social appearance it also made it possible for individuals to make their way into Spanish society through activities and behaviors that were in tune with new forms of sociability. Sure, Portillo's musicians encompassed men from different castes but he made sure that they always performed wearing clerical frocks and wigs.[123] The wearing of frocks no doubt caused the indignation of some pundits, who saw these musicians as mere street vendors, slackers, convent acolytes, and others that had not even received the tonsure. Nevertheless, Jesuit authorities advocated the use of frocks so as not to compromise the formality of these musicians.

Portillo's circuit included not only services in the smaller churches of different monastic orders (not surrogate to cathedral authority) but also celebrations either at the Profesa or in the houses of important personalities who liked to sponsor rituals "for this or that saint."[124] And indeed, there was a reason for Portillo and Jesuit authorities to enforce dress code. Some of the most important families of the New Spanish aristocracy attended rituals at the parish of the Casa Profesa, and some of the most important events of the city's high society took place there.[125] Although there is no direct evidence, it would not be unreasonable to think that Portillo's interest in taking over the chapelmastership of the Profesa was the possibility to develop relationships in this distinguished milieu. Records show that he eventually enjoyed the favor of individuals such as Ambrosio Eugenio de Melgarejo Santaella (mayor and judge of the supernumerary crime court of Mexico), his son Antonio Eugenio Melgarejo Santaella (rector of the university), Miguel de Berrio y Zaldívar (marqués de Jaral de Berrio and conde de San Mateo Valparaíso), and even the viceroy, Carlos Francisco de Croix (marqués de Croix, viceroy 1766–1771).

For cathedral musicians, their knowledge of music and career as church ministers—the product of a lifetime of service for some of them—were means to establish a discourse of status that allowed them to claim certain privileges. This was something to which Portillo very likely aspired and institutional affiliation was indeed necessary. His incursion into the Profesa in 1765 was a move in that direction, although it was short-lived. Known for being an antiroyalist group, the Jesuit order was expelled from all Spanish territories in 1767 by Charles III. The king did not take lightly the fact that the Jesuits answered only to papal authority, and that they thought that the church should administer its own financial assets. With the excuse of the Esquilache Revolt (*motín de Esquilache*, a social revolt allegedly planned and instigated by the Jesuits in which people demonstrated against socioeconomic conditions in Spain) the monarch ousted what he considered an obstacle to the implementation of economic reforms, in which the administration of ecclesiastical resources featured prominently.

After the Jesuits left Mexico City, the Oratorio de San Felipe Neri was quick to occupy the parish of the Casa Profesa, and in 1771 Viceroy de Croix officially gave the building to this congregation. The Oratorio did not have plans to keep the music chapel but this was not necessarily bad for Portillo. First, he was able to secure the protection of Miguel de Berrio y Zaldívar and Ambrosio Eugenio de Melgarejo Santaella, both of whom advocated his being hired in different places. This became most evident when administrator del Águila (with the help of the Campusanos) was able to secure the continued performance of cathedral musicians in services held at the Convent of Capuchin Nuns. According to a royal decree (see below), the convent had the right to choose which musicians were hired for services. Given that things were going well after hiring the cathedral's chapel (which was likely to become the mainstay ensemble) Berrio y Zaldívar and Melgarejo Santaella started to pressure the nuns to hire Portillo instead.[126]

These individuals quite possibly promoted Portillo's name within their circle, and it is very likely that, because of his singing, he became a person *de pública voz y fama* (of public voice and fame). After all, even viceroy de Croix spoke well of him and of his talent. Given that Portillo was institutionally unaffiliated since the closure of the Jesuit parish the viceroy tried to persuade one of the canons to hire him again in the cathedral. Specifically, de Croix asked the chapter "why don't your illustrious lordships introduce a great voice and ability that there is in Mexico, someone called Portillo, that people tell me sings divinely, given that there is not one single good voice in the choir."[127] The canons, of course, did not welcome Portillo back. But these proofs of support did keep the chapel on its toes and on the lookout for the continuing competition between both ensembles, because, as del Águila said, "first dead than beaten by Portillo" (*primero muerto que vencido por Portillo*).[128]

Such were the political heights that Portillo reached, which served him well to make his ensemble even more competitive. The institutional connection that he needed came along soon enough and he did not hesitate to make use of it right away. His acquaintance with Melgarejo Santaella senior enabled Portillo to establish a relationship with his son, Antonio Eugenio, who was rector of the university. Records show that Portillo enjoyed the patronage of the Melgarejo family as their protégé at the parishes of San Miguel and the royal hospital.[129] However, it was under Antonio Eugenio's protection that Portillo made a bold move: he wrote directly to the king asking for his permission to allow him and the musicians that Portillo considered pertinent

> to attend and serve all of the events of the royal university, giving this group the title of chapel of this royal university, and to me of chapelmaster of it . . . so that [this chapel] shall enjoy—as chapel of your majesty's university, and thus, as royal chapel—all of the privileges, honors, and prerogatives that the royal chapel in Madrid has, for which [this chapel] may attend events at any church or convent . . . inside or outside of the city, without obstacles from any prelate, organization, or person of any rank or hierarchy.[130]

Portillo's intentions with this letter were very clear: (1) to get approval from the highest authority for the affiliation of his chapel to an important social institution in order to claim social privilege; and (2) to debase to position of the cathedral's music chapel as the leading music group in the viceroyalty. According to Portillo, his initiative was inspired by the king's royal decree from June 2, 1755, in which he gave the Convent of Capuchin Nuns the privilege to overlook the exclusivity that the cathedral chapel had to perform at their services. The convent—which was surrogate to cathedral authority—was thus free to hire whatever musicians it pleased.[131] The news traveled fast and Jerusalem, del Águila, and the chapel's deputies responded to the matter promptly.

> The chapelmaster, deputies and administrator of the chapel of this holy metropolitan church, in the name of all of its members, before your illustrious lordship, with all due veneration, we say that it has come to our attention that the Royal University submitted a petition presented by Don Antonio Portillo—expelled musician from this holy church— in which he asks to be named chapelmaster of said Royal University asking the king, our lord, to approve the formation of this ensemble under the title of Royal Chapel, all of which is cause of dishonor for the chapel of this holy church, for which we petition, under the protection of your illustrious lordship . . . to give us permission to use the necessary recourse at the royal court through [the chapter's agent in Spain] Don José Miranda . . . to present our merits in service to the king, our lord, the high court, this noble city, and its public, which are just and protected by your illustrious lordship, all of which promises our success [in this matter] (see appendix 5.11).[132]

It is possible that Antonio Eugenio, as rector, introduced and pushed for the approval of Portillo's petition by university officials, not all of whom agreed with the singer's requests entirely. The petition was sent to the king with the rector's endorsement, nonetheless. The royal court took a while to respond but this did not stop Portillo from presenting himself as interim chapelmaster of the university.[133] He even signed receipts for payment at the royal hospital as "chapelmaster of the university and of the parish of San Miguel," places where Portillo received the patronage of the Melgarejo family. This shows that Melgarejo's protection largely accounted for the singer's overconfidence to use these credentials prematurely, with which "he is able to take over all events, leaving this [cathedral] chapel without obvenciones."[134] The situation had become quite complicated politically, and this moved cathedral musicians to outline in their letter to the king the list of calidades—a certification of merits of sorts—that made them worthy of their corporate privileges.

> This music chapel is comprised of thirty individuals, *decent men*, fifteen of them criollos of known lineage, all alumni of the Colegio de Infantes, who before being admitted gave full information about their legitimate birth, purity of blood, and about their descent from old Christians, according to the bylaws of the Colegio, of which five are presbyters and two are on their way to this rank. The other fifteen are European who have been summoned by the illustrious and venerable dean and

chapter for the service of this holy church. Others have come requesting accommodation [for employment], which they accomplished due
to their dexterity and ability, after a rigorous examination and scrutiny
of their lives and customs (see appendix 5.13).[135]

As part of this certification (addressed in Chapter 2, see appendix 2.3) the
music chapel also outlined all of the services that the ensemble provided to
the king and its royal administration, as well as to the city and its public. These
included services to commemorate the king's birthday and the birth of princes,
to observe official royal proclamations, and other events pertaining to the royal
family (such as funerals). The ensemble also participated in services at the viceroyal palace, as well as in civic celebrations and in cathedral rituals to commemorate civic events. Last, cathedral musicians mentioned their work teaching at the
music school founded by archbishop Juan Antonio de Vizarrón y Eguiarreta in
the orphanage of San Miguel de Bethlen (spelled Belem in this document), and
in the Real Colegio de San Ignacio de Vizcaínas. These services were part of a
large certification of merits to the exclusive privilege to perform in venues that
were surrogate to the authority of the highest prelate in the viceroyalty. With
this document cathedral musicians attempted to position the music chapel as
the foremost ensemble in New Spain, politically parallel to the king's royal chapel (more by inference than by decree), and therefore, of higher status than any
other group.

What seems interesting is that, in order to legitimize this position, the music
chapel started by making mention of calidades that could place it indisputably
above Portillo's ensemble. These were, first and foremost, the "known lineage"
(of public voice and fame) and purity of blood of their Spanish members, who
had given full testimony of their descent from old Christians as required by the
bylaws of the Colegio de Infantes. Membership with this institution gave corporate validity to their limpieza de sangre, and in consequence, to their status
claims. More interesting is that the chapel mentioned the clerical rank of some of
its members as a credential that added weight to the "Spanishness" of the group.
This brought legitimacy to the membership of other European musicians, whose
claim to be "decent men" (a Spanish trope of status) was the result of their corporate identity within the chapel and within the cathedral as a Spanish institution.
Musical dexterity and knowledge (corroborated by a "rigorous examination")
were also important, and the chapel was very careful to outline how all of these
calidades placed the ensemble on a plane quite apart from Portillo's.

Jerusalem sent a separate letter to accompany the chapel's certification of
merits in which he stated why Portillo was not qualified to be chapelmaster.
Among other things, Jerusalem mentioned that neither Portillo nor any of the
musicians had proper musical knowledge as required by an institution like the

university. Such knowledge, Jerusalem added, was something that cathedral musicians proved to have through the appropriate examinations.[136] The canons agreed with Jerusalem on this point; they mentioned that Portillo usually assigned someone to merely mark the beat (*hechar el compás*) while he just sang from memory.[137] Jerusalem also stated that Portillo did not have proper knowledge of music because he came from the theater (omitting Portillo's time in the Colegio), which put in question his social class, and thus, his calidad.[138] This remark resonated with the opinion of all chapel members about Portillo's musicians, whose calidad and status could be inferred from their lack of music knowledge, lack of institutional affiliation, and from their race. Therefore, the "decency" of the music chapel—a group comprised of "decent men"—was a social quality that resulted from the alleged musical knowledge of its members and their affiliation with a Spanish institution. Just as important was the fact that half of its members were Spaniards of proven limpieza, of which half were clerics. These attributes consolidated the Spanish character of the music chapel's corporate political identity. "Decency," therefore, became a racialized discourse of status through which cathedral musicians claimed a privileged position over other individuals "who are not our equals. They might be very good men, but not *decent* to so many white men and cleric gentlemen in the chapel."[139]

Epilogue

Further Considerations on Race and Music Culture

The answer from the royal council to the plea from cathedral musicians arrived on April 29, 1769. Seemingly, the body of evidence submitted by the chapelmaster, the administrator, and the deputies had a positive effect. The monarch was convinced that neither Portillo nor his ensemble had merit to their pretensions. First, the cathedral's chapel presented evidence showing that the prelate and the high court supported their claims to performance privileges. Second, Portillo's background was suspicious at best: he was not only an alleged "musician from the theater" with no musical knowledge, but also an individual expelled from the church because of theft. It might seem puzzling at first to understand how the theater–knowledge argument held any weight at all, especially since Jerusalem himself could be accused of the same (that is, of being a theater musician without knowledge of music). Here one must be aware of the context of these facts.

Jerusalem arrived in New Spain as a theater musician, yes, but he tried to dissociate (himself and his family) from that environment. He not only tried to find accommodation in the cathedral for himself but also for his son, Salvador. Moreover, his daughter, María Michaela Jerusalem Sisto, became a novice at the Convent of Conceptionist Nuns in 1760. And while it is not clear whether she received music training at the school of San Miguel de Bethlen in order to be a musician nun (*música religiosa,* a training that would allow her to work at a convent as a musician in lieu of a dowry), the fact that Antonia Sisto (her mother) asked for a loan to the cathedral chapter in order to cover the cost of the professing ceremony suggests this as a possibility.[1]

Affiliation with Spanish institutions was a means of social mobility, and Jerusalem knew that. Regarding music, it is true that he did not comply with traditional cathedral standards as far as notions of knowledge were concerned. However, it is possible that by undergoing the scrutiny of an examination, and by relying on his compositional skills to fulfill expectations (especially, being able to write the type of works needed in a cathedral, and not just short arias and lyric music for the theater, as some said), Jerusalem endorsed a notion of musical knowledge more in tune with the aesthetic and ideological shifts that transpired in New Spain during the second half of the eighteenth century. This interpretation might seem thin, but it does explain a lot in this context. Jerusalem had been a theater musician, yes, and proficient in música moderna, just like Portillo. However, the latter's credentials (and thus, his all-around social appearance) were rather dubious not only because of his lack of musical knowledge (allegedly he only sang from memory and did not even conduct the ensemble) but also because of the people who surrounded him (Mulattoes, Mestizos, Chinos)—also, he was a thief. Support of the chapel's claim by archbishop Francisco Antonio de Lorenzana added further weight to their case, and the king, therefore, ruled in favor of the prelate. In the royal decree the king disapproved Antonio Eugenio Melgarejo Santaella's support of Portillo's chapel in the university, and ordered him to dissolve it immediately.[2] After this episode, Portillo's competition continued for approximately six years, although in minor form. For the most part, his activity remained relegated to small events at places where he still enjoyed the favor of elite personalities, like the Melgarejo family and Berrio y Zaldívar (e.g., the Convent of Capuchin Nuns, or the parish of the Hospital Real). In cathedral records, his name disappears after 1775 and one wonders if this was because of death or because musicians finally deserted him.[3]

The altercation with Portillo was perhaps the most heated contestation of privilege that cathedral musicians faced, but this was largely because of the corporate character that the situation assumed. The work of historians addressed in previous chapters shows that the racial system of castes had grown unstable by the mid-eighteenth century (especially in the middle classes), and the continuous attempts of individuals of mixed race to compete for performance spaces with cathedral musicians corroborates that. If the high court ruled in favor of the cathedral's chapel in every instance (up until 1753, when we have notice of the last recorded case) it was because of the weight that the music chapel had as a Spanish corporation (affiliated to the most important New Spanish religious institution, and an extension of its clergy), which legitimized the racialized claims to status and privilege made by its members. Just like university students and individuals with positions in Spanish institutions, the social quality of musicians (i.e., their calidad)—as well as the validity of their claims—was inferred from their institutional credentials and not the other way around (see Chapter 3). Institutional memberships were important means of social mobility, and therefore, an important component of status claims. For Portillo, his acquaintance with important personalities was in all probability a way to attain institutionalization, to thus elevate his position; his attempt to establish a "royal chapel" at the university (a probable institutional symbol of erudition in enlightened intellectual circles) makes this very plausible. Creating a corporation (a music chapel) with the support not only of elite individuals but also of a Spanish institution would have been an effective way to outrank cathedral musicians. The latter reacted very differently to Portillo's challenge than to other litigations ruled on by the high court. This was the first time in which the entire chapel drafted a certification of merits in which the limpieza de sangre and clerical background of some of its members appeared so emphatically documented. Unlike other cases when chapelmasters only asserted the ensemble's jurisdictional rights to perform, now there was a need to claim the "Spanishness" and social quality, and therefore, the status and privilege of the corporation.

One of the main reasons that made this conflict possible was that music, unlike other activities, was not bound to corporate guidelines of operation. Handcraft artists, instrument makers, and other artisans operated according to guild policies. Each guild had specific rules to regulate admission (some required limpieza de sangre for membership), training, and work within a certain profession. Through these guidelenes, guilds enjoyed exclusive privileges to manufacture certain goods or to control specific trades and activities. Nobody could become a master silver worker, for example, without first passing an exam supervised by the guild. Racial exclusivity was a general rule in the operation of guilds, which, needless to say, limited the exercise of certain professions to a group of individuals, who, above all, aimed to monopolize the economic implications of their trade (such as employment and the selling of services and products).[4]

Although, in principle, the music chapel operated according to similar racial principles, the institutional underpinnings of music set it apart from the manual arts. Music had traditionally adhered to a confessional framework of theoretical knowledge rooted in the quadrivium, which gave it intellectual undertones and placed it outside the realm of guilds.[5] In confessional institutions such as the cathedral and the university, music was considered one of the liberal arts, buttressed by notions of erudition. Although this explanation might seem to put music and all musicians in the city on a de facto socially high and privileged plane, it actually means that music occupied a very liminal territory. When notice of the conflict with Portillo's chapel at the university first reached the chapter, some canons did not know how to proceed. They thought this was a dispute among musicians and that the chapter should not intervene. After all, music was a liberal art, for which any capable musician could petition to be chapelmaster at the university. It was up to the king, the canons said, to decide whether to grant the appointment.[6] That is why the certification of merits by the chapel was important and why limpieza de sangre featured prominently at the beginning of the document. If there was to be a royal chapel it would have to be a group of individuals possessing higher credentials, and therefore, status than cathedral musicians.

Ultimately, this event shows that, while on the one hand music was an activity that lacked strict corporate definition, on the other, this lack of definition set it socially apart from mechanical and manual activities. Initially, this might convey the idea that even street musicians could claim higher status than blacksmiths and tailors, but one must not forget that there were implications in these pretensions that not every musician could fulfill, musical knowledge and institutional membership being perhaps the most important. Perceptions of music as a liberal art gave this activity an intellectual character in which issues of style in relation to other musics might have been relevant after 1750. Given that the incursion of trends in music of the estilo moderno eventually debased the importance of contrapuntal principles, approaches toward performance perhaps acquired more weight in defining the musicianship and knowledge of those who pledged to be professional musicians. However, these properties alone did not define the status of music performers. It would be easy to say that some sounds held a higher place than others (e.g., European serenades or concertos over zarambeques and jarabes), but a racialized sonic landscape cannot account for the ways in which individuals used music to define their social place, and how race figured in their efforts.

The certification of merits by the chapel is quite informative in this regard, because it shows that European music was not in itself a marker of race or status, but rather a single element in a complex profiling process that produced different identity imaginaries and positionings within them, even within one single Spanish institution. This was specially relevant to non-Spanish European musicians, who relied on the Spanish corporate character of the music chapel to claim "decency."

In the aftermath of this analysis one could say that "Spanish hegemony" prevailed in the end because, epistemologically, it did. The claims of cathedral musicians were grounded on the validity of a social profiling process in which blood, institutional membership, and knowledge were important attributes that reflected a "Spanish" notion of calidad. In this respect, the fact that non-Europeans claimed "decency" as a racialized discourse of status—that is, as members of a Spanish corporation—only adds weight to this epistemology. Ultimately, these claims rested on the perpetuation of a racial order and on the reproduction of colonialism. The disclaimer here is that this unilateral system of operation cannot be equated with social readings of *race* without essentializing social actors. Such analogy would be at odds with the diverse and highly politicized ways in which colonial subjects articulated their social and political profiles in relation to that system. Given that claims of "Spanishness" (even from among individuals of different racial backgrounds) were quite pervasive, one can only wonder if it is possible (and historically sound) to consider individuals strictly as Mulatto, Mestizo, Castizo, Chino, and so on, disregarding the strategies that they used to fashion their social identities. These self-fashionings might be different from how we want to see these individuals today (for example, quite a few people still think that Manuel Sumaya was Mestizo, regardless of the fact that he, in all probability, considered himself Spaniard). As mentioned in Chapter 1, one of the main purposes of this study is to consider race as a historically situated, and contextually specific social construction. It is true that New Spain had a hierarchical system of racial castes in place, although it should be clear by now that race was not defined by this framework as much as by how people moved in it. Such movement and the fluidity of this system make it difficult to apply racial labels rigidly and uniformly without social and overall historical distortion. "Spanishness" is one of such labels, which in the context of the present study poses an important question: what did it mean to be Spanish in eighteenth-century New Spain?

This book sought to address the complexity of this query by showing that "Spaniards" were far from being an economically, politically, or even racially consistent group. Race was a social construction, which, based on notions of lineage (genealogical, religious, of blood), enabled people to articulate diverse claims to social status. There were different racial imaginaries (e.g., decency, nobility) to which individuals aspired in order to define their social place among Spaniards, and thus, in society at large. In light of the nuances that surround the study of race, and of the importance that this construct had in New Spanish society, the present study focused on calidad, or social quality, to understand the different racialized discourses of status that cathedral ministers claimed. The certification of merits by the music chapel addressed in the last chapter is especially relevant to this final analysis. It was mentioned above that this document alluded quite strategically to the limpieza de sangre and clerical status of some musicians to stress the Spanish character of the ensemble (as a group of decent men). It was this racialization that connected "decency" to notions of Spanish belonging, as it was informed by attributes that helped people to dissociate themselves from the remainder of the Spanish caste, especially because individuals of mixed race increasingly claimed being Spanish. Non-Spanish European musicians endorsed "decency" not as Spaniards, but as members of a Spanish corporation, to thus rank above others. This suggests that while musicians sought to differentiate themselves from other persons, it is quite possible that such differentiation indeed existed between cleric and lay musicians inside the cathedral, especially since the ecclesiastical rank of the first was used to justify the claims of the latter.

Some scholars have recognized this tendency within the high clergy. It was because Mestizos and Mulattos claimed "Spanishness" in order to enter the university and the church that individuals with financial means pursued doctoral degrees. Such rank not only made them eligible for positions on the university's board of directors or for ecclesiastical benefices (e.g., a canonry). Ultimately, a doctorate was a means to dissociate this clerical elite from the growing number of bachiller degree holders and presbyters during the eighteenth century.[7] For those without resources at the cathedral, the degree of bachiller and the rank of presbyter made them eligible to join the cathedral choir—a group made up of canons with doctoral degrees, members of the chapter—which entailed them to the privilege of noble treatment in light of their calidades, and that possibly placed them above "decent people."

There are degrees of social difference that are materially tangible here, while others are rather vague. On the one hand, canons certainly held higher status than chaplains not only because of their education and rank but also because of their socioeconomic standing (in addition to their high paying benefices, they also came from families of means). On the other, while both presbyters and lay musicians were cathedral ministers, the first held higher ecclesiastical rank and had more education. However, both came from similar backgrounds (low and middle classes), and while a chaplaincy could give a presbyter extra income, the fact that both were members of the chapel makes one wonder how differences in status could be established between them. Here lies the importance of contextualization, and the chapel's certification of merits provides important clues. If the certification addressed presbyters (and their limpieza) first it was because their calidad legitimized the claims of lay members of the corporation. In the same fashion, the calidad of canons from the chapter legitimized the "noble" status of presbyters who were members of the choir, just as nobles of blood legitimized the desires for noble prerogatives in the upper stratum of nobles of privilege. This framework of association established a structure for the construction of race among Spaniards that hinged around perceptions of calidad. For this reason, one could say that calidad functioned as a hierarchical discourse of difference, and that the relationship between race and status was highly sensitive to this profiling factor. This does not mean that blood lacked currency or that it became unimportant in the articulation of status. The certifications of merits from Martín Bernárdez de Rivera and the music chapel precisely show the importance that limpieza had in claims of "nobility" and "decency." However, the fact that the latter comprised a collective effort, which included non-Spaniards, suggests that people could claim "Spanishness" by corporate association. "Decency" and "nobility" were no doubt status claims derived from a Spanish racial system of social and political organization. However, the fact that these claims (and even the diversity of efforts that existed to endorse these claims) related to different social positions within this system urges us to approach race as a context-specific social construction, sensitive to the desires of particular individuals. Chapter 3 mentioned that, recently, scholars in social history have addressed the need to consider how the Spanish race-power ideology influenced specific aspects of social life. There is a need to understand the ways in which the construction of "Spanishness" was linked to intimate domains of experience. In part, this study sought to answer that call by stressing that ways of thinking about music were susceptible to notions of "Spanishness," and that the social ambitions of musicians who subscribed to this notion ultimately rested on the reproduction of a colonial racial hierarchy. In this respect, the tensions surrounding the examination of Ignacio Jerusalem for the post of chapelmaster show that if a traditional paradigm of music aesthetics held institutional weight it was not out of obstinate and stodgy dislike for new trends. It was a system of music education that buttressed discourses of "Spanishness" among cathedral ministers—especially among those reared in the cathedral—for whom limpieza and institutional affiliation were important.

The revolt of musicians against Jerusalem after his appointment was not arbitrary either. Aesthetic changes altered perceptions of what music erudition was supposed to be by the mid-eighteenth century. This change produced new understandings of musicianship, and therefore, new ways of thinking about music. The efforts of individuals to use music as a strategy to define their social place, nonetheless, were sensitive to the dynamics of a highly unstable racial landscape. The activity of musicians of mixed race in their competition for Spanish benefits is only proof of that. In this regard, this case study showed how, like other Spanish corporations (e.g., the church, the university), the music chapel relied on race as a means to uphold its place, an effort in which calidad figured at the center.

This book attempted to highlight the connections that existed between Spanish claims of status and music, and the way in which the destabilization of the caste system—arguably one of the most characteristic phenomena in eighteenth-century New Spanish history—influenced music culture. Along these lines, the present book has sought to propose an understanding of Spanish *race* in relation to an aggregate of elements that composed an individual's social profile. Calidad acquired central importance in this understanding: it was a hierarchical gradation of difference, through which "Spanishness" acquired different hues. Ultimately, this view of race problematizes views of Spanish hegemony that essentialize racial classifications. It is not possible to consider the lives of people of mixed race as racial peripherals without ignoring the efforts of those who relied on their Spanish lineage (either from the paternal or maternal side) to negotiate their political identities. All of these nuances make it hard to advocate for a meta-narrative of race that is consistent with all the possible elements that influenced diverse modes of social operation. This case about cathedral musicians has aimed at highlighting such fluidity, as well as to show that music, as an activity, functioned as an institutional process of subject formation, and therefore, as a dynamic element in the production of colonial society.

APPENDIX

Introduction

1.1—*Con la venia de vuestra señoría, y de toda la capilla, como más antiguo de ella digo que tengo dos puntos que hablar:*

El primero es que el señor administrador no admita más de dos funciones, las cuales se podrán servir bien, pero en queriendo admitir tres o cuatro llama [personas] de afuera que no son de nuestro igual, sí serán muy hombres de bien, pero no decentes para tanto hombre blanco y señores sacerdotes de dicha capilla. ACCMM, Acuerdos de Cabildo, folder 4, ca. 1768.

Chapter 2

2.1—*Se continúa entre diferentes personas, y especialmente entre la gente común, el tener oratorio dentro de sus casas poniendo altares con muchas luces a devoción de los santos San Francisco, San Nicolás, Santa Rosa, y otros santos con el festejo y ruido de arpa y guitarra y danzas que hacen en los mismos oratorios bailando hombres y mujeres todo el día y la noche, frecuentando las casas en que se hacen estos festejos mucho concurso de gente.* AGN, Inquisición, vol. 1179, document 10, fol. 185r.

2.2—After being hired to play violin Antonio Palomino was told: *por ninguna causa ni motivo ha de tocar en el coliseo ni ha de asistir a cosas profanas ni a fandangos comunes ni a cosa que no sea muy decente, y [sólo] en casas en que concurran las correspondientes circunstancias de atención, respeto y urbanidad.* ACCM, Actas, book 41, fol. 176r, October 17, 1752.

2.3—*Relación jurada de los méritos que presenta la capilla de música de la santa iglesia metropolitana de México, reino de Nueva España, en servicio del rey, nuestro señor, Real Audiencia, nobilísima ciudad y público.*

Dicha capilla de música se compone de treinta sujetos, hombres decentes, los quince criollos de linaje conocido, hijos todos del Colegio de Nuestra Señora de la Asunción, quienes antes de ser admitidos con la beca dieron plena información de legitimidad, limpieza y descender de cristianos viejos, según previenen los estatutos de dicho Colegio, en los cuales hay en la actualidad cinco presbíteros y dos en vía. Los otros quince son europeos que han pasado desde los reinos de Castilla a esta Nueva España, los unos llamados por este muy ilustre señor venerable deán y cabildo para el servicio de esta santa iglesia catedral, y los otros han venido en solicitud de su acomodo, el que han conseguido por su destreza y habilidad, habiendo precedido antes un examen rigurosísimo y pesquisa de su vida y costumbres, con lo que han logrado su acomodo. ACCMM, Acuerdos de Cabildo, folder 4, ca. 1768.

2.4—*. . . que al tiempo de cuaresma salen diferentes turnos de música a concertar pasos y procesiones enteras sin ser su oficio, por lo que todos los turnos se componen de mozos que tienen diferentes oficios, como son calceteros, tiradores de oro, danzarines y un comediante y un calderero y un chino verdulero, y un ciego herrero y otros de color quebrado . . . y además que los tales son objeto de risa por los muchos solecismos y disparates que dicen siendo los actos tan santos, a que se añade los muchos ruidos y escándalos que causan los contenidos peleando entre sí sobre los conciertos con personas que no saben lo que hacen, todo lo cual es público y notorio en esta ciudad y en perjuicio de nosotros, siendo pobres sacerdotes, y otras personas virtuosas que desde su niñez estan ocupadas en servicio de la iglesia sin tener más ocupación que esta [la música] para sustentarse a sí y a sus obligaciones por estarlo ejerciendo todo el año, y los mencionados arriba nomás en este tiempo lo ejercitan.* ACCMM, Correspondencia, box 1, folder 8, March 12, 1662.

Chapter 3

3.1—*Tengo ya del suplicante hecho informe en otra ocasión en que he dicho que es suficiente en tocar el violín y la música italiana, que es la que ordinariamente tocan este género de instrumentos, y ahora digo lo propio: sólo añado que la decencia del coro y de un cabildo tan ilustre como el de esta santa iglesia pide y demanda que sus ministros no se ocupen en ministerios que puedan desdecir con entrar a servirla, cuya providencia toca a vuestra señoría, y lo demás que debo suponer en sus acertados dictámenes, quien en todo proveerá lo mejor.* ACCMM, Correspondencia, book 23, folder 3, May 19, 1730.

3.2—*La prerrogativa de nobleza no se puede negar a los españoles Americanos, porque estos tienen su origen, o de aquellos, que perdiendo noblemente las vidas y derramando su sangre conquistaron aquel nuevo mundo, rubricando con su propia púrpura la mejor ejecutoría de fidelidad a sus soberanos dueños; o de aquellos, que por nacer segundos en sus nobilísimas casas y no tener lo necesario para mantener con decencia el heredado lustre de sus mayores, se determinaron a pasar a las Indias, huyendo de la pobreza; o finalmente de aquellos que por sus virtudes, letras y prendas, merecieron que vuestra majestad y sus gloriosos predecesores les dieran los empleos políticos y militares de aquel reino, por cuya causa desde su raíz deben estimarse nobles.* Excerpt taken from *Representación político-legal que hace a nuestro señor soberano Don Felipe Quinto (que Dios guarde), rey poderoso de las Españas y emperador siempre augusto de las Indias: para que sirva declarar, no tienen los Españoles indianos óbice para obtener los empleos políticos y militares de la América; y que deben ser preferidos en todos, así eclesiásticos como seculares* (1725), in *Colección varia de papeles y asuntos curiosos de don Francisco López Portillo, del consejo de su majestad, oidor y de la Real Audiencia de Guadalajara en la Nueva Galicia,* Biblioteca Nacional de México, Fondo Reservado, Colección Lafragua, no. 413 LAF, fols. 123r–143v.

3.3—*Don Pedro Rodríguez Calvo, vecino de esta ciudad, marido legítimo de Doña María Ignacia Díaz Tirado, con el más humilde respeto y veneración parezco ante vuestras señorías y digo:*

Que entre los varios hijos legítimos que hemos tenido en nuestro matrimonio el uno de ellos es un niño nombrado Josef [sic] Ignacio Mariano de los Santos, de edad de nueve años y dos meses, quien por propia inclinación y amor que tiene al estado eclesiástico, ha pretendido y con toda ansia desea entrar en el Colegio de Infantes de esta santa iglesia metropolitana, a cuyo efecto tiene hechas las correspondientes diligencias, y según se me ha dicho es uno de los nominados para asistir el día de hoy a presencia de este ilustre y venerable cabildo para la votación de las cuatro becas vacantes de dicho colegio que han de hacer vuestras señorías en los más beneméritos. Por lo que respecta a la voz, o música, que es el principal objeto por que se reciben dichos niños, no juzgo al mío por el más despreciable, pues no lo hace muy mal aún en tan corta edad, más por su habilidad, capacidad y buena inclinación puede igualarse con el mejor de los propuestos, y en la ilustre y distinguida sangre que le asiste. ACCMM, Correspondencia, book 18, without a date.

3.4—*En la ciudad de México en 6 días del mes de junio de 1738 años, en conformidad de lo mandado por el decreto proveído al escrito de la vuelta de esta foja, Ciprián de Aguilera, para la información que tiene ofrecida y le esta mandada recibir, presentó por testigo al Br. Don Antonio de Puga, presbítero y capellán del Hospital del Amor de Dios, cita en esta dicha ciudad de quien estando presente, yo, el secretario del ilustrísimo venerable señor deán y cabildo de esta santa iglesia catedral metropolitana, recibí juramento que hizo in verbo sacerdotis tacto pectore, según derecho, so cargo del* cual ofreció decir verdad en lo que fue expresado, y siéndolo por el conocimiento de José de Aguilera y Doña Gregoria Pérez de Alzivia, padres del dicho Ciprián de Aguilera, sus calidades, vecindad [y] naturaleza del suplicante, su vida y costumbres y limpieza, dijo que conoció a los dichos padres del que le presenta de mucho tiempo, a quien está atento . . . por lo que sabe y le consta fueron españoles y vecinos de esta ciudad, limpios de toda mala raza, de judíos, moros, mezcla de otras ningunas castas, y que nunca oyó decir que los suso dichos ni sus ascendentes hubiesen sido castigados por el santo oficio de la Inquisición ni por otro tribunal eclesiástico ni secular, y que así mismo sabe fueron casados y velados según orden de nuestra santa madre iglesia, y que durante su matri-monio hubieron y procrearon por su hijo legítimo y de legítimo matrimonio al dicho Ciprián, criándolo, manteniéndolo y educándolo como tal su hijo, dándole siempre este título, y el expresado tratándoles y llamándoles de padres, y mediante la buena y cris-tiana educación con que lo criaron se ha mantenido y mantiene sin vicio alguno ni dar nota alguna de su persona, y que ha reconocido en él su aplicación a buenas costumbres, y que le consta ser el mismo que contiene la fe de bautismo que se le ha demostrado y leído, que así mismo sabe que es el que le presenta persona reconocida, honesta y vir-tuosa, por lo que no tiene impedimento canónico alguno que le impida su pretensión. Y que lo que lleva dicho es público y notorio y la verdad, so cargo del juramento que hecho lleva en que se afirmó y ratificó, siéndole leído, y lo firmó de que doy fe y de conocerle . . . Br. Antonio de Puga. Ante mi, Br. Juan Roldán de Aránguiz, secretario. ACCMM, Correspondencia, box 15, folder 14, June 6, 1738.

3.5—. . . habiéndose leído las cláusulas octava y novena de la fundación y las cali-dades de los que han de ser nombrados, que serán clérigos presbíteros que sepan bien el canto llano y sean buenos estudiantes, y a lo menos muy peritos en la latinidad, y pre-cisamente naturales y patrimoniales de esta Nueva España, virtuosos, modestos y de buen ejemplo, hijos legítimos españoles y no expuestos de alguna religión, prefiriendo los más doctos y nobles, y los que fueren de esta ciudad, y entre estos los más pobres, y que en estos nombramientos se tenga principal atención con los sacerdotes que fueren más antiguos en el seno de dicha santa iglesia en ministerios inferiores a los capellanes de coro . . . por la atención de que para la seguridad de este aumento haya muchos que entren a servir en ella en dichos ministerios inferiores . . . y que dichos ocho capellanes (segun la cláusula décima) han de gozar las honras, gracias y excepciones y premi-nencias que tienen y gozan, teniesen y gozaren los que son y fueren del coro de dicha santa iglesia, que nombrándolos con este título, y tratándoles de una misma forma y con el mismo asiento, siendo iguales en todo y por todo sin diferencia alguna, mas de en cuanto a la renta que ha de ser la que se les aplica en dicha fundacion de que son patronos perpetuos. ACCMM, Actas, book 24, fol. 40r, July 19, 1695.

3.6—Certificación de méritos dada por el Br. Don Juan Roldán de Aránguiz, sec-retario del muy ilustre señor venerable Deán y Cabildo de la Santa Metropolitana Iglesia Catedral de México a favor de Br. Don Martín Bernárdez de Rivera, presbítero, *capellán de coro de dicha santa iglesia, de mandato de dicho ilustre señor dean y cabildo.*

El bachiller Don Juan Roldán de Aránguiz, presbítero y secretario de el muy ilustre señor dean, cabildo de la santa iglesia metropolitana de México, certifico, doy fe y testimonio de verdad en cuanto puedo y debo que Don Martín Bernárdez de Rivera, clérigo presbítero de este arzobispado, se halla capellán de coro de la expresada santa iglesia y músico de su capilla, que fue colegial del colegio de nuestra señora de la asunción y señor San José de los infantes de dicho coro por el tiempo de nueve años y en el que se mantuvo con la mayor aceptación por haberse portado con particular esmero y juicio, cumpliendo en todo cuanto pertenece a dicho colegio con su obligación, por lo que mereció la atención de su rector y maestros, pues por el informe de estos, según el juramento que prestan, salió en derechura para la capilla sin detenerse en los empleos de librero [ni] acólito por su habilidad y aprovechamiento en la música como consta. Que después que salió de él, que ha más de diez años, se ha mantenido y mantiene en los ministerios referidos con la misma afirmación de los señores capitulares como de los ministros y demás, debiendo esto al arreglo y compostura de su modo y acciones y al buen ejemplo que como buen eclesiástico ha solicitado dar, sin que todo el tiempo de cerca de veinte años que ha que sirve a esta santa iglesia haya dado en ella motivo a queja alguna ni por sus empleos ni por su persona. Así mismo, certifico que su hermano, Don Pedro Bernárdez de Rivera, fue colegial del expresado colegio y ministro del coro de esta santa iglesia, y en la que fue el señor doctor y maestro Don Juan Bernárdez de Rivera medio racionero, racionero y juez hacedor, y el Br. Antonio Bernárdez de Rivera fue secretario de su venerable cabildo. Y para que así conste dónde y cómo convenga doy la presente a pedimento del dicho Don Martín Bernárdez de Rivera y de mandato del muy ilustre señor venerable dean y cabildo, que es fecha en la ciudad de México en 12 días del mes de noviembre de 1761, siendo testigos Don Diego Santos, Don Manuel Gutiérrez y Don José Orellana, presentes. En testimonio de fe lo firmó Br. Juan Roldán de Aránguiz, secretario. AHAM, Fondo Cabildo, Box 187, folder 21, December 4, 1761.

Chapter 4

4.1—*Así mismo, debajo del mismo juramento, declaro a vuestra señoría para descargo de mi conciencia y lo que pudiese acaecer, que el Br. Don Manuel Sumaya está tan eminente compositor de contrapunto que puede ser maestro de capilla en la real de su majestad, y tiene acabada una misa para el día de la Concepción de Nuestra Señora que oirá vuestra majestad siendo Dios servido, la cual con todo el estudio de mis tareas no pudiera darle todo el cumplimiento que en sí tiene.* ACCMM, Correspondencia, box 23, folder 2, November 22, 1709.

4.2—*Leído un escrito de Antonio de Salazar . . . representando el que se le dispense en lo mandado sobre que asista a la escoleta a la enseñanza de el contrapunto a todos los músicos y los niños infantes, y a uno o dos sujetos para el ministerio de sochantre, por las razones que expresa en dicho escrito: su corta salud y no ser necesario que todos los cantores hayan de saber contrapunto para ser diestros; hallarse con sesenta años de edad y casi ciego.* ACCMM, Actas, book 26, fol. 336v, January 10, 1710.

4.3—*. . . y el Br. Don Manuel de Cárdenas con 200 pesos, a quien acudiendo vuestra señoría sido servido aplicarle este salario porque se adelantase en el canto de órgano para que pudiese ser sochantre cuando hubiese falta de él en el coro, desde hoy hasta el día que recibió dicha renta no ha tomado una tan sola lección.* ACCMM, Correspondencia, box 23, folder 2, November 22, 1709.

4.4—*[A] todos los músicos y profesores . . .* (illegible) *hacemos saber como en esta dicha santa iglesia está vaca la plaza de maestro de capilla por muerte de Antonio de Salazar, su último poseedor; y por cuanto conviene y es necesario elegir y nombrar persona de toda suficiencia en dicha facultad y que pueda hacer y haga todas las composiciones que se ofrezcan para el canto del coro según y como lo han hecho y debido hacer los maestros que han estado en dicha santa iglesia, por tanto para que tuviese y tenga su debido efecto nuestra pretensión, mandamos dar y despachar esta nuestra carta de edicto convocatorio: Por cuyo tenor convocamos, llamamos y emplazamos a todos los músicos compositores que quisieren hacer oposición al magisterio de capilla y del coro de dicha santa iglesia para que parezcan ante nos dentro de quince días perentorios primero siguiente a el de la fijación de este nuestro edicto para hacer las demostraciones de su suficiencia y pericia en dicho arte, y fechas les haremos y guardaremos su justicia prefiriendo a el que lo tuviere para elegir y nombrarle en el dicho magisterio y posesión de dicha plaza con la renta de quinientos pesos y con el respectivo correspondiente en las obvenciones. Y para que llegue a noticia de todos mandamos dar y dimos el presente firmado de nos y sellado con nuestro sello y refrendado de nuestro infraescripto secretario que es fecho en nuestra sala capitular a siete días del mes de mayo de mil setecientos y quince años.* ACCMM, Edictos, box 2, folder 37, May 7, 1715.

4.5—*Atendiendo a que por la jubilación del bachiller Don Domingo Dutra y Andrade se halla vacante la plaza y ministerio de capilla de el coro de esta dicha santa iglesia metropolitana, y siendo preciso el nombrar sujeto que obtenga dicho empleo: Por el tenor del presente citamos y llamamos a todas las personas inteligentes en el canto llano y figurado, y especialmente en la ciencia y arte de la música, y en la composición de villancicos, versos y demás papeles de ella que quisieren hacer oposición a dicho ministerio de maestro de capilla comparezcan en la secretaría de cabildo de la dicha santa iglesia dentro del término de sesenta días que asignamos por último perentorio, en cuyo empleo gozará la renta de 500 pesos anuales y las obvenciones correspondientes y emolumentos acostumbrados: Y para que llegue a noticia de todos los inteligentes en dicha facultad de música y composición y quisieren hacer oposición a dicho magisterio, mandamos despachar el presente edicto convocatorio el que se fije en esta dicha*

nuestra santa iglesia metropolitana y en la de los obispados sufragáneos de la Puebla
de los Ángeles, Valladolid, Oaxaca y Guadalajara, que es fecho en la sala capitular
de ella, firmado de nos, sellado con el sello de dicha santa iglesia y refrendado del
infraescripto secretario de cabildo, en la ciudad de México en nueve de enero de 1750.
ACCMM, Canonjías, book 1, January 9, 1750.

4.6—Yo, Don Ignacio Jerusalem, maestro de capilla de esta santa iglesia por erección,
puesto ante la grandeza de vuestra señoría ilustrísima, con el respeto y veneración que
debe, dice: que ha mucho tiempo que la capilla le está usurpando los privilegios que
debe gozar, y así suplica a vuestra señoría ilustrísima se sirva de mandar al admin-
istrador de dicha capilla que en todas las funciones de capilla, media capilla, tandas
grandes o chicas, haga presente al maestro, asista o no asista, que es privilegio que
gozan los maestros de capilla en todas partes, por los papeles que ministran para las
funciones, teniendo vuestra señoría ilustrísima presente que otros individuos llevan
más que el maestro, siendo así que el maestro lleva los papeles que ha trabajado para
el lucimiento de dichas funciones. Esto es menester se modifique mandando vuestra
señoría ilustrísima al administrador ponga al maestro la parte de papeles que le cor-
responde, como también el que ninguno lleve papeles a las funciones, que sólo toca
al maestro por privilegio. Por tanto, a vuestra señoría ilustrísima suplica rendidam-
ente se digne conceder como pide en que recibirá bien y merced. Ignacio Jerusalem.
ACCMM, Correspondencia, book 17, without a date.

Chapter 5

5.1—De aquí inferirá vuestra señoría cómo el haber alborotado a los músicos para lo
que toca a las fiestas del santísimo sacramento no es otro caso que ver cómo pueden,
sacando diversos artículos, ponerme mal con vuestra señoría para atarme las manos y
estos mis calumniadores entrar a saco roto y acabarlo todo a título de piedad, teniendo
estos salarios de a 300 pesos y algunos de ellos tan codiciosos que no tienen que acaban
de entrar en esta santa iglesia y que han empezado por donde sus mismos maestros
acabaron, pues 300 pesos en esta santa iglesia no los ha dado nunca [sic], sin que
puedan dar méritos de muchos años con tan poca veneración a este ilustre cabildo que
quieren venir a darle leyes. . . ACCMM, Correspondencia, book 10, June 1727.

5.2—En breve quedé convencido por experiencia propia, de que para la práctica de
la música, de nada sirve la teoría de las matemáticas; y si yo conservase las primeras
lecciones de contrapunto que hice según las reglas que intenta sacar de los numeros el P.
Kirker, tendría el documento más decisivo de la presente cuestión, y el más propio para
hacer tapar los oídos o hacer reír a los hombres más estúpidos. Y aunque entonces ya
me ocurría alguna sospecha de que nada absolutamente tienen que ver con la música

las matemáticas, sin embargo deseché como vano tal pensamiento, considerando que a lo menos la teoría de la música sería una parte de ellas, como otras muchas cosas semejantes que estas ciencias contienen, tan inútiles a la práctica de las artes como las sutilezas de la escuela aristotélica. Eximeno, *Del origen y reglas de la música,* pp. 5–6.

5.3—*Si fue en el cantar me pareció muy bien, si por lo que ejecuta como por ser con un estilo muy moderno. Esto lo compruebo con más seguridad y experiencia (la que no necesitaba) en que habiendo concurrido con él en casa de Don Francisco Reyna, en donde asistieron varios sujetos de distinción, como muchos aficionados y profesores, tocó desde las cinco de la tarde hasta las once de la noche dichos instrumentos, así a solo obligado como en concierto . . . lo que ejecutó con una libertad, gusto y destreza tan distinta de lo que hizo el día de la prueba que nos sorprendió y tuvimos que confesar todos su habilidad.* ACCMM, Actas, book 44, fol. 220r, October 10, 1760.

5.4—*Pero [el motivo] que antes me había animado a emprender [esta composición métrica], fue principalmente la consideración de que entre las artes y ciencias que varios ingenios antiguos y modernos han tratado en poemas didácticos, era de extrañar hubiese estado como desairada la música, pareciendo este olvido tanto más injusto, cuanto su hermana la poesía ha merecido que Horacio, Vida, Boileau y otros poetas hayan explicado su doctrina en verso.* Iriarte, *La música, poema,* p. ii.

5.5—*Luego dijo el señor Castillo que el motivo principal de haber pedido este cabildo era para proponer y representar que los ministros, capellanes y músicos ocurrían por sus mesadas, que era una lástima el verlos así por sus enfermedades como por sus cortedades, que su señoría consultaba a este venerable cabildo de dónde se habían de dar, pues hasta los más de los señores capitulares las querían y que la fábrica que las suplía ya se sabía cómo estaba sin dinero alguno.* ACCMM, Actas, book 37, fol. 182v, May 21, 1745.

5.6—*Luego se leyó un escrito de Don Ignacio Jerusalem, maestro de capilla de esta santa iglesia, por sí en nombre de los músicos que la componen, en que dice que es notoria la gran decadencia que tienen las obvenciones fuera de esta santa iglesia, así por la cortedad del comercio como por la universal pobreza de México, pues cuando antes se daban 100 y 200 pesos por repetidas profesiones de religiosos, entierros y honras, pues si se reconocen los libros apenas se hallarán dos o tres de estas en los dos últimos años, pues considerándose cómo en una mitad de la renta el fondo de dichas obvenciones ahora ha bajado a menos de una tercera parte, que a esto se agregaba el que los músicos y sirvientes de las parroquias: los religiosos principalmente de la Merced, San Francisco y Santo Domingo, y fuera de estos un gran número de volantes de mulatos cantores, se han introducido a cantar y oficiar las funciones que la capilla de esta santa iglesia, o toda, o la mitad, o en tercios, de seis y ocho, que llaman tandas, reduciendo a un vilísimo precio la obvención de la asistencia. Y que aunque se ha disimulado esta viciosa introducción ha sido porque no se atribuyese a codicia o ambición en dichos músicos, pero que habiendo llegado ya a tanto exceso hacen presente a este venerable cabildo el derecho que asiste a la capilla para que no puedan otros que los que la componen cantar en función alguna como está resuelto por la Real Audiencia y providenciado por los ilustrísimos señores arzobispos y por este venerable cabildo en sede vacante.* ACCMM, Actas, book 41, fol. 89r, February 22, 1752.

5.7—*Que estando mandado por vuestra señoría ilustrísima el que todas las obvenciones de los músicos se pongan en el libro de ellas (y que corre a cargo del bachiller Don Martín Vásquez) según y cómo las pagaren sin defraudar de ellas, imponiéndoles [a los músicos] varias penas por su transgresión. Y esto no ha tenido efecto, pues más frecuentemente se hacen las llamadas sangonautlas [sic], no sólo de ocho o diez pesos como las hacían antes, sino hasta de cuarenta o cincuenta como sucedió la semana pasada que hubo dos entierros, uno en la Casa Profesa y otro en el convento de nuestro padre San Francisco, y no se puso cosa alguna de ellos en el libro. Por lo que ocurrimos a la justificación de vuestra señoría ilustrísima suplicándole se sirva de dar la más severa providencia para que esto se remedie. Pues siguiendo como van los músicos llegará el tiempo de que ninguna obvención se ponga en el libro, con perjuicio notable que resulta a la Congregación de Nuestra Señora de la Antigua . . . a la fábrica espiritual, a nosotros, y aún algunos de dichos músicos que se quejan de esto mismo, como lo declarará el bachiller Don Joseph [sic] González, porque a las dichas sangonautlas no van todos, sino sólo aquellos que son de la parcialidad de los que las ejecutan, concurriendo a ello así el maestro de capilla como el dicho bachiller Vásquez que debían y pudieran estorbarlos, por lo que a vuestra señoría ilustrísima suplicamos se sirva mandar como llevamos pedido, que es justicia.* ACCMM, Correspondencia, box 1, folder 9, April–May, 1749.

5.8—*Con este motivo se conferenció con difusión sobre que los libros del coro y los papeles del archivo de la música andaban por ahí y hasta vendiéndose, pues se decía que el bachiller Don Vicente Santos tenía ya ajustada la música . . . y que así Alacio como Aguilar tenían en su poder muchísimos papeles de música pertenecientes a esta santa iglesia y otros varios tenían también, porque el archivo de música estaba sin cuidado alguno y las llaves que tenía Don Ignacio Jerusalem como maestro de capilla se las daba a cualquiera, por lo que se experimentaba tanto desorden y que pedía esto todo el correspondiente remedio, pues Jerusalem no se daba la correspondiente estimación de su ejercicio ni cumplía con su obligación de maestro en la composición de villancicos para maitines que se cantan en esta santa iglesia para lo que tiene asignado en dichos maitines su renta . . . y otras varias expresiones que sobre el asunto se hicieron.* ACCMM, Actas, book 40, fol. 242r, May 21, 1751.

5.9—*Y además de esto se ha de servir la grandeza de este venerable cabildo, por la protección con que atiende a sus ministros, interesar su súplica al ilustrísimo señor arzobispo, nuestro prelado, para que se sirva mandar en los conventos de su fijación que, o canten las religiosas solas, o con la capilla de esta santa iglesia, o la capilla sola, como se ha ejecutado antes con gran satisfacción de las religiosas músicas de los* conventos, sin que estas permitan, como lo están permitiendo (no sin grave nota) el que los religiosos de las expresadas órdenes, otros particulares y los mulatos oficien en sus iglesias, y que su señoría ilustrísima se sirva, favoreciéndoles, de dar las providencias que hallare por más convenientes para moderar los expresados abusos y reintegrar a la capilla de esta santa iglesia en sus privilegios y posesión en que estaba de oficiar todas las misas, entierros, honras, y funciones de música en todos los conventos de la filiación de su señoría ilustrísima, como en los demás de los regulares. ACCMM, Actas, book 41, fol. 89r, February 22, 1752.

5.10—. . . bachiller Don Gabriel Francisco Aguilar, administrador interino de la capilla de esta santa iglesia, en que dice que de tres meses a esta parte se ha mantenido la dicha capilla en una gran quietud sin concurrir con los de la calle a zangonautlas, y que sólo perturban esta paz los ayudantes del coro, los acólitos y libreros, pues en perjuicio de la capilla se han unido con los de la calle no sólo a hacer zangonautlas, sino a andarse metiendo a las casas al ajuste de las funciones, estorbando que vengan a la capilla. ACCMM, Actas, book 45, fol. 167v, February 19, 1762.

5.11—El maestro de capilla, diputados y administrador de la capilla de esta santa iglesia metropolitana, en nombre de todos sus individuos que la componen, ante vuestra señoría ilustrísima, con la más debida veneración, decimos que por cuanto ha llegado a nuestra noticia que el claustro de la Real Universidad de esta corte proveyó una petición presentada por Don Antonio Portillo, músico expulso de esta santa iglesia, la que se dirigió a que el claustro le nombrase maestro de capilla de dicha Real Universidad, y que se impetrase su conformación al rey, nuestro señor, con título de capilla real, y resultar todo lo proyectado en sumo deshonor y grave perjuicio de la capilla de esta santa iglesia, por lo que nos acojemos bajo el poderoso amparo y protección de vuestra señoría ilustrísima como súbditos que somos y ministros de esta santa iglesia, suplicando rendidamente se digne concedernos su licencia para hacer el ocurso necesario a la corte por mano de Don José Miranda, apoderado de vuestra senoría ilustrísima, a quien le remitiremos poder bastante para el negocio presente y los que en adelante se ofrecieren a la dicha capilla, juntamente las instrucciones hechas sobre el asunto por letrado, y porque dichas instrucciones citan varios autos ejecutoriados y algunos decretos dados por V.S.I. = suplicamos a V.S.I. se sirva mandar el que su secretario nos lo dé, como así mismo autorize los cortos méritos que presentamos en servicio del rey, nuestro señor, Real Audiencia, nobilísima ciudad, y público, y siendo nuestras pretenciones tan justas, amparadas, protegidas y fomentadas de vuestra señoría ilustrísima por mano del referido Miranda, su apoderado, nos prometemos el más feliz éxito, protestando, como protestamos en nombre de todos los individuos de la capilla que en la actualidad existen y en adelante fueren, subrogar los gastos que el negocio o los negocios pertenecientes ocasionaren con nuestras rentas y obvenciones, rata por cantidad, cada uno según su renta. ACCMM, Acuerdos de Cabildo, folder 4, 1768.

GLOSSARY

Bachiller (degree)—This was the first degree that the university conferred and that enabled individuals to follow a profession in one of the major areas of study, such as canon law. Consequently, a person holding this degree was referred to as bachiller (e.g., Br. Manuel Sumaya).

Cacique—An indigenous person who ruled over one of the principalities or towns outside a major city.

Calidad—An aggregate of attributes (e.g., employment, institutional rank, personal connections) that gave an all-encompassing impression of a person's social reputation and image, and thus defined one's status among Spaniards.

Capellanía (chaplaincy)—There were two types of chaplaincies. One type consisted in singing a set number of masses every year for the soul of a deceased person. The other type consisted in singing plainchant in the choir during religious services.

Casta—Translated as caste, this term denoted groups used to classify individuals—and therefore, organize society—according to a person's lineage.

Copla—A Spanish popular song that usually featured love themes. It was written in eight rhymed verses divided in two strophes. In each strophe the first verse rhymed with the fourth, and the second verse rhymed with the third.

Criollo—A Spanish person who was born and/or raised in Spanish America.

Décima—A Spanish popular song written in strophes of ten verses and that was sometimes improvised. Of these verses the first rhymed with the fourth and fifth; the second with the third; the sixth, with the seventh and tenth; and the eighth with the ninth.

Fuero—According to historian María Elena Martínez, this term was used in Spain to refer to community charters, each with its own code of laws. The term, however, also referred to the particular judicial status of a specific group (e.g., the military, the clergy), as well as to its prerogatives.

Gente decente—Elusive in its definition, gente decente denoted a milieu primarily characterized by the Spanish lineage and privileges of its members. It was not so much a class as it was a conglomeration of groups with legal exemptions and benefits.

Gente de razón—In a very general sense, this was a term that denoted a person's sensibility and acculturation to Spanish mannerisms and social behavior.

Jamaica—Public dance events usually held outdoors where it was customary to hear popular tunes and songs such as seguidillas and jarabes.

Jarabe—A popular couples dance influenced by Spanish dances, such as the *jota* or the *zapateado*.

Limpieza de sangre—"Purity of blood" referred to the absence of Jewish, Moorish, or black ancestry.

Mayorazgo—A legal measure to institutionalize a family's estate. The purpose of a mayorazgo was to consolidate all of the assets of a family (e.g., lands, titles, money) in order to perpetuate the longevity of the estate itself. The mayorazgo forbade the dismemberment of the estate upon the death of the family's patriarch, at which time the entire estate was inherited by the oldest child (usually male, in order to preserve the family's last name in connection with the estate).

Mayordomo—An individual hired to administer the treasury. He was charged with recording all income and expenses as well as keeping detailed records of every transaction.

Mestizo—A person of Spanish and indigenous ancestry.

Mozos de coro—See seises.

Mulatto—A term referring to a person of Spanish and black ancestry. Eventually the term was applied in a very general manner to any person with partial black ancestry.

Música especulativa—In the scope of this book, this term refers to a person's acquired intellectual capacity to understand music from a theoretical basis, as well as to the ability to communicate such understanding to others. This was the notion that writers like Pedro Cerone, Andrés Lorente, and Pablo Nassarre used to describe this term in their treatises.

Música práctica—In the scope of this book, this term refers to a person's practical ability to compose and perform music. This was the notion that writers like Pedro Cerone, Andrés Lorente, and Pablo Nassarre used to describe this term in their treatises.

Nobleza de privilegio (nobility of privilege)—A distinction granted by the king to individuals in light of their service in specific areas, such as the military or metallurgy, for example.

Nobleza de sangre (nobility of blood)—The most coveted type of noble status among Spaniards because it implied that a person's lineage (sanguine, familial, racial) could be traced back for generations, since "time immemorial."

Obvenciones—In addition to their salary, cathedral musicians received these payments (obvenciones) for their performance in churches that were surrogate to the authority of the cathedral.

Oratorio—This book uses this term to refer to a designated room inside a home where people set an altar on a table with a sacred image on it. This was supposed to be a room for prayer, and sometimes, to celebrate Mass or other rituals when a person, for some reason, could not go to church.

Patitur—A benefit that the cathedral chapter granted to musicians, which allowed them to be absent from work with pay during illness.

Probanza—The name given to the process for proving one's purity of blood.

Pulque—Known before the arrival of the Spaniards to Mexico, this was a fermented beverage made out of maguey juice.

Pulquería—These could be either locales in a building or stalls were people could buy and drink pulque.

Real Audiencia—The high court was a royal tribunal and it was the most important governing body in New Spain.

Sarao—Along with the *tertulia*, these were evening social gatherings, typical at the houses of notable individuals, where people enjoyed music and engaged in conversation.

Seguidillas—Popular Spanish tunes that accompanied lyrical texts of either four or seven verses. Of these, the last one always rhymed with the second one (if the stanza had four verses) or with the fifth one (if the stanza had seven verses).

Seises—Translated literally as "six," the *seises* was the group of choirboys (six originally, although the number grew with time) trained musically and liturgically in Spanish cathedrals.

Tepache—A fermented beverage made out of the flesh and rind of the pineapple.

Tepachería—A locale or stall where people could buy and drink Tepache.

Tertulia—A recreational social gathering where people met to chat.

Zangonautla (sangonautla)—This term was used to refer to the activity of musicians who contracted performance events independently. Such contracting was not allowed, as the chapelmaster was the one responsible for procuring such performances in a way that would benefit the entire music chapel and not just a few individuals.

NOTES

Introduction

1. There is no precise date for this document. However, its tenor relates to situations and events that developed in the cathedral around 1768–69. The context of this letter is addressed in Chapter 5. Letter from Ignacio Pedroza to the chapter. ACCMM, Acuerdos de Cabildo, folder 4, ca. 1768.
2. ACCMM, Actas, book 33, fol. 174v, April 24, 1736.
3. *Oxford English Dictionary*, December 2013, http://www.oed.com/view/Entry/53985?rskey=uQrRoT&result=1#eid
4. Small, *Musicking*, pp. 8–9.
5. Goffman, *The Presentation of Self*, p. 141.
6. Davies, "Making Music, Writing Myth," p. 64.
7. Baker and Knighton, *Music and Urban Society*, pp. i, xviii.
8. The conceptual approach to music culture in this case study is also influenced by scholar Tia DeNora. See DeNora, *After Adorno*, pp. 44–45.

Chapter 1

1. Seminario de Música en la Nueva España y el México Independiente, "Presentación," http://musicat.unam.mx/v2013/index.html (accessed June 6, 2014).
2. Stevenson, *Renaissance and Baroque*, p. 131.
3. Stevenson, *Music in Mexico*, p. 101; *Music in Aztec and Inca*, p. 204.
4. Stevenson, *Music in Aztec and Inca*, p. v.
5. Béhague, Review of *Music in Aztec and Inca*, p. 120.
6. Baker, *Imposing Harmony*, pp. 178–179.
7. Depending on the place there could be always exceptions to what seems to have been a rule otherwise. Recent cases have been documented in Cuzco (Peru), Manila (Philippines), and Mexico City. See Baker, *Imposing Harmony*, pp. 7, 84, 178, 238; Irving, "Employment, Enfranchisement, and Liminality," p. 125; and Nava Sánchez, "El cantor mulato Luis Barreto," pp. 105–120.
8. Baker and Knighton, *Music and Urban Society*, p. xviii.
9. Béhague, Review of *Renaissance and Baroque Musical Sources*, pp. 211–213.
10. Stevenson, *Renaissance and Baroque Musical Sources*, p. 1.
11. These articles are "Sixteenth and Seventeenth Century Resources in Mexico," parts I, II, and III published in 1954, 1955, and 1978, respectively.
12. Baker, "The Resounding City," p. 15; *Imposing Harmony*, p. 189.
13. See "Baroque Music in Oaxaca Cathedral: Mexico's Most Memorable Indian Maestro," *Inter-American Music Review* 2, no. 1 (1979), pp. 179–204.

14. Saavedra, "Chávez, Revueltas" (essay presented at the Colloquium Series, Music Department, Northwestern University, Fall 2006). See also Paz, *The Labyrinth of Solitude*, p. 88.

15. Stevenson, *Music in Mexico*, pp. 2, 6.

16. March, "Latin American Music," p. 1.

17. March, "Latin American Music," p. 2.

18. Stevenson, "Latin American Archives," p. 19.

19. As Stevenson notes, this in fact did not happen after all. Stevenson, "Latin American Archives," p. 19.

20. Stevenson, "From Archive to Print," p. 3.

21. Stevenson, "Early Peruvian Music," p. 6.

22. See Stevenson, "The Last Musicological Frontier," pp. 49–54; and "The First New World Composers," pp. 95–106.

23. Davies, "The Italianized Frontier," pp. 64, 66.

24. Baker, "Polychorality, Ethnicity, and Status," pp. 260–262.

25. Irving, *Colonial Counterpoint*, pp. 3–5.

26. Martínez, *Genealogical Fictions*, p. 5.

27. Carrera, *Imagining Identity in New Spain*, p. 120.

28. Martínez, *Genealogical Fictions*, pp. 2–6.

29. Martínez, *Genealogical Fictions*, p. 12.

Chapter 2

1. Baker, "The Resounding City," p. 2.

2. Marichal, *La bancarrota del virreinato*, p. 17; Van Young, *La crisis del orden colonial*, pp. 21–24.

3. González Obregón, *Las calles de México*, pp. 15–16.

4. González Obregón, *Las calles de México*, pp. 63–68.

5. Marín López, "Music, Power and the Inquisition," p. 48.

6. González Obregón, *Las calles de México*, pp. 13–14, 61.

7. Rubio Mañé, *El virreinato, IV*, p. 232.

8. Calvo, "Ciencia, cultura y política ilustradas," p. 99.

9. Rubial García, *La plaza, el palacio y el convento*, p. 49; Viqueira Albán, *¿Relajados o reprimidos?*, p. 229; González Obregón, *Las calles de México*, pp. 68, 99.

10. Although not shown here, there are eighteenth-century screen paintings of saraos in which more elaborate chamber music took place. Violins, harpsichords, flutes, and bass viols are seen commonly in ensemble. Some records found in ecclesiastical archives also indicate that church musicians were often invited to perform at such gatherings. ACCMM, Actas, book 44, fol. 220r, October 10, 1760; book 45, fol. 78r, July 24, 1761; book 54, fol. 239r, July 4, 1780.

11. Viqueira Albán, *¿Relajados o reprimidos?*, pp. 230–231.

12. Marín López, "Music, Power and the Inquisition," pp. 46–49; Sánchez Reyes, "Oratorios domésticos," p. 546.

13. When the musician Juan de Esquivel asked for a salary raise in 1698 the cathedral chapter asked him to stop rehearsing zarambeques and profane songs (*sones*) and to focus on learning the eight chant tones instead. ACCMM, Actas, book 25, fol. 16r, June 17, 1698. See also Marín López, "Music, Power and the Inquisition," p. 49.

14. Viqueira Albán, *¿Relajados o reprimidos?*, pp. 171, 211, 213.

15. Viqueira Albán, *¿Relajados o reprimidos?*, pp. 162–163.

16. Viqueira Albán, *¿Relajados o reprimidos?*, pp. 161–162.

17. Sánchez Reyes, "Oratorios domésticos," p. 539.

18. AGN, Inquisición, vol. 1179, document 10, fol. 185r.

19. Sánchez Reyes, "Oratorios domésticos," p. 546; Robles Cahero, "Inquisición y bailes populares," p. 37.

20. Robert McCaa and Michael M. Swann summarized the debate in McCaa and Swann, "Social Theory and the Log-Linear Approach," no. 76. See also McCaa, "*Calidad, Clase*, and Marriage in Colonial Mexico," pp. 477–478; Seed, "Social Dimensions of Race," pp. 602–604.

21. Martínez, *Genealogical Fictions*, p. 54.

22. See Patricia Seed's notion of "social race" in Seed, "Social Dimensions of Race," p. 574; Gonzalbo Aizpuru, *Familia y orden colonial*, p. 14; McCaa, "*Calidad, Clase,* and Marriage in Colonial Mexico," pp. 477–478.

23. Gonzalbo Aizpuru, *Familia y orden colonial*, pp. 127–128, 134.

24. Brading, *Miners and Merchants*, p. 20.

25. Chance and Taylor, "Estate and Class," p. 483; Seed, "Social Dimensions of Race," p. 603.

26. Seed, "Social Dimensions of Race," pp. 602–604.

27. Seed, "Social Dimensions of Race," pp. 572–573; Gonzalbo Aizpuru, *Familia y orden colonial*, p. 14.

28. Lucas Alamán, *Historia de Méjico*, pp. 1, 19. In Brading, *Miners and Merchants*, p. 20.

29. Martínez, *Genealogical Fictions*, p. 238.

30. Gonzalbo Aizpuru, *Familia y orden colonial*, p. 156; Aguirre Salvador, *El mérito y la estrategia*, p. 103; Aguirre Salvador et al., *La universidad novohispana*, pp. 62–64.

31. Cope, *The Limits of Racial Domination*, pp. 21–26; Martínez, *Genealogical Fictions*, p. 242; Aguirre Salvador, *El mérito y la estrategia*, p. 115.

32. Kicza, *Colonial Entrepreneurs*, pp. 14, 28; Aguirre Salvador, *El mérito y la estrategia*, p. 88.

33. See Martínez, *Genealogical Fictions*, pp. 25–26.

34. In the aftermath of the expulsion of Jews and Moors from Castile and Aragon in the late fifteenth century, the accreditation of individuals by means of their proof of purity of blood became a measure derived from a monarchal anxiety for social and political stability. The concept of a racial estate and racialized corporate membership was an integral part of the cultural baggage that Spain brought to America and that was still in operation in the eighteenth century. Mcalister, "Social Structure and Social Change," p. 353; Martínez, *Genealogical Fictions*, pp. 1–2.

35. Aguirre Salvador et al., *La universidad novohispana*, pp. 62–63.

36. Aguirre Salvador, *El mérito y la estrategia*, p. 115; Florescano and Gil Sánchez, "La época de las reformas borbónicas," pp. 202–203.

37. This suggests that institutional affiliation and rank alone did not provide an individual with impressive professional credentials; context of operation also added distinction to occupation as an attribute of social quality. Taylor, *Magistrates of the Sacred*, pp. 86–88; Menegus Bornemann and Aguirre Salvador, *Los indios, el sacerdocio y la universidad*, pp. 123, 129.

38. Martínez, *Genealogical Fictions*, pp. 240, 244; Aguirre Salvador, *El mérito y la estrategia*, p. 87; Aguirre Salvador et al., *La universidad novohispana*, pp. 62–63; Mcalister, "Social Structure and Social Change," p. 353.

39. ACCMM, Actas, book 43, fol. 260r, October 6, 1758; Torres Medina, "La capilla de música de la catedral de México," pp. 167, 180.

40. When violin player Gabriel de Córdoba asked for permission to travel for three months with the conde de San Mateo de Valparaíso, the canons saw no objection, in part because musicians improved their skills from playing with him. Years later, the chapter also agreed to hire Manuel Delgado as second violin while allowing him to remain in the service of the conde's widow. ACCMM, Actas, book 45, fol. 78r, July 24, 1761; book 54, fol. 239r, July 4, 1780.

41. ACCMM, Actas, book 41, fol. 176r, October 17, 1752.

42. Viqueira Albán, *¿Relajados o reprimidos?*, p. 74.

43. Enríquez, "¿Y el estilo galante en la Nueva España?," p. 180; Viqueira Albán, *¿Relajados o reprimidos?*, pp. 57, 60; Spell, "The Theater in New Spain," p. 140.

44. Viqueira Albán, *¿Relajados o reprimidos?*, p. 53.

45. *Gente de razón* translates as "people of reason": people of different race in tune with Spanish cultural mannerisms, habits, and customs. Viqueira Albán, *¿Relajados o reprimidos?*, p. 72.

46. Viqueira Albán, *¿Relajados o reprimidos?*, pp. 15–16.

47. Alzate y Ramírez, *Obras*, p. 55.

48. Viqueira Albán, *¿Relajados o reprimidos?*, pp. 77–78; 90–92. A well-cited incident involved Eusebio Vela, one of the better-known theater playwrights and impresarios of the first half of the eighteenth century. Having paid a debt that Vela had incurred with a local merchant, he was issued a receipt for the money paid back. In the receipt, however, the payer was referred to as "Eusebio Vela" and not as "Don Eusebio Vela," for which the playwright went to confront

the merchant for this disrespectful audacity. María y Campos, *Los payasos, poetas del pueblo*, pp. 124–129.

49. Peña Muñoz, "El teatro novohispano en el siglo XVIII," pp. 25–26; Viveros, "El teatro como instrumento educativo," p. 177; Leonard, "The Theater Season of 1791–1792," p. 352; "The 1790 Theater Season," p. 107.

50. ACCMM, Actas, book 40, fol. 196v, February 20, 1751; book 41, fol. 3r, June 9, 1751.

51. ACCMM, Actas, book 34, fol. 76r, June 28, 1737.

52. ACCMM, Actas, book 35, fol. 283r, July 28, 1741; book 36, fol. 93r, August 13, 1741.

53. ACCMM, Actas, book 37, fol. 227r, August 25, 1745; fol. 235r, September 7, 1745; book 44, fol. 147r, May 9, 1760.

54. ACCMM, Actas, book 38, fol. 106r, July 15, 1746; book 45, fol. 84v, August 8, 1761.

55. ACCMM, Actas, book 45, fol. 76r, July 24, 1761.

56. ACCMM, Actas, book 38, fol. 96r, May 27, 1746; fol. 106r, July 15, 1746.

57. ACCMM, Actas, book 38, fol. 106r, July 15, 1746; book 40, fol. 91r, August 3, 1750.

58. ACCMM, Actas, book 45, fol. 84v, August 8, 1761.

59. ACCMM, Actas, book 45, fol. 84v, August 8, 1761.

60. Another important benefit was membership in the Congregación de Nuestra Señora de la Antigua, a confraternity established in 1648 for all of those who worked in the cathedral. For an extended account about the benefits and obligations that the confraternity stipulated, see Marín López, "Música y músicos entre dos mundos," pp. 78–85; and Torres Medina, "La capilla de música de la catedral de México," pp. 140–159.

61. Each peso was divided into 8 reales or *tomines*, and each one of these eight parts was further divided in 12 *granos*. Thus, a peso consisted of 96 granos or 8 reales. See Schwaller, *Orígenes de la riqueza*, p. 20.

62. In a letter to the chapter (possibly from 1754, as the document mentions 1753 as "the past year") chapelmaster Ignacio Jerusalem mentioned that such privilege had been granted to the cathedral music chapel by the high court in 1679. ACCMM, Acuerdos de Cabildo, folder 4, ca. 1754.

63. ACCMM, Acuerdos de Cabildo, folder 4, ca. 1768. Torres Medina, "La capilla de música de la catedral de México," pp. 83–84.

64. Mcalister, "Social Structure and Social Change," p. 353.

65. Torres Medina, "La capilla de música de la catedral de México," p. 6.

66. ACCMM, Correspondencia, box 23, folder 3, February 11, 1721; Actas, book 42, fol. 10v, August 29, 1753.

67. ACCMM, Acuerdos de Cabildo, folder 4, ca. 1768. Raúl Torres Medina gives 1768 as a probable date for this document, in connection with the dispute that cathedral musicians had with the university regarding the formation of a music chapel at this institution that could rival or surpass the status of the cathedral ensemble. Such altercation was resolved through a royal decree in favor of cathedral musicians in 1769. This document and its context are discussed in more detail in Chapter 5. Torres Medina, "La capilla de música de la catedral de México," p. 83. See also Tate Lenning, *Reales cédulas*, pp. 225–227.

68. Records show this to be the case throughout the eighteenth century. For instance, José Salvatierra was examined in "violin performance and in music" (ACCMM, Correspondencia, book 18, January 21, 1778). Juan Baptista Sánchez was also "examined in music and made a demonstration of his voice" (ACCMM, Actas, book 41, fol. 29v, September 18, 1751). Of José Pissoni, the chapter said that he was "very intelligent in music and has proficiency in violin, trumpet and clarín" (ACCMM, Actas, book 40, fol. 218r, March 23, 1751). When examining Juan Rodríguez, the chapter was told that "as far as instrumental proficiency in violin he is capable, and as musician he needs more study" (ACCMM, Actas, book 36, fol. 5v, September 28, 1741). Moreover, when the choirboy Francisco Cerezo was ready to audition for a post as instrumentalist in the chapel, the chapter asked the chapelmaster to examine him "in music and in his instrument" (ACCMM, Actas, book 33, fol. 213v, September 18, 1736).

69. Each year boys were tested on *gramática, música y propiedades* (grammar, music, and properties). These labels alluded to knowledge of Latin, music principles (counterpoint is the specific element that records highlight), and a child's proficiency in either singing or playing an instrument (i.e., his performance abilities). ACCMM, Actas, book 33, fol. 153r, January 27, 1736; book 39, fol. 351v, January 10, 1749; book 40, fol. 28v, January 12, 1750.

70. Vizarrón y Eguiarreta, *Escuela de música*, p. 3. Document found in ACCMM, Correspondencia, book 30, fol. 300r.

71. *Exposición de la música eclesiástica y alivio de sochantres y expocisión de la música antigua y de la música viadana* (México: Doña María de Rivera, 1747). See Medina, *La imprenta en México, volume V*, pp. 28, 63. Also Spell, "The Theater in New Spain," p. 148.

72. Davies, "The Italianized Frontier," pp. 304–305.

73. ACCMM, Acuerdos de Cabildo, folder 4, ca. 1768

74. Vizarrón y Eguiarreta, *Escuela de música*, p. 5.

75. Vizarrón y Eguiarreta, *Escuela de música*, pp. 3, 5.

76. *Libro de la erección y fundación del collegio*, fol. 5v.

77. Aguirre Salvador, *El mérito y la estrategia*, pp. 17–18, 69.

78. Nassarre, *Escuela música*, p. 58; Cerone, *El melopeo y maestro*, p. 65.

79. Cerone, *El melopeo y maestro*, pp. 10, 17, 75.

80. Stevenson, *Christmas Music*, p. 27.

81. *"[el contrapunto] es preciso para saber componer y hacer música."* ACCMM, Actas, book 40, fol. 71r, May 25, 1750.

82. ACCMM, Actas, book 26, fol. 336v, January 10, 1710.

83. AHAM, Fondo Cabildo, box 128, folder 3, ca. 1790.

84. "... and due to the absences and sickness [of chapelmaster Antonio de Salazar], Don Manuel Sumaya shall attend as instructor [of the escoleta] every Monday and Thursday of the year to teach counterpoint because of his known proficiency." ACCMM, Actas, book 26, fol. 336v, January 10, 1710. See also Estrada, *Música y músicos*, p. 113.

85. ACCMM, Actas, book 40, fol. 16v, November 28, 1749.

86. ACCMM, Actas, book 38, fol. 106r, July 15, 1746.

87. ACCMM, Correspondencia, box 1, folder 8, February 1, 1669; Actas, book 26, fol. 336v, January 10, 1710.

88. ACCMM, Actas, book 40, fol. 242r, May 21, 1751.

89. ACCMM, Actas, book 40, fol. 89r, July 23, 1750.

90. Mark Brill has shown that even in the early eighteenth century Cerone's treatise was a theoretical base that Salazar used to gauge the knowledge of chapelmaster candidates in other cathedrals. Ortiz, "La musa y el melopeo," p. 247; Brill, "Carrasco or Mathías?," pp. 231–232.

91. Davies, "The Italianized Frontier," p. 307.

92. ACCMM, Actas, book 38, fol. 129r, October 14, 1746.

93. ACCMM, Actas, book 40, fol. 196v, February 20, 1751; fol. 242r, May 21, 1751.

94. ACCMM, Actas, book 41, fol. 74v, February 1, 1752; fol. 87v, February 22, 1752.

95. Letter from Ignacio Jerusalem to the chapter asking for support to uphold his privileges as chapelmaster. ACCMM, Correspondencia, book 17, without a date.

96. ACCMM, Actas, book 42, fol. 105v, October 17, 1754.

97. *Pompa, solemnidad, y grandeza* (pomp, solemnity, and grandiosity) are the most common attributes that canons used to describe ritual and ceremony in archival records. The following sources are just some examples: ACCMM, Actas, book 4, fol. 262v, June 19, 1601; book 5, fol. 122v, May 12, 1609; book 44, fol. 200v, August 29, 1760; Ordo, book 2, fol. 35r, 1754. See also Stevenson, *Christmas Music*, p. 8; Russell, *From Serra to Sancho*, pp. 99, 169, 173, 397; Davies, *Santiago Billoni*, p. xi.

98. Ramos-Kittrell, "Dynamics of Ritual and Ceremony," pp. 127–128.

99. ACCMM, Actas, book 25, fol. 156v, February 16, 1700; book 27, fol. 26r, January 7, 1711; fol. 51r, April 18, 1711; Correspondencia, box 23, folder 2, November 22, 1709.

100. Brading, *Miners and Merchants*, pp. 97, 100; García Cárcel, *Historia de España siglo XVIII*, p. 316.

101. Ramos-Kittrell, "Dynamics of Ritual and Ceremony," pp. 121–126; 147–150.

102. Ramos-Kittrell, "Dynamics of Ritual and Ceremony," pp. 163–165, 172.

103. ACCMM, Actas, book 37, fol. 182v, May 21, 1745.

104. Brading, *Miners and Merchants*, p. 100; Ramos-Kittrell, "Music, Liturgy, and Devotional Piety in New Spain," p. 94. Raúl Torres Medina mentions that cathedral finances had a marked recovery in the second half of the eighteenth century, and that petitions for loans decreased considerably in this period. The situation was quite different from 1700 to roughly 1745, however, when petitions for loans and salary increases were quite numerous.

See Ramos-Kittrell, "Dynamics of Ritual and Ceremony," chapter IV. Also Torres Medina, "La capilla de música de la catedral de México," pp. 145–146.

105. ACCMM, Actas, book 39, fol. 346v, January 7, 1749.

106. For an extensive account of zangonautlas at the cathedral of Mexico see Roubina, *El responsirio "Omnes Morienmini . . .,"* pp. 25–48.

107. Brading, *Miners and Merchants*, p. 100; Ramos-Kittrell, "Dynamics of Ritual and Ceremony," pp. 58–59. In a letter to the canons from 1752, chapelmaster Ignacio Jerusalem complained about the decline and income from obvenciones, on the one hand, because of the widespread poverty of New Spain, and on the other, because more and more ensembles (either from other convents or itinerant groups of mixed-race musicians) competed for these opportunities charging lower fees than the cathedral, and therefore, devaluing performances. This letter is discussed in Chapter 5 (see appendix 5.6). ACCMM, Actas, book 41, fol. 89r, February 22, 1752.

108. ACCMM, Actas, book 41, fol. 105v, April 28, 1752; book 45, fol. 167v, February 19, 1762. See also Torres Medina, "La capilla de música de la catedral de México," p. 247.

109. ACCMM, Correspondencia, box 1, folder 8, March 12, 1662.

110. ACCMM, Actas, book 41, fol. 89r, February 22, 1752.

111. Letter from Ignacio Pedroza to the chapter. ACCMM, Acuerdos de Cabildo, folder 4, ca. 1768.

112. ACCMM, Actas, book 38, fol. 96r, May 27, 1746.

113. Answer from Juan Baptista del Águila to accusations from the chapel. ACCMM, Acuerdos de Cabildo, folder 4, ca. 1768–1769.

114. Castro Santa-Anna, *Diario de Sucesos* in *Documentos para la historia de Méjico*, VI, p. 217.

115. Answer from Juan Baptista del Águila to accusations from the chapel. ACCMM, Acuerdos de Cabildo, folder 4, ca. 1768–1769. Given that Portillo was dismissed in 1754 and that the music chapel started to deal with Portillo's ensemble as potential competitor for music performances it is quite possible that this document was drafted after 1764. This coincides with the fact that Ambrosio Eugenio de Melgarejo Santaella, referred to as "judge" (*oidor*) in the same document, began such appointment on January 31, 1764. See Mayagoitia, "Los rectores del ilustre y real colegio," p. 310.

116. Letter from Juan Ignacio de la Rocha to the chapter. ACCMM, Acuerdos de Cabildo, folder 4, February 13, 1769. See also Mayagoitia, "Los rectores del ilustre y real colegio," pp. 312–313.

117. Tate Lenning, *Reales cédulas*, pp. 225–227.

118. Answer from Juan Baptista del Águila to accusations from the chapel. ACCMM, Acuerdos de Cabildo, folder 4, ca. 1768–1769.

119. Aguirre Salvador, *Por el camino de la letras*, p. 22.

120. After auditioning Benito Martino, a violin player from Rome looking for a position in the chapel, Manuel Sumaya remarked that Martino was "adept in Italian music, but in the music that we esteem in Spain he is not." This was not a big shortcoming, Sumaya wrote, as Martino could have been brought up to date "in the use of our music." Considering that there is no record of Sumaya ever having visited Spain, his use of the words "we esteem in Spain" and "our music" alludes less to a geographical connection than to a cultural sense of "we-ness" that Sumaya possibly associated with the paradigm of music education that had affiliated him to the cathedral since childhood. ACCMM, Correspondencia, box 23, folder 3, March 3, 1721.

Chapter 3

1. Martínez, "The Language, Genealogy, and Classification of 'Race,'" pp. 31, 34.

2. Martínez, "The Language, Genealogy, and Classification of 'Race,'" pp. 36–37.

3. Martínez, "The Language, Genealogy, and Classification of 'Race,'" p. 33; "Interrogating Blood Lines," p. 201; Hering Torres, "Color, pureza, raza," pp. 459–460.

4. Hernández Franco, *Cultura y limpieza de sangre*, pp. 15–17; Martínez, "Interrogating Blood Lines," p. 202.

5. Archivo del Sagrario Metropolitano de México (ASMM), book of Spanish baptisms, box 10, vol. 26, fol. 26r; in Olmos, "El Magisterio de Capilla de Manuel de Sumaya," pp. 29–30.

6. ACCMM, Correspondencia, box 23, folder 3, May 19, 1730.

7. Martínez, review of *El peso de la sangre: Limpios, Mestizos y Nobles en el mundo hispánico*, p. 1631.

8. L. N. Mcalister relates this notion to a report to the king from the *Consejo de Indias*: "It is undeniable that in those kingdoms [of America] any Spaniard who comes to them, who acquires some wealth, and who is not engaged in a dishonorable occupation, is regarded as noble." Mcalister, "Social Structure and Social Change," p. 357.

9. Martínez, *Genealogical Fictions*, pp. 79, 305-n35.

10. Liebman, *The Jews in New Spain*, pp. 92–93; Martínez, *Genealogical Fictions*, pp. 145, 148.

11. Martínez, *Genealogical Fictions*, p. 3.

12. Brading, *Miners and Merchants*, pp. 19–20.

13. Humboldt, *Ensayo político*, pp. 76, 90; in Brading, *Miners and Merchants*, p. 109.

14. Ladd, *The Mexican Nobility at Independence*, p. 20.

15. Domínguez Ortiz, *La clase de los conversos*, p. 75.

16. *Probanza* was the Spanish name for the process of proving one's purity of blood. Martínez, *Genealogical Fictions*, p. 74.

17. Martínez, *Genealogical Fictions*, p. 355-n39; Ladd, *The Mexican Nobility at Independence*, p. 17.

18. Martínez, *Genealogical Fictions*, pp. 49, 283.

19. *Carta de Hidalguía, 1743–1744*, DeGolyer Library, Southern Methodist University, A1992.1847c, fols. 81v–84r.

20. *Carta de Hidalguía, 1743–1744*, DeGolyer Library, Southern Methodist University, A1992.1847c, fols. 87v–133r.

21. Nutini, *The Wages of Conquest*, pp. 222–224.

22. A *mayorazgo* was an institution fostered by the ancient regime that allowed a family to keep an array of joint goods (like titles and properties) in a way that such array could not be divided among family members. The oldest male child in the family was usually the heir of the mayorazgo. In this way, the core of the mayorazgo did not diminish but could only increase.

23. Ventura Beleña, *Copias a la letra*, p. 289.

24. Nobles had to pay two types of tribute. One was the *lanza*, a feudal obligation of military service to the king. A noble, however, could be allowed to pay the king a yearly sum of money instead of maintaining an army of soldiers. In 1631, the sum was set at 531 pesos; by the nineteenth century it had increased to 800. The other tax was the *media annata*, which was imposed on the creation and succession of noble titles. Originally, the tax represented half the income produced by the lands given by the king to the noble person, and this was collected the year the noble died. After 1631, however, the crown required cash payments: a new noble paid 3,660 pesos for his bestowed privileges; the heirs paid 1,220 pesos to succeed to a parent's title, and a niece, nephew, cousin, or sibling paid 2,440 pesos for a transverse succession. Ladd, *The Mexican Nobility at Independence*, pp. 60–61.

25. Ladd, *The Mexican Nobility at Independence*, pp. 19–20; Kicza, *Colonial Entrepreneurs*, p. 42; Nutini, *The Mexican Aristocracy*, p. 284.

26. Ladd, *The Mexican Nobility at Independence*, pp. 6–7; Aguirre Salvador, *El mérito y la estrategia*, p. 91.

27. Martínez, *Genealogical Fictions*, pp. 136–140.

28. Some criollos could achieve high office, although a lot depended on their connections in Madrid and Mexico City. See Brading, *Miners and Merchants*, p. 243.

29. It is interesting to notice that allusions to guitar or vihuela playing in these paintings appear predominantly in depictions of lower castes. In contrast, violin music playing seems to have been represented mostly as a "Spanish" sort of activity. It would be a speculation to say that these representations alluded to specific genres or types of music (which could be attributed to certain racial groups). Nevertheless, the racialization of music as an activity in terms of the instruments depicted in each caste is certainly interesting.

30. Martínez, *Genealogical Fictions*, pp. 242–243; Carrera, *Imagining Identity in New Spain*, pp. 49–50.

31. Tanck de Estrada, "Tensión en la torre de marfil," pp. 32–33, 51.

32. *Instrucciones que los virreyes de Nueva España dejaron*, p. 259.

33. Rubio Mañé, *El virreinato, IV*, pp. 153–154, 222–223.

34. Aguirre Salvador, *El mérito y la estrategia*, pp. 17, 63, 69, 88. See also *Por el camino de las letras*, p. 22.

35. Carrera, *Imagining Identity in New Spain*, pp. 126, 139.

36. Konetzke, *Colección de documentos, volume 3*, pp. 813–814, 832; Ladd, *The Mexican Nobility at Independence*, pp. 17–18.

37. *Representación político-legal*, fols. 123r–143v, in López Portillo, *Colección varia de papeles* (miscellany of manuscript documents, without a date). Biblioteca Nacional de México (BNM), Fondo Reservado, Colección Lafragua, no. 143 LAF. See also Aguirre Salvador, *El mérito y la estrategia*, pp. 93, 53-n64.

38. Icaza Dufour, *La abogacía en el reino de Nueva España*, pp. 107–108.

39. Aguirre Salvador, *El mérito y la estrategia*, p. 95; Ladd, *The Mexican Nobility at Independence*, p. 7; Brading, *Miners and Merchants*, p. 210.

40. *Representación politico-legal*, fols. 123r–143v; in López Portillo, *Colección varia de papeles*. See also Brading, *Miners and Merchants*, p. 210.

41. Brading, *Miners and Merchants*, p. 103.

42. Brading, *Miners and Merchants*, pp. 211, 213–214.

43. Not to be confused with a bachelor degree nowadays, the degree of *bachiller* was the first degree that the university conferred and that enabled individuals to follow a profession. The degree also made individuals eligible to enter the university guild, through which a person could join the university council and be involved in issues pertaining university policies. Aguirre Salvador, *El mérito y la estrategia*, p. 72; Álvarez Sánchez, "La población de bachilleres," p. 24.

44. Farriss, *La corona y el clero en el México colonial*, p. 161.

45. Maravall, *Estado moderno y mentalidad social, volume II*, pp. 107–108.

46. Such was the case of bachiller Isidro de Sariñana, whose father, Benito Ángel de Sariñana, had served as mayor "and in other honorific positions, as a noble person (como persona noble)." Or the father of bachiller Manuel de Ávila y Mutio, who considered himself a "noble Spaniard" due to his work as a surgeon (hardly a prestigious occupation) and accountant at the hospital of Jesús Nazareno. See Aguirre Salvador, *El mérito y la estrategia*, pp. 101–102.

47. Álvarez Sánchez, "La población de bachilleres," pp. 24–26, 36.

48. Martínez, *Genealogical Fictions*, pp. 240, 244; Aguirre Salvador, *El mérito y la estrategia*, pp. 87, 103; Aguirre Salvador et al., *La universidad novohispana*, pp. 62–63; Mcalister, "Social Structure and Social Change," p. 353.

49. Brading, *Miners and Merchants*, pp. 213–214.

50. There were two main types of chaplaincies. One of these consisted in singing a set number of Masses every year for the soul of a diseased patron. The other was a position to sing plainchant in the choir during the divine office. Both of these chaplaincies are discussed in more detail below. For students seeking advanced degrees, sponsorship from individuals of prominent social standing was a way of establishing connections for future professional development under the sponsor's tutelage. It was customary for the coat of arms of the sponsor to be imprinted at the top of the student's graduating diploma.

51. Taylor, *Magistrates of the Sacred*, pp. 94–97.

52. Aguirre Salvador, *El mérito y la estrategia*, pp. 289–291; Taylor, *Magistrates of the Sacred*, pp. 98, 121–124.

53. Carvajal Ávila, "El Colegio de Infantes," pp. 156–157.

54. Carvajal Ávila, "El Colegio de Infantes," pp. 156–157.

55. Based on the work of José López-Calo, Celina Becerra Jiménez suggested that the cathedrals of Granada and Seville (and not Seville alone) provided a teaching model based on plainchant and counterpoint that New Spanish cathedrals followed in Mexico City, Guadalajara, and Valladolid (today Morelia, Michoacan). See López-Calo, *La música de la catedral de Granada*, p. 100; Becerra Jiménez, "Enseñanza y ejercicio de la música," p. 43; and Carvajal Ávila, "El Colegio de Infantes," p. 161; Durán Moncada, "La escoleta de música," p. 130.

56. Marín López, "La enseñanza musical," pp. 10–12.

57. Carvajal Ávila, "El Colegio de Infantes," p. 159.

58. Turrent, "Los actores del ritual sonoro," pp. 36–37.

59. Turrent, "Los actores del ritual sonoro," p. 188.

60. ACCMM, Actas, book 29, fols. 76v–77r, August 3, 1717; book 40, fol. 28v, January 12, 1750.

61. ACCMM, Obras Pías, book 3, fols. 6v–7r, 1725. See also Sánchez Rodríguez, "Los infantes de la catedral," pp. 168–174.

62. Aguirre Salvador, El mérito y la estrategia, p. 69.

63. ACCMM, Libro de la erección y fundación del collegio, fol. 6r. See also Actas, book 44, fol. 89v, January 9, 1760.

64. Although it is not possible to establish a parallel with cathedrals in Spain without historical distortion, it is interesting to note that the cathedral of Seville (sister church to Mexico City's cathedral) had a similar structure. The cathedral chapter in Seville grew concerned about the social well-being of choirboys, and for this reason they funded scholarships so that, after serving as choirboys, youths could continue studies in liberal arts and theology. Limpieza de sangre became an important requisite for entering choirboys, given that the ultimate aim was for children to enter the church. Bejarano Pellicer, El mercado de la música, pp. 54–56.

65. ACCMM, Actas, book 4, fol. 251r, November 14, 1600; Libro de la erección y fundación del collegio, fol. 5v. See also Marín López, "La enseñanza musical," p. 13.

66. ACCMM, Actas, book 27, fol. 85v, August 14, 1711.

67. ACCMM, Libro de la erección y fundación del collegio, fol. 5r.

68. ACCMM, Correspondencia, book 18, without a date.

69. ACCMM, Correspondencia, box 15, folder 14, June 6, 1738.

70. Thus far, exact biographical information about Manuel Sumaya's early years remains inexact. Regarding his admission as choirboy, scholars have relied on information provided by Jesús Estrada, who suggests that Sumaya entered the cathedral at around 1690. Nevertheless, records in the cathedral sacrarium show that the misplacement of his baptism record was corrected in 1691, making it possible that Sumaya auditioned as choirboy in that year. Alice Ray Catalyne suggests that Sumaya ended his term as choirboy in 1694, and given that the term to serve as choirboy was six years, one surmises that Sumaya might have been admitted to the cathedral in 1687. Craig H. Russell echoes the opinions of Estrada and Catalyne regarding Sumaya's admission and graduation as choirboy, respectively. Russell further supports this information by referring to the substantial contribution of Robert Stevenson to biographical studies of New Spanish composers. However, as none of these authors provides accurate archival reference to these facts, I use the year 1690 as an approximation to when Sumaya might have entered the cathedral. Estrada, Música y músicos, p. 106; Olmos, "El magisterio de capilla de Manuel de Sumaya," pp. 30–31; Catalyne, "Manuel de Zumaya," 102; Russell, "Manuel de Sumaya," pp. 91–92; see also Russell, "Zumaya, Manuel de," Grove Music Online, 2007–2011, http://www.oxfordmusiconline.com/subscriber/article/grove/music/31064?q=sumaya&hbutton_search.x=0&hbutton_search.y=0&hbutton_search=search&source=omo_gmo&search=quick&pos=1&_start=1#firsthit.

71. Archivo del Sagrario Metropolitano de México (ASMM), book of Spanish baptisms, box 10, vol. 26, fol. 26r. In Olmos, "Manuel de Sumaya en la Catedral de México," Palabra de Clío— Blog de la Asociación de Historiadores Mexicanos Palabra de Clío, July 16, 2010, http://palabradeclio.blogspot.com/2010/07/manuel-de-sumaya-en-la-catedral-de.html. See also "El magisterio de capilla de Manuel de Sumaya," pp. 29–30.

72. Estrada, Música y músicos, pp. 106–107. Robert Stevenson also adds that the chapter tried to aid Sumaya so that he would not join a mendicant order. Stevenson, "Mexico City Cathedral Music," p. 130.

73. ACCMM, Actas, book 36, fol. 33v, January 19, 1742. Although his audition occurred in 1742, a document dated January 15, 1751, mentions that, at that point, Rivera had completed eight years in the Colegio, which means that he was admitted in 1743. ACCMM, Actas, book 40, fol. 171v, January 15, 1751.

74. ACCMM, Actas, book 40, fol. 28v, January 12, 1750.

75. ACCMM, Actas, book 43, fol. 260r, October 6, 1758. See also Torres Medina, "La capilla de música de la catedral de México," p. 167.

76. ACCMM, Actas, book 40, fol. 171v, January 15, 1751.

77. ACCMM, Actas, book 30, fol. 9r, January 30, 1722; book 32, fol. 179r, January 27, 1733; book 37, fol. 67r, July 30, 1744.

78. ACCMM, Actas, book 33, fol. 153r, January 27, 1736.

79. I use the word "choir" to refer to the group of individuals comprising canons, members of the chapter, who, with the chaplains and succentors, performed plainchant during the divine office.

80. ACCMM, Correspondencia, book 18, without a date.

81. ACCMM, Correspondencia, box 15, folder 18, January 19, 1742.

82. ACCMM, Actas, book 36, fol. 197r, August 9, 1743.

83. ACCMM, Acuerdos de Cabildo, folder 4, June 25, 1784.

84. ACCMM, Actas, book 54, fol. 295r, September 26, 1781.

85. ACCMM, Actas, book 36, fol. 33v, January 19, 1742.

86. ACCMM, Actas, book 40, fol. 140v, October 30, 1750.

87. ACCMM, Actas, book 38, fol. 30v, January 14, 1746.

88. ACCMM, Actas, book 27, fol. 41v, February 10, 1711.

89. ACCMM, Actas, book 32, fol. 144v, October 24, 1732.

90. ACCMM, Actas, book 27, fol. 18v, November 18, 1710; book 32, fol. 104r, July 1, 1732; book 44, fol. 286r, January 21, 1761.

91. ACCMM, Actas, book 33, fol. 33r, June 22, 1734.

92. ACCMM, Actas, book 27, fol. 186r, August 3, 1712; book 33, fol. 14v, April 6, 1734; fol. 45v, September 24, 1734; fol. 137v, November 15, 1735.

93. Each of the ranks (subdeacon, deacon, and presbyter) assigned clerics duties but also restrictions. Subdeacons assisted deacons, who were licensed to preach. Only presbyters—full priests—were allowed to officiate at Mass, however. See Taylor, *Magistrates of the Sacred*, p. 93.

94. ACCMM, Correspondencia, book 18, without a date.

95. ACCMM, Actas, book 38, fol. 30r, January 14, 1746; book 40, fol. 160r, December 16, 1750.

96. ACCMM, Actas, book 25, fol. 16r, June 17, 1698; fol. 152v, February 12, 1700.

97. ACCMM, Actas, book 40, fol. 171v, January 15, 1751; book 41, fol. 124r, July 4, 1752.

98. ACCMM, Actas, book 27, fol. 178r, July 30, 1712. Although some priests in poor towns could be ordained because of their knowledge of an indigenous language (*a título de idioma*, which enabled them to be ordained without a bachiller degree) the prelate required future priests to show that they had some sort of solvency. One alternative was to become priest by having a chaplaincy (*a título de capellanía*), which meant that the chaplaincy would pay an amount of money to the person every year. The other one was to demonstrate some other type of solvency (*a título de suficiencia*), which was either personal wealth or some other sort of income, like a salary for performing with the cathedral music chapel. See Taylor, *Magistrates of the Sacred*, p. 95.

99. For example, on September 3, 1737, he submitted a Credo as part of a series of choirbooks he was writing for the cathedral (although we do not know for which festivities), and that the chapter paid him 20 pesos. Moreover, on December 9 of the same year he presented a series of finished choirbooks to the chapter, which paid to him 2 pesos per folio, while he continued writing a gradual for the liturgy of the common of saints. Records also show that Peñalosa is the one who wrote the books with the offices for Santa Isabel and San José, both major rituals in the Hispanic liturgy. ACCMM, Actas, book 34, fol. 103v, September 3, 1737; fol. 143v, December 9, 1737; book 35, fol. 6v, December 13, 1737. Fábrica Material, book 7, not foliated, July 24, 1748; Fábrica Espiritual, book 6, not foliated, April 16, 1749; September 9, 1749; September 23, 1749; October 15, 1749.

100. ACCMM, Actas, book 33, fol. 77r, March 8, 1735.

101. ACCMM, Actas, book 33, fol. 188v, June 19, 1736.

102. ACCMM, Actas, book 33, fol. 210r, September 11, 1736.

103. *Statuta ecclesiae mexicanae*, p. 18. ACCMM, Capellanías, box 1, folder 3, March 17, 1767. Thus far the actual document of foundation for the Lorenzana chaplaincies has not been found, so there is no way to know exactly when these positions were established. Moreover, due to financial constraints, the cathedral chapter opted to cancel two of the Lorenzana chaplaincies in 1735, so not all fourteen positions were always in operation. ACCMM, Actas, book 33, fol. 74r, March 3, 1735.

104. On two occasions, the cathedral chapter prompted chapelmaster Antonio de Salazar to teach counterpoint to all musicians and choirboys. Salazar, however, considered that not

all singers needed to know counterpoint and he hoped to teach only those interested in composition or in a position in the choir (like succentors). Regardless of Salazar's opinion, the canons continued to enforce the study of counterpoint among all cathedral musicians. ACCMM, Actas, book 26, fol. 336v, January 10, 1710; book 27, fol. 57r, May 19, 1711.

105. ACCMM, Actas, book 26, fol. 166v, June 21, 1708.

106. For instance, in 1709, chapelmaster Antonio de Salazar wrote a letter to the canons saying that Sumaya was an "eminent composer of counterpoint who can be chapelmaster in the king's royal chapel." ACCMM, Correspondencia, box 23, folder 2, November 22, 1709. See also Stevenson, "Mexico City Cathedral Music," p. 130; *Music in Mexico*, pp. 149–153; Estrada, *Música y músicos*, p. 116; Russell, "Manuel de Zumaya," pp. 92–95.

107. In addition to Franco and López Capillas, Antonio Rodríguez Mata is the only other example of a musician known to have had a position in the chapter. See Reyes Acevedo, "El testamento de Francisco López Capillas," p. 94. Although Juan Hernández (chapter secretary) was chapelmaster between 1586 and 1620, his position seems to have been *ad interim*. His was not the case of a musician rising to a post in the chapter but rather of a member of the chapter fulfilling the duties of a chapelmaster while the cathedral was in need of such a person.

108. In Chapter 4 we address the appointment of Ignacio Jerusalem to the cathedral chapelmastership in 1750. Documents show that because of all of the doubts surrounding Jerusalem's examination for this post, the chapter decided to appoint him only until a better candidate appeared. After all, the canons noted, the chapelmastership was not an ecclesiastical benefice, and therefore, was neither exclusive nor assigned in perpetuity. ACCMM, Actas, book 40, fol. 91r, August 3, 1750.

109. See Aguirre Salvador, *El mérito y la estrategia*, p. 231; Brading, *Church and State*, p. 116.

110. ACCMM, Actas, book 33, fol. 74r, March 3, 1735; fol. 77r, March 8, 1735.

111. Depending on their abilities, some individuals could earn as little as 70 pesos. ACCMM, Fábrica Espiritual, box 1, folder 14, July 28, 1732; January 21, 1733.

112. In his petition asking to be placed in a violin vacancy in the music chapel, José Salvatierra mentioned that such an appointment would help him find the place in the church to which he had always aspired. If appointed, Salvatierra could then devote time to the study of moral theology, the only impediment he had to be ordained at that point. ACCMM, Correspondencia, box 18, without a date.

113. Taylor, *Magistrates of the Sacred*, p. 98.

114. Geoffrey Baker has alluded to a similar situation in Cuzco, Peru. See Baker, *Imposing Harmony*, p. 92.

115. ACCMM, Acuerdos de Cabildo, folder 4, June 25, 1784.

116. ACCMM, Correspondencia, book 18, without a date.

117. ACCMM, Actas, book 26, fol. 166v, June 21, 1708.

118. ACCMM, Actas, book 33, fol. 77r, March 8, 1735.

119. ACCMM, Actas, book 24, fol. 40r, July 19, 1695.

120. ACCMM, Actas, book 41, fol. 258v, March 24, 1743.

121. ACCMM, Actas, book 44, fol. 150v, May 10, 1760.

122. ACCMM, Actas, book 45, fol. 63r, July 3, 1761; Correspondencia, book 17, without a date.

123. Archivo Histórico del Arzobispado de México (AHAM), Fondo Cabildo, box 187, folder 21, 1761.

124. Martínez, *Genealogical Fictions*, p. 141.

125. Martínez, *Genealogical Fictions*, pp. 123–128.

Chapter 4

1. By "music poetics" I am referring to Richard Taruskin's definition of *poetics* as a principle related to the making of an artwork, in which stylistic issues and compositional approaches (in the case of music) are as important as their realization in performance practice. Taruskin, *The Oxford History*, p. 13.

2. Stevenson, *Christmas Music*, p. 27.

3. ACCMM, Actas, book 38, fol. 96r, May 27, 1746.

4. Russell, "The Mexican Cathedral Music of Ignacio de Jerusalem," p. 102.
5. Feijóo y Montenegro, *Teatro crítico universal*, p. 300.
6. Davies, *Santiago Billoni*, p. ix; "The Italianized Frontier," p. 63.
7. Dietz, "Fortunes and Misfortunes," p. 87; Davies, "The Italianized Frontier," pp. 64–65; Carreras, "From Literes to Nebra," p. 8
8. In his advocacy for a less cathedral-centric study of colonial music practices, Geoffrey Baker mentions that "focusing excessively on an institution that blocked opportunities for indigenous advancement, has reduced the role of indigenous musicians in urban institutions to that of permanent underlings." Baker, *Imposing Harmony*, pp. 178–179.
9. Baker, *Imposing Harmony*, p. 189; Irving, "Employment, Enfranchisement, and Liminality," p. 119.
10. This label was possibly inspired by Jesús Estrada, who mentioned that, upon his death, Jerusalem's music "was admired by those intelligent in music and was considered a miracle." Estrada, *Música y músicos*, p. 146. See, for example, the article published by the magazine *Proceso*, "Tras la huella de Jerusalém en México," on May 2010 (http://www.proceso.com.mx/?p=106260).
11. Stevenson, "Ignacio Jerusalem," pp. 57–61; Russell, *From Serra to Sancho*, p. 349. See also Russell, "The Mexican Cathedral Music of Ignacio Jerusalem," p. 101; "Newly Discovered Treasures," p. 5; Lee Blodget, "From Manuscript to Performance," p. 15.
12. One of the canons, Francisco Jiménez Caro, even endorsed the admission of Jerusalem's son, Salvador, in the Colegio the Infantes, due to Jerusalem's capacities. However, there is no record that Salvador was ever admitted. ACCMM, Actas, book 38, fol. 96r, May 27, 1746.
13. This is something that the chapter always kept in mind when hiring musicians: *que es preciso tener presente lo adelantado y exquisito que está el arte de la música*. ACCMM, Actas, book 45, fol. 76r, July 24, 1761.
14. Robert Stevenson mentions that the group consisted of twelve individuals. However, new research shows that the whole group counted eighteen people, including Jerusalem's wife, Antonia, and his two children, Salvador and Isabel. Stevenson, "Ignacio Jerusalem," pp. 59–61; Gembero Ustárroz, "Migraciones de músicos," pp. 34–35, 37.
15. In the case of Jerusalem, documents show that Cárdenas did not hold an exclusivity clause. However, it is not known for how long Jerusalem continued working at the Coliseo after he was admitted to the cathedral. ACCMM, Actas, book 38, fol. 106r, July 15, 1746. See also Stevenson, "Ignacio Jerusalem," p. 57.
16. ACCMM, Actas, book 26, fol. 336v, January 10, 1710.
17. Letter from Guillermo de Carvajal to the cathedral chapter. ACCMM, Correspondencia, box 1, folder 8, February 1, 1669. Stevenson, "Mexico City Cathedral Music," p. 122.
18. The issue of marriage was especially sensitive for foreign immigrants who came to Spanish America. In the event that a man was married he was expected to come to New Spain with his wife. Otherwise, authorities expected the person to show a legitimate proof of why he had traveled without his spouse. This was done in order to prevent individuals from marrying again, and thus, of committing bigamy, which was a serious crime. The chapter's concerns related to their efforts to instill norms of proper moral behavior in the music chapel, especially considering that scandals involving infidelity or sexual affairs out of wedlock were common among people in the theater. See Nunn, *Foreign Immigrants*, pp. 70–71.
19. ACCMM, Actas, book 38, fol. 106r, July 15, 1746.
20. During a chapter meeting the canons commented on Jerusalem's "intelligence in all types of music, as he was the only composer in the city." ACCMM, Actas, book 38, fol. 106r, July 15, 1746.
21. ACCMM, Actas, book 36, fol. 152v, February 15, 1743; book 38, fol. 110v, September 29, 1746. The canons also agreed in that, as far as music was concerned, Dutra y Andrade was in charge of merely marking the beat: *pues tiene determinado [el cabildo] el que el dicho Don Domingo heche el compás en el coro*. ACCMM, Actas, book 38, fol. 129r, October 14, 1746.
22. Documents relevant to the endowment for the feast of Saint Peter, for example, stipulate the donor's wish to have new villancicos performed every year, for which the endowment allocated 10 pesos to pay the chapelmaster or assistant composer for writing these pieces. During Dutra y Andrade's time it seems that the music chapel performed previously composed villancicos. ACCMM, Actas, book 41, fol. 74v, February 1, 1752.

23. ACCMM, Actas, book 33, fol. 113r, July 29, 1735.
24. ACCMM, Actas, book 38, fol. 129r, October 14, 1746.
25. ACCMM, Actas, book 38, fol. 129r, October 14, 1746.
26. Estrada, *Música y músicos*, p. 129.
27. Aguirre Salvador, *El mérito y la estrategia*, pp. 18, 68; "El perfil de una élite académica," p. 51; Álvarez Sánchez, "La población de bachilleres," pp. 24–26, 36.
28. Martínez, "The Language, Genealogy and Classification of 'Race,'" pp. 31, 34; Mcalister, "Social Structure and Social Change," p. 353.
29. Brill, "The Oaxaca Cathedral 'Examen de oposición,'" p. 18.
30. Enríquez, "¿Y el estilo galante en la Nueva España?," p. 179.
31. ACCMM, Actas, book 25, fol. 152v, February 12, 1700.
32. AHAM, Fondo Cabildo, CL 48, 1700–1706, fols. 10r–19v.
33. ACCMM, Correspondencia, box 23, folder 2, November 22, 1709.
34. ACCMM, Actas, book 26, fol. 336v, January 10, 1710.
35. Musicologist Javier Marín López has mentioned that, for this reason, the musical style of Latin polyphony in Spanish cathedrals acquired social value and probably projected Spanish notions of calidad. See Marín López, "Ideología, hispanidad, y canon," pp. 69–72.
36. Davies, "Villancicos from Mexico City," p. 236.
37. "Ya La Gloria Accidental", ACCMM, Archivo de Música, A0090, ca. 1715. See also Catalyne, "Manuel de Zumaya," p. 118.
38. ACCMM, Actas, book 40, fol. 186r, February 9, 1751; book 41, fol. 176r, October 17, 1752; book 44, fol. 21r, May 4, 1759; book 45, fol. 76r, July 24, 1761. See also the letter from Juan Baptista del Águila to the cathedral chapter, ACCMM, Correspondencia, box 23, folder 6, ca. 1745–1746; and *Lista de los maestros que han tenido las escoletas de los infantes desde el año de 1770 hasta el presente*, AHAM, Fondo Cabildo, box 128, folder 30, ca. 1785.
39. ACCMM, Actas, book 40, fol. 71r, May 25, 1750.
40. For example, Pedro Cerone wrote: "The part that in music is called rhythm (*rítmica*) pertains to composition, and counterpoint is its principle." Andrés Lorente echoed this statement by saying that "counterpoint is the basis (*principio*), root and foundation of it, and from it [people] learn general rules to later do beautiful things (*primores*) in music." Cerone, *El melopeo y maestro*, p. 565; Lorente, *El porqué de la música*, p. 274; Stevenson, *Christmas Music*, pp. 27–28.
41. Geoffrey Baker has shown that Cerone's and Lorente's writings also circulated in Peru. See Baker, *Imposing Harmnony*, pp. 182–184. For information on music treatises circulating in New Spain see Lemmon, "Towards an Inventory," pp. 131–139; Leonard, "On the Mexican Book Trade, 1683," pp. 403–435; Saldívar, *Historia de la música*, pp. 129–140.
42. Mario A. Ortiz mentions that Sor Juana Inés de la Cruz was heavily influenced by Cerone, more so than by Lorente. Mark Brill has also shown that in the early eighteenth century Cerone's treatise was a theoretical base to gauge the examination of chapelmasters by personnel at the cathedral of Mexico. Ortiz, "La musa y el melopeo," p. 247; Brill, "Carrasco or Mathías?," pp. 231–232.
43. Cerone establishes this distinction in *El melopeo y maestro*. Later on, Lorente (heavily influenced by Cerone) gave a succinct definition for both fields saying that música teórica referred to the "understanding of music's logic or reason and being able to explain it . . . música práctica means composing songs and melodies in music" (*música teórica es comprender su razón y saberla dar . . . música práctica es el componer canciones y melodías en la música.*) Cerone, *El melopeo y maestro*, pp. 1–2; Lorente, *El porqué de la música*, p. 2. See also Nassarre, *Escuela música*, p. 8.
44. *Que todo debe el compositor gobernarlo con el entendimiento, mediante la especulación, para que la práctica sea con toda propiedad.* Nassarre, *Escuela música*, p. 58.
45. Cerone, *El melopeo y maestro*, p. 65.
46. *. . . estaba medianamente instruído en la [música] teórica y en la práctica.* ACCMM, Correspondencia, book 18, January 16, 1781.
47. ACCMM, Correspondencia, book 18, January 21, 1778.
48. ACCMM, Actas, book 41, fol. 29v, September 18, 1751.
49. ACCMM, Actas, book 40, fol. 218r, March 23, 1751.
50. ACCMM, Actas, book 33, fol. 213v, September 18, 1736.

51. ACCMM, Actas, book 36, fol. 5v, September 28, 1741.

52. ACCMM, Actas, book 41, fol. 2v, June 9, 1751.

53. Marín López, "Música y músicos," p. 542-n49.

54. Cerone, *El melopeo y maestro*, p. 565.

55. Cerone, *El melopeo y maestro*, p. 483.

56. Cerone, *El melopeo y maestro*, p. 565.

57. Lorente, *El porqué de la música*, p. 233.

58. Nassarre, *Fragmentos músicos*, p. 31.

59. Nassarre, *Fragmentos músicos*, p. 64.

60. Fiorentino, "canto llano, canto de órgano," pp. 150–152.

61. Given that his comment departs from a commentary by Nassarre, Russell is possibly alluding to the author's explanation that canto de órgano was called such because the organ "is always guided by such music" (i.e., canto de órgano). Nassarre, *Fragmentos músicos*, p. 32.

62. Russell, *From Serra to Sancho*, p. 67-n65.

63. ACCMM, Actas, book 26, fol. 336v, January 10, 1710.

64. ACCMM, Correspondencia, box 23, folder 2, November 22, 1709.

65. ACCMM, Actas, book 37, fol. 241r, September 18, 1745.

66. ACCMM, Actas, book 36, fol. 80r; July 10, 1742; book 40, fol. 176r, January 16, 1751.

67. ACCMM, Actas, book 27, fol. 41v, February 10, 1711; fol. 73v, July 17, 1711; book 32, fol. 113v, July 29, 1732.

68. ACCMM, Actas, book 33, fol. 153r, January 27, 1736; book 39, fol. 351v, January 10, 1749; book 40, fol. 28v, January 12, 1750.

69. ACCMM, Actas, book 40, fol. 28v, January 12, 1750.

70. ACCMM, Actas, book 33, fol. 14v, April 6, 1734.

71. ACCMM, Actas, book 38, fol. 30v, January 14, 1746.

72. ACCMM, Actas, book 37, fol. 241r, September 18, 1745.

73. ACCMM, Actas, book 40, fol. 160r, December 16, 1750.

74. A petition by José Salvatierra, who applied for a violin position, mentions that his eight years as choirboy and nine years as acolyte were "his short merits . . . to find the place in the church that he has aspired to for so long." Letter from José Salvatierra to the cathedral chapter, ACCMM, Correspondencia, book 18, not foliated, without a date.

75. In 1712, Salazar made an inventory of music books that he had bought for use in cathedral services. The inventory lists twenty-five volumes that encompass polyphonic works by these composers. A previous document from 1711 also shows that these were the common materials used to teach choirboys. Moreover, Sumaya composed music along these aesthetic lines and included it in choirbooks with music by Hernando Franco and Francisco Guerrero (some of the music from these choirbooks was first published by Steven Barwick, in 1982). These volumes have been catalogued as choirbooks P03 and P04 by the Seminario de Música en la Nueva España y el México Independiente. The website indicates that some of these books were possibly written in 1731 (P10), 1774 (P08), and 1781 (P12). Seminario de Música en la Nueva España y el México Independiente, "Proyecto Musicat: Libros de coro, polifonía," http://musicat.unam.mx/nuevo/polifonia.html. Also, ACCMM, Actas, book 27, fol. 41v, February 10, 1711; Fábrica Espiritual, book 3, fol. 1r, March 12, 1717; *inventario de los libros del Coro que se hizo por el señor Doctor Don Gerónimo López de Arbizu, 1712*, AHAM, Fondo Cabildo, box 185, folder 63, September 22, 1712. See also Barwick, *Two Mexico City Choirbooks of 1717* (Carbondale: Southern Illinois University Press, 1982). To this date, the most complete catalogue and codicological study of the cathedral's polyphony choirbook collection is Marín López's *Los libros de polifonía de la catedral de México: Estudio y catálogo crítico* (Jaén, Spain: Universidad de Jaén—Sociedad Española de Musicología, 2012). Recently, scholars have shown that this repertoire held currency not only in Mexico City but also in other ecclesiastical centers in New Spain. See Marín López, "Música local e internacional," pp. 89–90.

76. See also Davies, "The Italianized Frontier," p. 307.

77. ACCMM, Fábrica Espiritual, book 4, fol. 3r, June 2, 1747; book 6, not foliated, August 2, 1749; Fábrica Material, book 7, not foliated, April 29, 1748.

78. ACCMM, Actas, book 40, fol. 16v, November 28, 1749.

79. ACCMM, Canonjías, book 1, not foliated, January 9, 1750.

80. ACCMM, Actas, book 40, fol. 56v, April 7, 1750; fol. 71r, May 25, 1750.

81. *Y en su vista . . . sobre si era o no a propósito dicho Jerusalem para maestro, pues los músicos no le tenían respeto ni se le tendrían nunca por manosearse demasiado con ellos, lo que era necesario tener presente.* ACCMM, Actas, book 40, fol. 16v, November 28, 1749.

82. Juan Pedro Viqueira Albán mentions that professionalism and discipline were qualities considerably lacking among Coliseo personnel during the eighteenth century. It was not until 1786 that a new ordinance (which recapitulated tenets of ordinances from 1725, 1763, 1765, 1779 and 1780) attempted for the first time to curb the lack of discipline and professionalism among Coliseo actors and musicians. Among other things, the ordinance mandated individuals to attend rehearsals and to arrive to the theater punctually whenever there was a performance. This resonates with complaints by the canons who said that Jerusalem was lazy because he failed to show up to teach musicians. ACCMM, Actas, book 40, fol. 28v, January 12, 1750. See Viqueira Albán, *¿Relajados o reprimidos?*, pp. 77–79.

83. ACCMM, Actas, book 40, fol. 83v, June 30, 1750.

84. *. . . pues aunque sea notoria la aptitud y suficiencia del dicho Don Ignacio no se debe faltar a esta solemnidad ni a este preciso auto de examen una vez que hubo convocación.* ACCMM, Actas, book 40, fol. 71r, May 25, 1750.

85. ACCMM, Edictos, box 2, folder 37, May 7, 1715.

86. Brill, "Carrasco or Mathías?," p. 233.

87. Brill, "Carrasco or Mathías?," pp. 229–230.

88. Brill, "Carrasco or Mathías?," p. 231.

89. Brill, "Carrasco or Mathías?," p. 233.

90. Brill, "Carrasco or Mathías?," p. 243.

91. Brill, "Carrasco or Mathías?," p. 243,

92. Baker, *Imposing Harmony*, pp. 182–183; Irving, *Colonial Counterpoint*, pp. 47, 313-n18; Marín López, *Los libros de polifonía*, p. 354.

93. Although some scholars have shown that other cathedrals—such as the one in Valladolid (today Morelia), Michoacan—used Andrés Lorente's *El porqué de la música*, the influence of Cerone on this writer cannot be denied, especially in his exposition of Cerone's theoretical approach. For information about other music treatises used in Michoacan (in addition to Lorente's book), see Carvajal Ávila, El Colegio de Infantes," pp. 189–191.

94. Carreras, "La policoralidad como identidad," pp. 87–122. In Hernández Mateos, "Maestrazos de contrapunto," p. 204.

95. Brothers, "Musical Learning," pp. 2821–2825.

96. Marín López, *Los libros de polifonía*, pp. 88-n219, 351–354.

97. Stevenson, "Sor Juana Inés de la Cruz's Musical Rapports," p. 1; Arias, "Cerone as Historian," p. 108.

98. Hannas, "Cerone, Philosopher and Teacher," p. 421; Ortiz, "La musa y el melopeo," p. 261.

99. Ortiz, "La musa y el melopeo," p. 249.

100. Wingell, "Medieval Music Treatises," p. 159.

101. Miranda, "Éxtasis de luz y fe," p 276.

102. Stevenson, "El Melopeo," p. 484.

103. Miranda, "Éxtasis de luz y fe," p 276.

104. Cerone, *El melopeo y maestro*, pp. 1–2, 40, 89. See also Arias, "Cerone as Historian," p. 98.

105. ACCMM, Correspondencia, box 23, folder 2, March 9, 1700.

106. AHAM, Fondo Cabildo, box 185, folder 63, September 22, 1712. Petition by Hernando Franco to the chapter to buy a book of Masses by Francisco Guerrero, AHAM, Fondo Cabildo, box 183, folder 25, without foliation, without a date. According to Javier Marín López, some of the inscriptions seen on the cover page of the petition suggest that the request happened before February 24, 1580. See Marín López, "Por ser como es tan excelente música," pp. 209–226.

107. ACCMM, Canonjías, book 1, January 9, 1750.

108. Aguirre Salvador, *El mérito y la estrategia*, pp. 69–70.

109. This is something to which the canons alluded during a conflict that the music chapel had with another ensemble. As shown in Chapter 5, another ensemble was seeking affiliation with the university in order to compete for status with the cathedral group. At first, the

chapter did not want to intervene in the debacle because they thought they did not have jurisdiction. It was up to the king, the canons said, to decide whether to affiliate an ensemble with the university or not. After all, music was a liberal art and only the king could appoint someone to take on such activity at the university. ACCMM, Actas, book 49, fol. 187r, December 6, 1768.

110. Maravall, *Estado moderno y mentalidad social, volume II*, pp. 107–108.

111. ACCMM, Actas, book 30, fol. 9r, January 30, 1722.

112. ACCMM, Fábrica Espiritual, box 1, folder 14, July 28, 1732; Actas, book 33, fol. 25r, May 14, 1734.

113. ACCMM, Actas, book 32, fol. 216v, June 19, 1733.

114. ACCMM, Actas, book 36, fol. 240v, December 20, 1743; book 38, fol. 155r, January 18, 1747; book 39, fol. 351v, January 10, 1749; book 40, fol. 69v, May 23, 1750.

115. ACCMM, Actas, book 25, fol. 32v, January 9, 1699; Correspondencia, box 23, folder 2, November 22, 1709.

116. ACCMM, Actas, book 38, fol. 153v, January 13, 1747. See also Estrada, *Música y músicos*, p. 112.

117. ACCMM, Actas, book 33, fol. 83v, March 22, 1735; fol. 153r, January 27, 1736.

118. ACCMM, Actas, book 40, fol. 69v, May 23, 1750; fol. 89r, July 23, 1750; Correspondencia, book 18, August 22, 1774.

119. The piece was named after the incipit of the text, which is *A la milagrosa escuela de Pedro*. The webpage of the Seminario de Música en la Nueva España y el México Independiente shows this piece with the call number A2161.01. See Seminario de Música en la Nueva España y el México Independiente, "Proyecto Musicat: Catálogo del archivo de música de la catedral de México," http://musicat.unam.mx/nuevo/adabi_dg.php?sig=2-A2161-1&busquedas=YToxOntzOjEwOiJjb21wb3NpdG9yIjtzOjMwOiJKRVVJVU0FMRU0sIElnbmFjaW8W8gKDE3MDctMTc2OSkiO30=. On February 2005, I found the documents pertinent to Jerusalem's examination as *autos formados para la oposición y exámen de la plaza de maestro de capilla de la del coro de esta santa iglesia metropolitana y que obtuvo Don Ignacio Hierusalem*, ACCMM, Canonjías, book 1, no. 65, fols. 97r–133v. In 2007, Fernando Zamora and Jesús Alfaro Cruz published a much needed transcription of these documents. See Zamora and Alfaro Cruz, "El examen de oposición," pp. 12–23.

120. ACCMM, Actas, book 40, fol. 89r, July 23, 1750.

121. Marín López, "Dinámicas de género," pp. 14–15. I want to thank professor Javier Marín López for sharing so generously a copy of this article while it was still in press.

122. ACCMM, Actas, book 40, fol. 89r, July 23, 1750.

123. *Y en lo que toca a lo práctico, por la experiencia que tengo en lo presente, y en el tiempo que ha que está en la iglesia, y porque me he informado de personas inteligentes que le han manejado mucho tiempo, compone en cosas cortas, no en obras como las que necesita esta iglesia.* ACCMM, Canonjías, book 1, no. 65, fol. 105r.

124. *Diósele un canto llano para que hiciese un concierto como es costumbre en todas las catedrales y lo hizo según su modo de entender, no como debe ser.* ACCMM, Canonjías, book 1, no. 65, fol. 104r.

125. *. . . y que era cierto que le faltaba la práctica del canto de coro, pues en la que se había ejercitado era en aria y lírico para teatros.* ACCMM, Actas, book 40, fol. 91r, August 3, 1750.

126. *. . . aunque los sinodales no le expresaron la especie de contrapunto, por haber varios, formó contrapunto general, cuya inteligencia da a conocer la facilidad con que puede hacer los particulares y específicos.* ACCMM, Canonjías, book 1, no. 65, fols. 107r-107v.

127. *. . . y que para este género de composición se sirven en otras partes de otro modo de contrapunto por haber distintos como son las fugas, los cánones, los pasos forzados, las carreras . . . sin embargo soy de sentir que ha cumplido plenamente y suficientemente sobre este particular el examinante, según y conforme se le ha mandado por los examinadores.* ACCMM, Canonjías, book 1, no. 65, fol. 112r.

128. *. . . en lo que toca a lo teórico, así en lo que yo pregunté como en lo que oí de mis compañeros, en algunas cosas respondió, en otras no pudimos quedar satisfechos.* ACCMM, Canonjías, book 1, no. 65, fol. 105r.

129. ... *en lo que toca a lo teórico, preguntando lo necesario que se necesita, algunas cosas respondió, otras dejó por no tener costumbre de catedral.* ACCMM, Canonjías, book 1, no. 65, fol. 104r.

130. ... *digo señor, que un maestro de capilla de una catedral debe ser un compendio de las habilidades de los músicos, de suerte que lo que otro ignora el maestro sepa, y lo que otro sabe el maestro no ignore. Esto en Jerusalem no se verifica, porque en lo que preguntaron mis compañeros algunas cosas respondió y otras no respondió ... A las pocas preguntas que yo le hice sólo una me respondió, en todas las demás no acertó.* ACCMM, Canonjías, book 1, no. 65, fol. 106r.

131. *En punto de música especulativa o teórica es cierto que nos fue, y aún hoy nos es, muy difícil formar concepto cabal de hasta dónde pueda extenderse su comprensión y suficiencia, pues en muchas cosas ni el examinado entendía lo que se le preguntaba, ni los examinadores lo que él les respondía, viéndose en la precisión uno de nosotros, algo inteligente de la lengua italiana, a traducir las preguntas y las respuestas para que ellos entre sí pudiesen entenderse y concordasen.* ACCMM, Canonjías, book 1, no. 65, fols. 100r–103v.

132. *Por esta confusión y causa, en la última concurrencia que fue para calificar las obras de contrapunto y composición ejecutadas por el mencionado opositor, se le mando por nosotros que allá a su modo y como pudiese explicase lo que tenía entendido de la música ... Con efecto hízolo así, y con voces y palabras mestizas y no bien perceptibles discurrió, explicó y expuso por un buen rato de tiempo las principales y más sustanciales reglas de la música armónica, o canto llano, y también algunas de la cromática, o canto figurado, de el contrapunto, concierto y composición, diciendo a lo último que así se enseñaba y aprendía la música en su tierra de Italia y demás naciones extranjeras, y que no se necesitaba de más discursos ni libros antiguos para comprender, enseñar y aprender perfectamente la música que lo que el llevaba dicho, y algunas pocas cosas más, por ser la verdadera ciencia de la música solo la arreglada ejecución de ella.* ACCMM, Canonjías, book 1, no. 65, fols. 100r–103v.

133. ACCMM, Actas, book 40, fol. 91r, August 3, 1750.

134. The chapter mentioned that the chapelmastership was not an ecclesiastical benefice (*beneficio eclesiástico*) and therefore was not an appointment assigned in perpetuity. Specifically, the canons mentioned that the chapelmastership was not *colativo*, alluding to a *colación canónica*. A colación was a set of rights, privileges, and remuneration given to a cleric for his service in a given post, usually assigned in perpetuity. Given that the chapelmastership had been an appointment held by clerics it is possible that the chapter needed to stress that such post was not an ecclesiastical benefice, unlike a chaplaincy, for example. ACCMM, Actas, book 40, fol. 91r, August 3, 1750.

135. ACCMM, Actas, book 41, fol. 60v, January 7, 1752.

136. Ramos-Kittrell, "Dynamics of Ritual and Ceremony," pp. 147–150.

137. Torres Medina, "La capilla de música de la catedral de México," p. 82. Answer from Juan Baptista del Águila to accusations from the music chapel, ACCMM, Acuerdos de Cabildo, folder 4, ca. 1768–1769.

138. ACCMM, Actas, book 40, fol. 242r, May 21, 1751.

139. ACCMM, Actas, book 41, fol. 74v, February 1, 1752.

140. ... *[los músicos] se han enconado en su contra tratándole con palabras de menosprecio y provocativas, y aún faltándole al respeto y obediencia que como a tal maestro de capilla se le debe, pues habiendo mandado que asistiesen la noche del domingo a los maitines de San Pedro Nolasco en su convento de la Merced ... no lo ejecutaron ... y antes sí fueron ha procurar deslucir dichos maitines haciendo mofa de los que asistieron.* ACCMM, Actas, book 41, fol. 74v, February 1, 1752.

141. Letter from Ignacio Jerusalem to the chapter, ACCMM, Correspondencia, book 17, without a date.

142. Estrada, *Música y músicos*, p. 143; Russell, *From Serra to Sancho*, p. 384-n40.

143. Craig Russell has written extensively about this service and has edited the score for the acclaimed recording by the choral ensemble Chanticleer, originally released by Teldec in 1998. According to Russell, Jerusalem originally composed a first version of the service (excerpts) in 1756, later completing the full service in 1764 and revising it in 1765. Russell, "The Splendor of Mexican Matins: Sonority and Structure in Jerusalem's Matins for the Virgin of Guadalupe," *Institute of Sacred Music, Yale University—Colloquium Journal*, volume 4 (Autumn 2007) http://www.yale.edu/ism/colloq_journal/vol4/contents.html.

144. Russell, *From Serra to Sancho*, p. 385-n43.

145. Davies, "'Mexican Minerva'" (essay presented at the annual meeting of the American Musicological Society, Pittsburgh, PA, November 8, 2013).

146. *Que habiéndose oído y expresádose que era cierto que de pocos años a esta parte se habían puesto las funciones de esta santa iglesia dilatadísimas, pues estas nuevas composiciones de música necesitaban de mucho tiempo, pues había gloria que pasaba de media hora y credo de tres cuartos, y que para no quitar la atención y devoción convendría el solicitar el que sin faltar al rito se acortasen, pues era cierto que estas últimas habían estado inaguantables.* ACCMM, Actas, book 44, fol. 200v, August 29, 1760.

147. *... la mucha música que hay en el archivo ... la que por su antigüedad o poco arte, o también por demasiado larga, no podrá ya acomodarse en estos tiempos en que abundan las composiciones modernas de gusto delicado, breves, y proporcionadas a la solemnidad de las funciones.* ACCMM, Actas, book 52, fol. 111r, January 22, 1774.

Chapter 5

1. Manuel Sumaya responds to accusations from the administrator of the chapel, Juan de Salibe, regarding obvenciones. ACCMM, Correspondencia, book 10, not foliated, June 1727. In Marín López, "Música y músicos entre dos mundos," vol. 3, p. 72.

2. Marín López, "Música y músicos entre dos mundos," vol. 3, p. 72.

3. *... contra la mucha honra que Vuestra Señoría me hace y dio en el título que me confirió de maestro, que con una oposición pública y públicos exámenes que con los honores con que la erección de esta Santa Iglesia me tiene mandado que me obedezcan en todo lo que fuere de mi oficio...* Marín López, "Música y músicos entre dos mundos," vol. 3, p. 72.

4. *... es apto en música italiana pero en la que estimamos en España, no.* ACCMM, Correspondencia, box 23, folder 3, February 11, 1721.

5. Murphy, *José de Torres's Treatise*, pp. 97–98.

6. *El suplicante toca diestramente el instrumento de violín y entiende la música de tocatas y demás de italianas composiciones. Esto es lo que de este sujeto se me pregunta y vuestra señoría decidirá en todo lo mejor.* ACCMM, Correspondencia, box 23, folder 3, May 19, 1730.

7. ACCMM, Fábrica Espiritual, box 1, folder 14, July 28, 1732; January 21, 1733; Actas, book 37, fol. 15r, March 13, 1744.

8. ACCM, Actas, book 45, fol. 76r, July 24, 1761. AHAM, Fondo Cabildo, box 128, folder 30, ca. 1780.

9. ACCMM, Actas, book 54, fol. 294r, September 18, 1781.

10. ACCMM, Actas, book 57, fol. 198v, October 7, 1791.

11. Aguirre Salvador, *El mérito y la estrategia*, pp. 18, 68; "El perfil de una élite académica," p. 51; Álvarez Sánchez, "La población de bachilleres," pp. 24–26, 36.

12. Becerra López, *La organización de los estudios*, p. 189. While in central Europe the advancement of secular thinking in science and philosophy had begun to shake the foundation of Aristotelian thought in different universities, in New Spain courses in Aristotelian philosophy, as well as oral examinations on rhetorical debate were standard curricular components. After passing this examination students were allowed to "expose and teach on the books by Aristotle," a mention that officially conferred the degree of *bachiller en artes*. AGN, Universidad, volume 358, fol. 553r, March 23, 1702; volume 156, fol. 49r, January 24, 1710; and fol. 63r, March 15, 1711.

13. Aguirre Salvador, *El mérito y la estrategia*, p. 262.

14. Beristáin y Souza, *Biblioteca hispanoamericana*, pp. 140–141.

15. *Memoria de los libros que quedaron por muerte del señor conde de San Mateo de Valparaíso, marqués de Jaral de Berrio, avaluados por Don Ignacio Villegas en 1o de febrero de 1780.* Archivo Histórico Banamex, Fondo Marqueses de Jaral de Berrio, Administración, Inventarios, MJB-01–010-073, P1F1A1E5/C01, fol. 21r, February 1, 1780.

16. *Memoria de los libros*, fols. 21v, 26v, 28v, 30r, and 34v.

17. Melgares Guerrero, "La biblioteca privada del 'marqués de Uribe,'" p. 1714.

18. Davies, "The Italianized Frontier," p. 307.

19. Eximeno, *Del origen y reglas de la música*, pp. 5–6.

20. Forrester, "An Introduction," p. 62.

21. Pollin, "Towards an Understanding of Antonio Eximeno," pp. 92–93. See also Eximeno, *Don Lazarillo Vizcardi. Sus investigaciones músicas con ocasión del concurso a un magisterio de capilla vacante* (Madrid: Imprenta de Rivadeneyra, 1872 and 1873).

22. ... *el nuevo sistema de Eximeno, fundado en la naturaleza, y la experiencia, que le manisfestó los verdaderos principios, y dictó las reglas de la armonía.* Eximeno, *Duda de don Antonio Eximeno*, p. v.

23. *Memoria de los libros*, fols. 54r–57r.

24. Calvo, "Ciencia, cultura y política ilustradas," pp. 86–87, 113; González Polo, *El palacio de los condes*, pp. 34, 56–57; Sánchez-Navarro Peón, *Memorias de un palacio*, pp. 160–162, 168–169.

25. Valdivia Sevilla, "Usos y prácticas musicales," p. 95.

26. Ruiz Torres, "La música en la Ciudad de México," pp. 527–528.

27. Consider for example the activity of violinist José Palomino among the high society of eighteenth-century Lisbon. During the inaugural session of the Aula de Música Teórica y Práctica of Francisco Inácio Solano in 1779, several musicians wrote and recited sonnets for the occasion. Scholar Cristina Fernandes considers these poetic and literary efforts reflections of the intellectual ambitions of musicians, which was in itself a typical attitude during the Enlightenment. See Fernandes, "De la etiqueta de la Real Cámara," pp. 146–147.

28. ACCMM, Actas, book 44, fol. 220r, October 10, 1760.

29. *Con que la música, decía yo entre mí, no es más que una prosodia para dar al lenguaje gracia y expresión.* Eximeno, *Del origen y reglas de la música*, p. 9.

30. Eximeno, *Del origen y reglas de la música*, p. 224. For an account about the ways in which Renaissance theorists attempted to synthesize views of music from mathematics and poetics (here referring to the study of literary forms), see Moyer, *Musica Scientia*, pp. 200, 206.

31. Eximeno, *Del origen y reglas de la música*, pp. 189–190.

32. Eximeno, *Del origen y reglas de la música*, pp. 189, 193, 258.

33. Moyer, *Musica Scientia*, p. 3. See also Palisca, *Humanism in Italian Renaissance*, pp. 369–371.

34. Lemmon, "Towards an Inventory," p. 133; Stevenson, *Music in Mexico*, p. 190; Saldívar, *Historia de la música*, p. 132.

35. Sánchez Flores, "José Ignacio Bartolache," p. 195.

36. Lemmon, "El archivo general de la nación," p.18; "Towards an Inventory," pp. 134–135.

37. Iriarte, *La música, poema*, p. ii.

38. Deans-Smith, "This Noble and Illustrious Art," pp. 70–71.

39. Deans-Smith, "This Noble and Illustrious Art," pp. 77–79.

40. Deans-Smith, "This Noble and Illustrious Art," pp. 79, 81.

41. Deans-Smith, "This Noble and Illustrious Art," p. 93.

42. Sigüenza y Góngora, *Triunfo parténico*, p. 137.

43. Leonard, *Baroque Times*, p. 140.

44. Leonard, *Baroque Time*, pp. 130, 136–140.

45. Davies, "'Mexican Minerva'" (essay presented at the annual meeting of the American Musicological Society, Pittsburgh, PA, November 8, 2013).

46. Minerva was the Roman goddess of wisdom and protector of the arts. After the second century B.C., she became virtually identified with the Greek goddess Athena, who was the virgin goddess of music, poetry, and wisdom.

47. Miranda, "Racial and Cultural Dimensions," pp. 267–268.

48. Miranda, "Racial and Cultural Dimensions," p. 266.

49. Brading, *Miners and Merchants*, pp. 23–24.

50. Florescano, *Precios del maíz*, p. 51.

51. Garner, "Precios y salarios," pp. 83, 85–86.

52. Miño Grijalva, *El mundo novohispano*, pp. 270, 381.

53. Ramos-Kittrell, "Dynamics of Ritual and Ceremony," pp. 82–85.

54. Ramos-Kittrell, *Music, Liturgy, and Devotional Piety*, pp. 88–89.

55. ACCMM, Actas, book 37, fol. 182v, May 21, 1745.

56. Russell, "The Splendor of Mexican Matins," Institute of Sacred Music—Yale University, http://ism.yale.edu/sites/default/files/files/The%20Splendor%20of%20Mexican%20Matins-1.pdf.

57. ACCMM, Actas, book 33, fol. 153r, January 27, 1736.

58. *En lo que toca a la composición, confieso sobra* ... ACCMM, Actas, book 40, fol. 89r, July 23, 1750.
59. ACCMM, Actas, book 32, fol. 266v, January 12, 1734.
60. ACCMM, Actas, book 33, fol. 54r, November 2, 1734.
61. ACCMM, Actas, book 33, fol. 133v, November 11, 1735.
62. ACCMM, Actas, book 33, fol. 173v, April 20, 1736.
63. ACCMM, Actas, book 33, fol. 153r, January 27, 1736.
64. *Informa el maestro que [Francisco Cerezo] tiene buenos principios y aplicación teórica, pero no aquella para constituirse sujeto ni dejarlo de la mano, y así se le debe encargar continúe enseñándolo, porque dejándolo no quede imperfecta la obra.* ACCMM, Actas, book 34, fol. 13r, November 6, 1736.
65. ACCMM, Actas, book 35, fol. 125v, August 29, 1738.
66. ACCMM, Actas, book 40, fol. 71r, May 25, 1750.
67. ACCMM, Actas, book 32, fol. 266v, January 12, 1734.
68. ACCMM, Actas, book 34, fol. 78r, July 2, 1737.
69. ACCMM, Actas, book 35, fol. 19r, December 23, 1737.
70. This incident occurred when Bernárdez de Rivera was already a choir chaplain. He asked to be pardoned a 50 pesos fine because this was the first time that this happened. He had done this because he had seen how his peers regularly attended similar functions. Given Bernárdez de Rivera's profile, the chapter pardoned the fine. ACCMM, Actas, book 44, fol. 150v, May 10, 1760.
71. Letter from Ignacio Jerusalem to the chapter asking for support to uphold his privileges. ACCMM, Correspondencia, book 17, without a date.
72. ACCMM, Actas, book 41, fol. 89r, February 22, 1752.
73. ACCMM, Actas, book 41, fol. 89r, February 22, 1752.
74. ACCMM, Actas, book 38, fol. 110v, July 29, 1746.
75. Estrada, *Música y músicos*, p. 129.
76. ACCMM, Actas, book 41, fol. 74v, February 1, 1752.
77. ACCMM, Actas, book 39, fol. 346v, January 7, 1749.
78. ACCMM, Correspondencia, box 1, folder 9, April–May 1749. I want to thank John Swadley for pointing me to this source and for candidly sharing his images of this document.
79. ACCMM, Correspondencia, box 1, folder 9, April–May 1749.
80. ACCMM, Correspondencia, box 1, folder 9, April–May 1749.
81. ACCMM, Correspondencia, box 1, folder 9, April–May 1749. The following information regarding the interviews of musicians occurred on May 7, 1749, and is drawn from the same source.
82. ACCMM, Correspondencia, box 1, folder 9, April–May 1749.
83. ACCMM, Actas, book 41, fol. 87v, February 22, 1752.
84. ... *sólo un gracioso obsequio sujetándose a lo que la liberalidad del que los convidó les quisiese voluntariamente dar.* ACCMM, Actas, book 41, fol. 74v, February 1, 1752.
85. ACCMM, Actas, book 41, fol. 74v, February 1, 1752.
86. ... *los dichos [músicos] se han enconado en su contra, tratándole con palabras de menosprecio y provocativas, y aún faltándole al respeto y obediencia que como a tal maestro de capilla se le debe.* ACCMM, Actas, book 41, fol. 74v, February 1, 1752.
87. ... *y antes sí fueron ha procurar deslucir dichos maitines haciendo mofa de los que asistieron.* ACCMM, Actas, book 41, fol. 74v, February 1, 1752.
88. ACCMM, Actas, book 41, fol. 74v, February 1, 1752.
89. ... *y que así como en esta santa iglesia se le paga respectivamente diez o cinco pesos por el derecho de asistencia con sus papeles, del mismo modo ajustó en dicha obención lo que le tocaron personales de sus papeles.* ACCMM, Actas, book 41, fol. 74v, February 1, 1752.
90. ACCMM, Actas, book 27, fol. 62v, June 26, 1711; fol. 63v, June 30, 1711.
91. ACCMM, Actas, book 40, fol. 242r, May 21, 1751.
92. ... *y sobre si era o no a propósito dicho Jerusalem para maestro, pues lo músicos no le tenían respeto ni se lo tendrían nunca por manosearse demasiado con ellos, lo que era necesario tener presente.* ACCMM, Actas, book 40, fol. 16v, November 28, 1749.
93. ACCMM, Actas, book 41, fol. 89r, February 22, 1752.

94. ACCMM, Actas, book 41, fol. 105v, April 28, 1752.

95. ACCMM, Actas, book 41, fol. 87v, February 22, 1752.

96. ACCMM, Actas, book 42, fol. 6r, August 14, 1753.

97. ACCMM, Actas, book 42, fol. 6r, August 14, 1753.

98. *… que si no fuera por los hábitos que trae y ser ministro de esta santa iglesia, que es lo que más le sirve, y en lo que más se fía para sus maldades, ya hubiera conocido de él y lo hubiera prendido el capitán Velásquez.* ACCMM, Actas, book 42, fol. 105v, August 17, 1754.

99. ACCMM, Actas, book 33, fol. 183v, May 18, 1736.

100. ACCMM, Actas, book 38, fol. 30r, January 14, 1746.

101. ACCMM, Actas, book 38, fol. 30r, January 14, 1746.

102. ACCMM, Actas, book 45, fol. 167v, February 19, 1762.

103. *… con la precisa e inviolable condición de que todos los años ha de hacer y componer nuevamente algo de lo que haga falta y sea necesario para esta santa iglesia.* ACCMM, Actas, book 45, fol. 93r, September 5, 1761.

104. Letter from Ignacio Jerusalem to the chapter asking for support to uphold his privileges. ACCMM, Acuerdos de Cabildo, folder 4, without a date.

105. ACCMM, Acuerdos de Cabildo, folder 4, October 1, 1768.

106. ACCMM, Acuerdos de Cabildo, folder 4, October 1, 1768.

107. As a matter of fact, the administrator's role as a liaison is what scholar Raúl Torres Medina identifies as the solution that musicians found to the internal political problems of the music chapel. See Torres Medina, "¿La solución al problema?," pp. 211–240.

108. ACCMM, Actas, book 45, fol. 167v, February 19, 1762.

109. ACCMM, Acuerdos de Cabildo, folder 4, August 20, 1768; October 1, 1768.

110. ACCMM, Acuerdos de Cabildo, folder 4, August 20, 1771; September 26, 1775; April 18, 1776.

111. *Ignacio Jerusalem pide se le dé cuenta con este escrito y los autos de la materia que cita.* ACCMM, Acuerdos de Cabildo, folder 4, without a date.

112. Casta paintings often depict Chinos as the offspring of a Morisco(a) and a Spaniard. A Morisco(a) was considered to be the offspring of a Mulatto(a) and a Spaniard.

113. ACCMM, Actas, book 45, fol. 167v, February 19, 1762. See also Torres Medina, "La capilla de música de la catedral de México," p. 230.

114. ACCMM, Actas, book 45, fol. 37v, May 5, 1761.

115. ACCMM, Actas, book 45, fol. 84v, August 8, 1761.

116. ACCMM, Actas, book 45, fol. 167v, February 19, 1762.

117. ACCMM, Actas, book 44, fol. 63r, October 9, 1759.

118. ACCMM, Actas, book 45, fol. 169r, March 2, 1762. Torres Medina, "La capilla de música de la catedral de México," p. 233.

119. Torres Medina, "La capilla de música de la catedral de México," p. 233.

120. Answer from Juan Baptista del Águila to accusations from the chapel. ACCMM, Acuerdos de Cabildo, ca. 1768–1769.

121. ACCMM, Acuerdos de Cabildo, ca. 1768–1769.

122. ACCMM, Acuerdos de Cabildo, ca. 1768–1769.

123. ACCMM, Actas, book 51, fol. 163v, February 1, 1772.

124. Answer from Juan Baptista del Águila to accusations from the chapel. ACCMM, Acuerdos de Cabildo, ca. 1768–1769.

125. Villalobos Jaramillo, *Los 100 sitios y monumentos*, p. 116.

126. Answer from Juan Baptista del Águila to accusations from the chapel. ACCMM, Acuerdos de Cabildo, ca. 1768–1769.

127. *Por qué no meten vuestras señorías a una gran voz y habilidad que hay en México en coro de catedral, un tal Portillo que me dicen canta divinamente, y no que no hay una voz de provecho en el coro.* ACCMM, Acuerdos de Cabildo, ca. 1768–1769.

128. ACCMM, Acuerdos de Cabildo, ca. 1768–1769.

129. ACCMM, Acuerdos de Cabildo, folder 4, February 13, 1769.

130. AGN, Universidad, volume 24, fol. 207v, November 14, 1768. In Torres Medina, "La capilla de música de la catedral de México," p. 237.

131. Tate Lenning, *Reales cédulas*, pp. 225–227.

132. Letter from the chapelmaster, chapel administrator, and deputies to the chapter. ACCMM, Acuerdos de Cabildo, folder 4, 1768.

133. Torres Medina, "La capilla de música de la catedral de México," p. 238.

134. ACCMM, Acuerdos de Cabildo, not foliated, February 13, 1769.

135. Certification of merits (*Relación jurada de méritos*) presented by the music chapel in service of the king, the high court, noble city, and public. ACCMM, Acuerdos de Cabildo, folder 4, ca. 1768.

136. Gembero Ustárroz, "El mecenazgo musical," p. 474-n42.

137. ACCMM, Actas, book 49, fol. 187r, December 6, 1768.

138. Gembero Ustárroz, "Ignacio de Jerusalem" (essay presented at the meeting Encuentro de Mexicanistas 2010. Educación, Ciencia y Cultura, Antwerp, Belgium, September 21, 2010).

139. ... *personas que no son de nuestro igual, sí serán muy hombres de bien, pero no decentes para tanto hombre blanco y señores sacerdotes de dicha capilla.* Letter from Ignacio Pedroza to the chapter. ACCMM, Acuerdos de Cabildo, folder 4, ca. 1768.

Epilogue

1. ACCMM, Actas, book 45, fol. 120r, October 27, 1761.

2. Tate Lenning, *Reales cédulas*, pp. 225–227.

3. Torres Medina, "La capilla de música de la catedral de México," pp. 243–244.

4. Arcila Farías, *Reformas económicas*, pp. 76, 83.

5. This was the tension that painters tried to negotiate in eighteenth-century New Spain. They considered that the art of painting was intellectually removed from the work done by artisans in other guilds. This was in part the reason that painters attempted to create an academy: this would be a center that would remove painting from the realm of guild activity and would position it as an intellectual endeavor, a stance that painters tried to legitimize by alluding to a connection between art and poetry. See Chapter 5.

6. ACCMM, Actas, book 49, fol. 187r, December 6, 1768.

7. The university also enforced a bull by Pope Martin V, which stated that doctoral candidates could shorten their time of candidacy given that they were nobles and had enough financial resources for graduation. Aguirre Salvador, *El mérito y la estrategia*, pp. 80–83.

BIBLIOGRAPHY

Primary Sources

ARCHIVO DEL CABILDO—CATEDRAL METROPOLITANA DE MÉXICO (ACCMM), MEXICO CITY

1. *Libro de erección y fundación del collegio de la asumpción de nuestra señora y patriarcha S.S. Joseph para los ymphantes de el choro de esta santa iglesia metropolitana de México* (1725).
2. Actas de Cabildo
   - Book 4, fol. 251r, November 14, 1600
   - Book 4, fol. 262v, June 19, 1601
   - Book 5, fol. 122v, May 12, 1609
   - Book 24, fol. 40r, July 19, 1695
   - Book 25, fol. 16r, June 17, 1698
   - Book 25, fol. 32v, January 9, 1699
   - Book 25, fol. 152v, February 12, 1700
   - Book 25, fol. 156v, February 16, 1700
   - Book 26, fol. 166v, June 21, 1708
   - Book 26, fol. 336v, January 10, 1710
   - Book 27, fol. 18v, November 18, 1710
   - Book 27, fol. 26r, January 7, 1711
   - Book 27, fol. 41v, February 10, 1711
   - Book 27, fol. 51r, April 18, 1711
   - Book 27, fol. 57r, May 19, 1711
   - Book 27, fol. 62v, June 26, 1711
   - Book 27, fol. 63v, June 30, 1711
   - Book 27, fol. 73v, July 17, 1711
   - Book 27, fol. 85v, August 14, 1711
   - Book 27, fol. 178r, July 30, 1712
   - Book 27, fol. 186r, August 3, 1712
   - Book 29, fols. 76v–77r, August 3, 1717
   - Book 29, fol. 342v, May 19, 1730
   - Book 30, fol. 9r, January 30, 1722
   - Book 32, fol. 104r, July 1, 1732
   - Book 32, fol. 113v, July 29, 1732
   - Book 32, fol. 144v, October 24, 1732
   - Book 32, fol. 179r, January 27, 1733

- Book 32, fol. 216v, June 19, 1733
- Book 32, fol. 266v, January 12, 1734
- Book 33, fol. 14v, April 6, 1734
- Book 33, fol. 25r, May 14, 1734
- Book 33, fol. 33r, June 22, 1734
- Book 33, fol. 45v, September 24, 1734
- Book 33, fol. 54r, November 2, 1734
- Book 33, fol. 74r, March 3, 1735
- Book 33, fol. 77r, March 8, 1735
- Book 33, fol. 83v, March 22, 1735
- Book 33, fol. 113r, July 29, 1735
- Book 33, fol. 133v, November 11, 1735
- Book 33, fol. 137v, November 15, 1735
- Book 33, fol. 153r, January 27, 1736
- Book 33, fol. 173v, April 20, 1736
- Book 33, fol. 174v, April 24, 1736
- Book 33, fol. 183v, May 18, 1736
- Book 33, fol. 188v, June 19, 1736
- Book 33, fol. 210r, September 11, 1736
- Book 33, fol. 213v, September 18, 1736
- Book 34, fol. 13r, November 6, 1736
- Book 34, fol. 76r, June 28, 1737
- Book 34, fol. 78r, July 2, 1737
- Book 34, fol. 103v, September 3, 1737
- Book 34, fol. 143v, December 9, 1737
- Book 35, fol. 6v, December 13, 1737
- Book 35, fol. 19r, December 23, 1737
- Book 35, fol. 125v, August 29, 1738
- Book 35, fol. 283r, July 28, 1741
- Book 36, fol. 5v, September 28, 1741
- Book 36, fol. 33v, January 19, 1742
- Book 36, fol. 80r, July 10, 1742
- Book 36, fol. 93r, August 13, 1742
- Book 36, fol. 152v, February 15, 1743
- Book 36, fol. 197r, August 9, 1743
- Book 36, fol. 240v, December 20, 1743
- Book 37, fol. 15r, March 13, 1744
- Book 37, fol. 40v, June 2, 1744
- Book 37, fol. 67r, July 30, 1744
- Book 37, fol. 182v, May 21, 1745
- Book 37, fol. 227r, August 25, 1745
- Book 37, fol. 235r, September 7, 1745
- Book 37, fol. 241r, September 18, 1745
- Book 38, fol. 30r, January 14, 1746
- Book 38, fol. 30v, January 14, 1746
- Book 38, fol. 96r, May 27, 1746
- Book 38, fol. 106r, July 15, 1746
- Book 38, fol. 110v, July 29, 1746
- Book 38, fol. 129r, October 14, 1746
- Book 38, fol. 153v, January 13, 1747
- Book 38, fol. 155r, January 18, 1747
- Book 39, fol. 346v, January 7, 1749
- Book 39, fol. 351v, January 10, 1749
- Book 40, fol. 16v, November 28, 1749

- Book 40, fol. 28v, January 12, 1750
- Book 40, fol. 56v, April 7, 1750
- Book 40, fol. 69v, May 23, 1750
- Book 40, fol. 71r, May 25, 1750
- Book 40, fol. 83v, June 30, 1750
- Book 40, fol. 89r, July 23, 1750
- Book 40, fol. 91r, August 3, 1750
- Book 40, fol. 140v, October 30, 1750
- Book 40, fol. 160r, December 16, 1750
- Book 40, fol. 171v, January 15, 1751
- Book 40, fol. 176r, January 16, 1751
- Book 40, fol. 186r, February 9, 1751
- Book 40, fol. 196v, February 20, 1751
- Book 40, fol. 218r, March 23, 1751
- Book 40, fol. 242r, May 21, 1751
- Book 40, fol. 245r, May 28, 1751
- Book 41, fol. 2v, June 9, 1751
- Book 41, fol. 3r, June 9, 1751
- Book 41, fol. 29v, September 18, 1751
- Book 41, fol. 60v, January 7, 1752
- Book 41, fol. 74v, February 1, 1752
- Book 41, fol. 87v, February 22, 1752
- Book 41, fol. 89r, February 22, 1752
- Book 41, fol. 105v, April 28, 1752
- Book 41, fol. 124r, July 4, 1752
- Book 41, fol. 176r, October 17, 1752
- Book 41, fol. 258v, March 24, 1743
- Book 42, fol. 6r, August 14, 1753
- Book 42, fol. 10v, August 29, 1753
- Book 42, fol. 105v, August 17, 1754
- Book 43, fol. 260r, October 6, 1758
- Book 44, fol. 21r, May 4, 1759
- Book 44, fol. 63r, October 9, 1759
- Book 44, fol. 89v, January 9, 1760
- Book 44, fol. 147r, May 9, 1760
- Book 44, fol. 150v, May 10, 1760
- Book 44, fol. 200v, August 29, 1760
- Book 44, fol. 220r, October 10, 1760
- Book 44, fol. 286r, January 21, 1761
- Book 45, fol. 37v, May 5, 1761
- Book 45, fol. 63r, July 3, 1761
- Book 45, fol. 76r, July 24, 1761
- Book 45, fol. 78r, July 24, 1761
- Book 45, fol. 84v, August 8, 1761
- Book 45, fol. 120r, October 27, 1761
- Book 45, fol. 167v, February 19, 1762
- Book 45, fol. 169r, March 2, 1762
- Book 49, fol. 187r, December 6, 1768
- Book 51, fol. 163v, February 1, 1772
- Book 52, fol. 111r, January 22, 1774
- Book 54, fol. 239r, July 4, 1780
- Book 54, fol. 294r, September 18, 1781
- Book 54, fol. 295r, September 26, 1781
- Book 57, fol. 198v, October 7, 1791

3. Acuerdos de Cabildo
- Folder 4, without a date; Ignacio Jerusalem asks the chapter to support the chapel's privileges, as they were upheld by the high court.
- Folder 4, ca. 1754, letter from Ignacio Jerusalem to the chapter.
- Folder 4, ca. 1768, letter from Ignacio Pedroza to the chapter.
- Folder 4, ca. 1768, *relación jurada de los méritos de la capilla de música de la santa iglesia catedral de México.*
- Folder 4, 1768, letter from the chapelmaster, chapel administrator, and deputies to the chapter.
- Folder 4, July 4, 1768, letter from Domingo Dutra y Andrade to the chapter.
- Folder 4, August 20, 1768, minutes of the meeting of the music chapel.
- Folder 4, October 1, 1768, report by the chapter's secretary about Ignacio Jerusalem's cathedral activity since 1750.
- Folder 4, December 6, 1768, report by Juan Ignacio de la Rocha to the chapter about the meeting of the music chapel on October 13, 1768.
- Folder 4, ca. 1768–1769, answer from Juan Baptista del Águila to accusations from the chapel.
- Folder 4, February 13, 1769, letter from Juan Ignacio de la Rocha to the chapter.
- Folder 4, August 20, 1771, minutes of the meeting of the music chapel.
- Folder 4, October 7, 1772, meeting of the music chapel to elect a new administrator.
- Folder 4, February 20, 1775, report of the meeting of the music chapel.
- Folder 4, September 26, 1775, meeting of the music chapel to elect a new administrator.
- Folder 4, April 18, 1776, meeting of the music chapel to elect a new administrator.
- Folder 4, June 25, 1784, petition by choir chaplains to the chapter to allow a deacon to serve in one of the Lorenzana chaplaincies.

4. Archivo de Música
- A0090, "Ya La Gloria Accidental"

5. Canonjías
- Book 1, no. 65, fols. 97r–133v, *autos formados para la oposición y exámen de la plaza de maestro de capilla de la del coro de esta santa iglesia metropolitana y que obtuvo Don Ignacio Hierusalem.*
- Book 1, January 9, 1750

6. Capellanías
- Box 1, folder 3, March 17, 1767

7. Correspondencia
- Book 10, June 1727, Manuel Sumaya responds to accusations from the administrator of the chapel, Juan de Salibe, regarding obvenciones.
- Book 17, without a date, letter from Ignacio Jerusalem to the chapter asking for support to uphold his privileges.
- Book 17, without a date, letter from Martín Bernárdez de Rivera to the chapter.
- Book 17, without a date, certification of merits of Martín Bernárdez de Rivera.
- Book 18, without a date, letter from José Salvatierra to the chapter.
- Book 18, without a date, letter from Pedro Rodríguez Calvo to the chapter.
- Book 18, without a date, letter from Francisco Álvarez de la Cadena to the chapter.
- Book 18, August 22, 1774, report by Manuel de Acevedo, Martín Vásquez de Mendoza and Martín Bernárdez de Rivera about the examination of Juan Pombo.
- Book 18, January 21, 1778, report by Pedro Navarro about the examination of José Salvatierra.
- Book 18, January 16, 1781, report by Matheo Tollis de la Rocca about the examination of Ignacio Rodríguez.
- Book 30, *Escuela de música en que perpetuamente hallen las niñas más desvalidas del Recogimiento y Casa de San Miguel de Bethlen de esta Ciudad de México dote y título para poder ser religiosas.* Mexico City: Doña María de Rivera, 1746.
- Box 1, folder 8, March 12, 1662, letter from Antonio Visencio to the chapter.
- Box 1, folder 8, February 1, 1669, letter from Guillermo de Carvajal to the chapter.

- Box 1, folder 9, April-May, 1749, report by the accountants Francisco Javier Gómez Beltrán and Juan José de Mier to the chapter about zangonautlas.
- Box 15, folder 14, June 6, 1738, information about the legitimacy, purity, life and customs of Ciprian de Aguilera.
- Box 15, folder 18, January 19, 1742, information about the legitimacy, purity, life, and customs of Timoteo Torres y Cuevas.
- Box 23, folder 2, March 9, 1700, letter from Antonio de Salazar to the chapter.
- Box 23, folder 2, November 22, 1709, report by Antonio de Salazar about earnings from obvenciones by every musician in the chapel.
- Box 23, folder 3, February 11, 1721, letter from Benito Martino to the chapter.
- Box 23, folder 3, March 4, 1721, agreement by the chapter to hire Benito Martino to play violin.
- Box 23, folder 3, May 19, 1730, letter from Antonio Rodríguez to the chapter.
- Box 23, folder 6, ca. 1745–1746, letter from Juan Baptista del Águila to the chapter.

8. Edictos
   - Box 2, folder 37, May 7, 1715
9. Fábrica Espiritual
   - Book 3, fol. 1r, March 12, 1717
   - Book 4, fol. 3r, June 2, 1747
   - Book 6, not foliated, April 16, 1749
   - Book 6, not foliated, August 2, 1749
   - Book 6, not foliated, September 9, 1749
   - Book 6, not foliated, September 23, 1749
   - Book 6, not foliated, October 15, 1749
   - Box 1, folder 14, July 28, 1732
   - Box 1, folder 14, January 21, 1733
10. Fábrica Material
    - Book 7, not foliated, April 29, 1748
    - Book 7, not foliated, July 24, 1748
11. Obras Pías
    - Book 3, fols. 6v–7r, 1725
12. Ordo
    - Book 2, fol. 35r, 1754

ARCHIVO GENERAL DE LA NACIÓN (AGN), MEXICO CITY

1. Inquisición
   - Volume 1179, document 10, fol. 185r
2. Universidad
   - Volume 24, fol. 207v, November 14, 1768
   - Volume 156, fol. 49r, January 24, 1710
   - Volume 156, fol. 63r, March 15, 1711
   - Volume 358, fol. 553r, March 23, 1702

ARCHIVO HISTÓRICO DEL ARZOBISPADO DE MÉXICO (AHAM), MEXICO CITY

1. Fondo Cabildo
   - Box 128, folder 30, ca. 1790, list of the music instructors at the Colegio de Infantes since 1770.
   - Box 183, folder 25, petition by Hernando Franco to the chapter to buy a book of Masses by Francisco Guerrero.
   - Box 185, folder 63, September 22, 1712, inventory of choirbooks gathered by Jerónimo López de Arbizu.
   - Box 187, folder 21, December 4, 1761, certification of merits of Martín Bernárdez de Rivera.
   - CL 48, 1700–1746

ARCHIVO HISTÓRICO BANAMEX (AHB), MEXICO CITY

1. Fondo Marqueses de Jaral de Berrio
   • Administración, Inventarios, MJB-01-010-073, P1F1A1E5/C01, fols. 21r, 21v, 26v, 28v, 30r, 34v, 54r–57r, February 1, 1780.

ARCHIVO DEL SAGRARIO METROPOLITANO DE MÉXICO (ASMM), MEXICO CITY

1. Book of Spanish baptisms
   • Box 10, vol. 26, fol. 26r

BIBLIOTECA NACIONAL DE MÉXICO (BNM), UNIVERSIDAD NACIONAL AUTÓNOMA DE MÉXICO, MEXICO CITY

1. Fondo Reservado
   • *Colección varia de papeles y asuntos curiosos de don Francisco López Portillo, del consejo de su majestad, oidor y de la Real Audiencia de Guadalajara en la Nueva Galicia.* Colección Lafragua, number 143 LAF

DEGOLYER LIBRARY, SOUTHERN METHODIST UNIVERSITY, DALLAS, TEXAS

1. *Carta de Hidalguía, 1743–1744,* A1992.1847c
2. *Collection of Documents regarding Limpieza de Sangre, 1619–1786,* A2002.0107c

Secondary Sources

Aguirre Salvador, Rodolfo. "El acceso al alto clero en el arzobispado de México 1650–1787." *Fronteras de la Historia* (Instituto Colombiano de Antropología e Historia) 9 (2008): 179–203.

Aguirre Salvador, Rodolfo et al. *La universidad novohispana en el Siglo de Oro: A cuatrocientos años de El Quijote.* Mexico City: Universidad Nacional Autónoma de México, 2006.

Aguirre Salvador, Rodolfo. "Los límites de la carrera eclesiástica en el arzobispado de México (1730–1747)." In *Carrera, linaje y patronazgo: Clérigos y juristas en Nueva España, Chile y Perú (siglos XVI–XVIII),* ed. Rodolfo Aguirre Salvador, 73–120. Mexico City: Universidad Nacional Autónoma de México, 2004.

Aguirre Salvador, Rodolfo. *El mérito y la estrategia: Clérigos, juristas y médicos en Nueva España.* Mexico City: Universidad Nacional Autónoma de México, 2003.

Aguirre Salvador, Rodolfo. "El perfil de una élite académica en la Nueva España del siglo XVIII: Los licenciados y doctores canonistas." In *Universitarios en la Nueva España,* ed. Armando Pavón Romero, 51–84. Mexico City: Universidad Nacional Autónoma de México, 2003.

Aguirre Salvador, Rodolfo. *Por el camino de las letras: El ascenso profesional de los catedráticos juristas de la Nueva España, siglo XVIII.* Mexico City: Universidad Nacional Autónoma de México, 1998.

Alamán, Lucas. *Historia de Méjico,* 5 volumes. Mexico City: Editorial Jus, 1942.

Álvarez Sánchez, Adriana. "La población de bachilleres en artes de la universidad mexicana (1701–1738)." In *Del aula a la ciudad: Estudios sobre la universidad y la sociedad en el México virreinal,* ed. Enrique González González, Mónica Hidalgo Pego, and Adriana Álvarez Sánchez, 23–53. Mexico City: Universidad Nacional Autónoma de México, 2009.

Alzate y Ramírez, José Antonio. *Obras: Periódicos, volumen 1.* Mexico City: Universidad Nacional Autónoma de México, 1980.

Arcila Farías, Eduardo. *Reformas económicas del siglo XVIII en Nueva España: II. Industria, minería y Real Hacienda.* Mexico City: Secretaría de Educación Pública, 1974.

Arias, Enrique Alberto. "Cerone as Historian." *Anuario Musical* 58 (2003): 87–110.

Baker, Geoffrey and Tess Knighton, eds. *Music and Urban Society in Colonial Latin America.* Cambridge: Cambridge University Press, 2011.

Baker, Geoffrey. "Polychorality, Ethnicity and Status in Colonial Cuzco, Peru." In *Polychoralities: Music, Identity and Power in Italy, Spain and the New World*, ed. Juan José Carreras and Iain Fenlon, 255–262. Venice: Fondazione Ugo e Olga Levi; Kassel: Edition Reichenberger, 2013.

Baker, Geoffrey. "The Resounding City." In *Music and Urban Society in Colonial Latin America*, ed. Geoffrey Baker and Tess Knighton, 1–20. Cambridge: Cambridge University Press, 2011.

Baker, Geoffrey. *Imposing Harmony: Music and Society in Colonial Cuzco*. Durham, NC: Duke University Press, 2008.

Bal y Gay, Jesús. *Tesoros de la música polifónica en México I: El códice del Convento del Carmen.* Mexico City: Instituto Nacional de Bellas Artes, 1952.

Barwick, Steven. *Two Mexico City Choirbooks of 1717.* Carbondale: Southern Illinois University Press, 1982.

Barwick, Steven. "Sacred Vocal Polyphony in Early Colonial Mexico." Ph.D. diss., Harvard University, 1949.

Becerra Jiménez, Celina G. "Enseñanza y ejercicio de la música en la construcción del ritual sonoro en la catedral de Guadalajara." In *Enseñanza y ejercicio de la música en México*, ed. Arturo Camacho Becerra, 21–69. Mexico City: Centro de Investigaciones y Estudios Superiores en Antropología Social, 2013.

Becerra López, José Luis. *La organización de los estudios en la Nueva España.* Mexico City: Editorial Cultura, 1963.

Béhague, Gerard. Review of *Renaissance and Baroque Musical Sources in the Americas*, by Robert Stevenson. *Anuario Interamericano de Investigación Musical* 10 (1974): 211–213.

Béhague, Gerard. Review of *Music in Aztec and Inca Territory*, by Robert Stevenson. *Musical Quarterly* 55, no. 1 (January 1969): 115–120.

Bejarano Pellicer, Clara. *El Mercado de la música en la Sevilla del Siglo de Oro.* Seville, Spain: Universidad de Sevilla—Fundación Focus-Abengoa, 2013.

Beristáin y Souza, José Mariano. *Biblioteca hispanoamericana setentrional, volumen 1.* Mexico City: Calle de Santo Domingo y esquina de Tacuba, 1816; facsimile edition by Fortino Hipólito Vera, Amecameca, Mexico: Tipografía del Colegio Católico, 1883.

Brading, David A. *Church and State in Bourbon Mexico: The Diocese of Michoacán, 1749–1810.* Cambridge: Cambridge University Press, 1994.

Brading, David A. *Miners and Merchants in Bourbon Mexico.* Cambridge: Cambridge University Press, 1971.

Brill, Mark. "Carrasco or Mathías? Plagiarism and Corruption in an Eighteenth-Century Examen de Oposición from the Oaxaca Cathedral." *Latin American Music Review* 26, no. 2 (Autumn–Winter 2005): 227–247.

Brill, Mark. "The Oaxaca Cathedral 'Examen de oposición': The Quest for a Modern Style." *Latin American Music Review* 26, no. 1 (Spring–Summer 2005): 1–22.

Brothers, Lester D. "Musical Learning in Seventeenth-Century Mexico: The Case of Francisco López Capillas." *Revista de Musicología* 16, no. 5, XV Meeting of the International Musicological Society: Mediterranean Music Cultures and their Ramifications, vol. 5 (1993): 2814–2834.

Calvo, Thomas. "Ciencia, cultura y política ilustradas (Nueva España y otras partes)." In *Las reformas borbónicas, 1750–1808, volumen 1,* ed. Clara García Ayluardo, 83–130. Mexico City: Fondo de Cultura Económica, 2010.

Campa, Gustavo E. *Escritos y composiciones musicales.* Mexico City: Imprenta de E. Murguía, 1917.

Carrera, Magali M. *Imagining Identity in New Spain. Race, Lineage, and the Colonial Body in Portraiture and Casta Paintings.* Austin: University of Texas Press, 2003.

Carreras, Juan José. "La policoralidad como identidad del 'Barroco musical español.'" In *Polychoralities: Music, Identity, and Power in Italy, Spain and the New World,* ed. Juan José Carreras and Iain Fenlon, 87–122. Venice: Fondazione Ugo e Olga Levi; Kassel: Edition Reichenberger, 2013.

Carreras, Juan José. "From Literes to Nebra: Spanish Dramatic Music between Tradition and Modernity." In *Music in Spain during the Eighteenth Century,* ed. Malcom Boyd and Juan José Carreras, 7–16. Cambridge: Cambridge University Press, 1998.

Carvajal Ávila, Violeta Paulina. "El Colegio de Infantes del Salvador y Santos Ángeles: Semillero de la tradición musical de la catedral de Valladolid de Michoacán." In *Enseñanza y ejercicio de la música en México*, ed. Arturo Camacho Becerra, 155–195. Mexico City: Centro de Investigaciones y Estudios Superiores en Antropología Social, 2013.

Castro Santa-Anna, José Manuel. "Diario de sucesos notables y comprende los años de 1754 a 1756." In *Documentos para la historia de Méjico, vol. VI*, ed. Manuel Orozco y Berra. Mexico City: Imprenta de Juan R. Navarro, 1854.

Catalyne, Alice Ray. "Manuel de Zumaya (ca. 1678–1756): Mexican Composer for Church and Theater." In *Festival Essays for Pauline Alderman*, ed. Burton L. Karson, 101–124. Provo, UT: Brigham Young University Press, 1976.

Catalyne, Alice Ray. "Music of the Sixteenth to the Eighteenth Centuries in the Cathedral of Puebla, Mexico." *Anuario* 2 (1966): 75–90.

Cerone, Pedro. *El melopeo y maestro: Tractado de musica theorica y pratica*. Naples: Juan Bautista Gargano and Lucrecio Nucci, 1613.

Chance, John K. and William B. Taylor. "Estate and Class in a Colonial City: Oaxaca in 1792." *Comparative Studies in Society and History* 19 (July 1977): 454–487.

Cope, Douglas R. *The Limits of Racial Domination: Plebeian Society in Colonial Mexico City, 1660–1720*. Madison: University of Wisconsin Press, 1994.

Davies, Drew Edward. "'Mexican Minerva': Myth and Erudition in a Coronation Ode for Charles III of Spain." Essay presented at the annual meeting of the American Musicological Society, Pittsburgh, PA, November 8, 2013.

Davies, Drew Edward. "Making Music, Writing Myth: Urban Guadalupan Ritual in Eighteenth-Century New Spain." In *Music and Urban Society in Colonial Latin America*, ed. Geoffrey Baker and Tess Knighton, 64–82. Cambridge: Cambridge University Press, 2011.

Davies, Drew Edward. *Santiago Billoni: Complete Works*. Middleton, WI: A-R Editions, 2011.

Davies, Drew Edward. "Villancicos from Mexico City for the Virgin of Guadalupe." *Early Music* 39, no. 2 (May 2011): 229–244.

Davies, Drew Edward. "The Italianized Frontier: Music at Durango Cathedral, Español Culture, and the Aesthetics of Devotion in Eighteenth-Century New Spain." Ph.D. diss., University of Chicago, 2006.

Deans-Smith, Susan. "'This Noble and Illustrious Art': Painters and the Politics of Guild Reform in Early Modern Mexico City, 1674–1768." In *Mexican Soundings: Essays in Honour of David A. Brading*, ed. Susan Deans-Smith and Eric Van Young, 67–98. London: Institute for the Study of the Americas, 2007.

De la Main, Ricardo. *Exposición de la música eclesiástica y alivio de sochantres y exposición de la música antigua y de la música viadana*. Mexico City: Doña María de Rivera, 1747.

DeNora, Tia. *After Adorno: Rethinking Music Sociology*. Cambridge: Cambridge University Press, 2003.

Dietz, Hanns-Bertold. "Fortunes and Misfortunes of Two Italian Composers in Early Eighteenth-Century Spain: Philipo Falconi and Francesco Corradini." *International Journal of Musicology* 7 (2000): 87–111.

Domínguez Ortiz, Antonio. *La clase de los conversos en Castilla en la edad moderna*. Granada: Universidad de Granada, 1955.

Durán Moncada, Cristóbal M. "La escoleta de música de la catedral de Guadalajara (1691–1750)." In *Enseñanza y ejercicio de la música en México*, ed. Arturo Camacho Becerra, 127–154. Mexico City: Centro de Investigaciones y Estudios Superiores en Antropología Social, 2013.

Enríquez, Lucero. "¿Y el estilo galante en la Nueva España?" In *Primer coloquio Musicat: Música, catedral y sociedad*, ed. Lucero Enríquez and Margarita Covarrubias, 175–191. Mexico City: Universidad Nacional Autónoma de México, 2006.

Estrada, Jesús. *Música y músicos en la época virreinal*. Mexico City: Secretaría de Educación Pública, 1980.

Eximeno, Antonio. *Don Lazarillo Vizcardi. Sus investigaciones músicas con ocasión del concurso a un magisterio de capilla vacante*, 2 volumes. Madrid: Imprenta de Rivadeneyra, 1872–1873.

Eximeno, Antonio. *Duda de don Antonio Eximeno sobre el ensayo fundamental práctico de contrapunto del m.r.p.m. fray Juan Bautista Martini.* Translated by Francisco Antonio Gutiérrez. Madrid: Imprenta Real, 1797.

Eximeno, Antonio. *Del origen y reglas de la música, con la historia de su progreso, decadencia y restauración.* Translated by Francisco Antonio Gutiérrez. Madrid: Imprenta Real, 1796.

Farriss, Nancy M. *La corona y el clero en el México colonial, 1579–1821: La crisis del privilegio eclesiástico.* Mexico City: Fondo de Cultura Económica, 1995.

Feijóo y Montenegro, Benito Jerónimo. *Teatro crítico universal.* Madrid: Joaquín Ibarra, 1778.

Fernández, Teodisio. "Magia y milagros en el teatro novohispano del siglo XVIII." *Anales de literatura hispanoamericana* 21 (1992): 165–178.

Fernandes, Cristina. "De la etiqueta de la Real Cámara a las nuevas sociabilidades públicas y privadas: La actividad del violinista y compositor José Palomino en Lisboa (1774–1808)." *Revista de Musicología* 36, nos. 1–2 (2013): 141–170.

Fiorentino, Giuseppe. "Canto llano, canto de órgano y contrapunto improvisado: El currículo de un músico professional en la España del renacimiento." In *Francisco de Salinas: Música, teoría y matemática en el Renacimiento,* ed. Amaya García Pérez and Paloma Otaola González, 147–160. Salamanca: Ediciones Universidad de Salamanca, 2014.

Fisher, Andrew B. and Matthew D. O'Hara, eds. *Imperial Subjects: Race and Identity in Colonial Latin America.* Durham: Duke University Press, 2009.

Florescano, Enrique and Isabel Gil Sánchez. "La época de las reformas borbónicas y el crecimiento económico, 1750–1808." In *Historia general de México, volumen 2,* ed. Alejandra Moreno Toscano, Andrés Lira, Luis Muro, Enrique Florescano, Isabel Gil Sánchez, Luis Villoro, and Jorge Alberto Manrique, 199–301. Mexico City: El Colegio de México, 1977.

Florescano, Enrique and Isabel Gil Sánchez. *Precios del maíz y crisis agrícolas en México (1708–1810): Ensayo sobre el movimiento de los precios y sus consecuencias económicas y sociales.* Mexico City: El Colegio de México, 1969.

Forrester, Donald W. "An Introduction to Seventeenth-Century Spanish Music Theory Books." *Journal of Research in Music Education* 21, no. 1 (Spring 1973): 61–67.

García Cárcel, Ricardo. *Historia de España siglo XVIII: La España de los borbones.* Madrid: Cátedra, 2002.

Garner, Richard L. "Precios y salarios en México durante el siglo XVIII." In *Economías coloniales: Precios y salarios en América Latina, siglo XVIII,* ed. Lymann Johnson and Enrique Tandeter, 81–118. Mexico City: Fondo de Cultura Económica, 1992.

Gembero Ustárroz, María. "Ignacio de Jerusalem y la capilla de música de la Universidad de México en el siglo XVIII: Europeos, novohispanos, identidad e intereses institucionales en conflicto." Essay presented at the meeting Encuentro de Mexicanistas 2010. Educación, Ciencia y Cultura, Antwerp, Belgium, September 21, 2010.

Gembero Ustárroz, María. "Migraciones de músicos entre España y América (siglos XVI–XVIII): Estudio preliminar." In *La música y el Atlántico: Relaciones musicales entre España y Latinoamérica,* ed. María Gembero Ustárroz and Emilio Ros-Fábregas, 17–58. Granada: Universidad de Granada, 2007.

Gembero Ustárroz, María. "El mecenazgo musical de Juan de Palafox (1600–1659), Obispo de Puebla de los Ángeles y virrey de Nueva España." In *Palafox: Iglesia, cultura y estado en el siglo XVII,* ed. Ricardo Fernández Gracia, 463–496. Pamplona: Universidad de Navarra, 2001.

Goffman, Erving. *The Presentation of Self in Everyday Life.* New York: Bantam Doubleday Dell Publishing Group, 1959.

Gonzalbo Aizpuru, Pilar. *Familia y orden colonial.* Mexico City: El Colegio de México, 1998.

González Obregón, Luis. *La calles de México,* 2 volumes. Mexico City: Ediciones Botas, 1941.

González Polo, Ignacio. *El palacio de los condes de Santiago de Calimaya.* Mexico City: Universidad Nacional Autónoma de México, 1973.

Green, Otis H. and Leonard A. Irving. "On the Mexican Book Trade in 1600: A Chapter in Cultural History." *Hispanic Review* 9, no. 1 (January 1941): 1–40.

Hannas, Ruth. "Cerone, Philosopher and Teacher." *Musical Quarterly* 21 (1935): 408–422.

Hering Torres, Max S. "Color, pureza, raza: La calidad de los sujetos coloniales." In *La cuestión colonial*, ed. Heraclio Bonilla, 451–469. Bogota: Universidad Nacional de Colombia, 2011.

Hernández Franco, Juan. *Cultura y limpieza de sangre en la España moderna*. Murcia: Universidad de Murcia, 1997.

Hernández Mateos, Alberto. "'Maestrazos de contrapunto, rutineros maquinales, chabacanos seguidilleros': La recepción polémica del pensamiento de Antonio Eximeno en el *Diario de Madrid* (1796–1804)." *Revista de Musicología* 36, nos. 1–2 (2013): 189–224.

Herrera y Ogazón, Alba. *El arte musical en México*. Mexico City: Departamento editorial de la Dirección general de las bellas artes, 1917.

Humboldt, Alexander von. *Ensayo político sobre el reino de la Nueva España*, ed. Juan Ortega y Medina. Mexico City: Editorial Porrúa, 1966.

Icaza Dufour, Francisco. *La abogacía en el reino de Nueva España: 1521–1821*. Mexico City: Editorial Porrúa, 1998.

Illari, Bernardo. "The Slave's Progress: Music as Profession in Criollo Buenos Aires." In *Music and Urban Society in Colonial Latin America*, ed. Geoffrey Baker and Tess Knighton, 186–207. Cambridge: Cambridge University Press, 2011.

Instrucciones que los virreyes de Nueva España dejaron a sus sucesores, volumen 1. Mexico City: Imprenta de Ignacio Escalante, 1873.

Iriarte, Tomás de. *La música, poema*. Madrid: Imprenta Real de la Gazeta, 1779.

Irving, David R. M. "Employment, Enfranchisement and Liminality: Ecclesiastical Musicians in Early Modern Manila." In *Music and Urban Society in Colonial Latin America*, ed. Geoffrey Baker and Tess Knighton, 117–131. Cambridge: Cambridge University Press, 2011.

Irving, David R. M. *Colonial Counterpoint: Music in Early Modern Manila*. New York: Oxford University Press, 2010.

Israel, Jonathan I. *Race, Class, and Politics in Colonial Mexico, 1610–1670*. London: Oxford University Press, 1975.

Kicza, John E. *Colonial Entrepreneurs: Families and Business in Bourbon Mexico City*. Albuquerque: University of New Mexico Press, 1983.

Konetzke, Richard, ed. *Colección de documentos para la historia de la formación social de Hispanoamérica, 1493–1810, volumen 3*. Madrid: Consejo Superior de Investigaciones Científicas, 1962.

Ladd, Doris M. *The Mexican Nobility at Independence, 1780–1826*. Austin: University of Texas Press, 1976.

Laird, Paul R. *Towards a History of the Spanish Villancico*. Warren, MI: Harmonie Park Press, 1997.

Lee Blodget, Sherrill Bigelow. "From Manuscript to Performance: A Critical Edition of Ignacio de Jerusalem's Los Maitines de Nuestra Señora de la Concepción (1768)." D.M.A. thesis, University of Arizona, 2008.

Lemmon, Alfred E. "El archivo general de la nación mexicana, un fondo musical." *Heterofonía Revista Musical* 13, no. 2 (June 1980): 13–18.

Lemmon, Alfred E. "Towards an Inventory of Music Theory Books in Colonial Mexico." *Anuario Musical* 23–25 (1980): 131–139.

Leonard, Irving A. *Baroque Times in Old Mexico*. Ann Arbor: University of Michigan Press, 1959.

Leonard, Irving A. "The Theater Season of 1791–1792 in Mexico City." *Hispanic American Historical Review* 31, no. 2 (May 1951): 349–364.

Leonard, Irving A. "The 1790 Theater Season of the Mexico City Coliseo." *Hispanic Review* 19, no. 2 (April 1951): 104–120.

Leonard, Irving A. "On the Mexican Book Trade, 1683." *Hispanic American Historical Review* 27, no. 3 (August 1947): 403–435.

Liebman, Seymour B. *The Jews in New Spain: Faith, Flame, and the Inquisition*. Miami, FL: University of Miami Press, 1970.

López-Calo, José. *La música en la catedral de Granada en el siglo XVI, volumen I*. Granada: Fundación Rodríguez Acosta, 1963.

Lorente, Andrés. *El porqué de la música*. Alcalá de Henares: Nicolás de Xamarés, 1672.

Maravall, José Antonio. *Estado moderno y mentalidad social (siglos XV a XVII)*, 2 volumes. Madrid: Revista de Occidente, 1972.

March, Barbara. "Latin American Music Today." *Inter-American Music Bulletin* 21 (January 1961): 1–4.

María y Campos, Armando. *Los payasos, poetas del pueblo (El circo en México): Crónica ilustrada con reproducciones de programas de la época y viñetas de los mismos, de la colección del autor.* Mexico City: Ediciones Botas, 1939.

Marichal, Carlos. *La bancarrota del virreinato: Nueva España y las finanzas del imperio español, 1780–1810.* Mexico City: El Colegio de México, Fideicomiso Historia de las Américas, and Fondo de Cultura Económica, 1999.

Marín López, Javier. "Dinámicas de género en un repertorio singular: Las antífonas de la O 'en contrapunto' de la catedral de México." In *De música y cultura en la Nueva España y el México independiente: Testimonios de innovación y pervivencia*, ed. Lucero Enríquez. Mexico City: Universidad Nacional Autónoma de México, in press.

Marín López, Javier. *Los libros de polifonía de la catedral de México: Estudio y catálogo crítico.* Jaén, Spain: Universidad de Jaén—Sociedad Española de Musicología, 2012.

Marín López, Javier. "Music, Power and the Inquisition in Vice-regal Mexico City." In *Music and Urban Society in Colonial Latin America*, ed. Geoffrey Baker and Tess Knighton, 43–63. Cambridge: Cambridge University Press, 2011.

Marín López, Javier. "Ideología, hispanidad, y canon en la polifonía latina de la Catedral de México." *Resonancias* no. 27 (2010): 57–77.

Marín López, Javier. "Música local e internacional en una catedral novohispana de provincias: Valladolid de Michoacán (ss. XVII-XVIII)." In *Música y catedral: Nuevos enfoques, viejas temáticas*, ed. Jesús Alfaro Cruz and Raúl Torres Medina, 87–93. Mexico City: Universidad Autónoma de la Ciudad de México, 2010.

Marín López, Javier. "La enseñanza musical en la catedral de México durante el período virreinal." *Música y Educación* 76, no. 4 (December 2008): 8–19.

Marín López, Javier. "Una desconocida colección de villancicos sacros novohispanos (1689–1812): El Fondo Estrada de la catedral de México." In *La música y el Atlántico: Relaciones musicales entre España y Latinoamérica*, ed. María Gembero Ustárroz and Emilio Ros-Fábregas, 311–357. Granada: Universidad de Granada, 2007.

Marín López, Javier. "Música y músicos entre dos mundos: La catedral de México y sus libros de polifonía (siglos XVI–XVIII)." Ph.D. diss., Universidad de Granada, 2007.

Marín López, Javier. "Por ser como es tan excelente música." In *Concierto barroco: Estudios sobre música, dramaturgia e historia cultural*, ed. Juan José Carreras and Miguel Ángel Marín, 209–226. Logroño: Universidad de La Rioja, 2004.

Martínez, María Elena. Review of *El peso de la sangre: Limpios, mestizos y nobles en el mundo hispánico*, ed. Nikolaus Böttcher, Bernd Hausberger, and Max S. Hering Torres. *American Historical Review* 117, no. 5 (December 2012): 1630–1632.

Martínez, María Elena. "The Language, Genealogy, and Classification of 'Race' in Colonial Mexico." In *Race and Classification: The Case of Mexican America*, ed. Ilona Katzew and Susan Deans-Smith, 25–42. Stanford, CA: Stanford University Press, 2009.

Martínez, María Elena. *Genealogical Fictions: Limpieza de Sangre, Religion, and Gender in Colonial Mexico.* Stanford, CA: Stanford University Press, 2008.

Martínez, María Elena. "Interrogating Blood Lines: Purity of Blood, the Inquisition, and Casta Categories in Early Colonial Mexico." In *Religion in New Spain*, ed. Susan Schroeder and Stafford Poole, 196–217. Albuquerque: University of New Mexico Press, 2007.

Mayagoitia, Alejandro. "Los rectores del ilustre y real colegio de abogados de México: La primera generación (1760–1783)." In *Carrera, linaje y patronazgo: Clérigos y juristas en Nueva España, Chile y Perú (siglos XVI–XVIII)*, ed. Rodolfo Aguirre Salvador, 267–319. Mexico City: Universidad Nacional Autónoma de México, 2004.

Maynez Champion, Samuel. "Tras la huella de Jerusalém en México." *Proceso* (May 2, 2010). http://www.proceso.com.mx/?p=106260.

Mcalister, L. N. "Social Structure and Social Change in New Spain." *Hispanic American Historical Review* 43, no. 3 (August 1963): 349–370.

McCaa, Robert. "Calidad, Clase, and Marriage in Colonial Mexico: The Case of Parral, 1788–90." *Hispanic American Historical Review* 64, no. 3 (August 1984): 477–501.

McCaa, Robert and Michael Swan. "Social Theory and the Log-linear Approach: The Question of Race and Class in Colonial Spanish America." *Syracuse Geography Discussion Paper Series* 76 (1982).

Medina, José Toribio. *La imprenta en México,* 5 volumes. Mexico City: Universidad Nacional Autónoma de México, 1989.

Melgares Guerrero, José Antonio. "La biblioteca privada del 'marqués de Uribe,' un ilustrado caravaqueño en las postrimerías del s. XVIII." *Estudios Románicos* 6 (1987–89): 1713–1718.

Menegus Bornemann, Margarita and Rodolfo Aguirre Salvador. *Los indios, el sacerdocio, y la universidad en Nueva España, siglos XVI–XVIII.* Mexico City: Universidad Nacional Autónoma de México, 2006.

Miño Grijalva, Manuel. *El mundo novohispano: Población, ciudades y economía, siglos XVII y XVIII.* Mexico City: El Colegio de México—Fondo de Cultura Económica, 2001.

Miranda, Gloria E. "Racial and Cultural Dimensions of 'Gente de Razón' Status in Spanish and Mexican California." *Southern California Quarterly* 70, no. 3 (Fall 1988): 265–278.

Miranda, Ricardo. "Éxtasis de luz y de fe: la policoralidad en la Nueva España a través de la obra de Juan Gutiérrez de Padilla." In *Polychoralities: Music, Identity and Power in Italy, Spain and the New World,* ed. Juan José Carreras and Iain Fenlon, 263–286. Venice: Fondazione Ugo e Olga Levi; Kassel: Edition Reichenberger, 2013.

Morales Abril, Omar. "El esclavo negro Juan de Vera: Cantor, arpista y compositor de la catedral de Puebla (florevit 1575–1617)." In *Música y catedral: Nuevos enfoques, viejas temáticas,* ed. Jesús Alfaro Cruz and Raúl Torres Medina, 43–59. Mexico City: Universidad Autónoma de la Ciudad de México, 2010.

Moyer, Ann E. *Musica Scientia: Musical Scholarship in the Italian Renaissance.* Ithaca, NY: Cornell University Press, 1992.

Murphy, Paul, ed. *José de Torres's Treatise of 1736 General Rules for Accompanying.* Bloomington: Indiana University Press, 2000.

Nassarre, Pablo. *Escuela música según la práctica moderna.* Zaragoza: Diego de Larumbe, 1724.

Nassarre, Pablo. *Fragmentos músicos repartidos en quatro tratados en que se hallan reglas generales y muy necesarias para canto llano, canto de órgano, contrapunto, y composición…* Madrid: Imprenta Real de Música, 1700.

Nava Sánchez, Alfredo. "El cantor mulato Luis Barreto: La vida singular de una voz en la catedral de México en el amanecer del siglo XVII." In *II coloquio Musicat: Lo sonoro en el ritual catedralicio: Iberoamérica, siglos XVI–XIX,* ed. Patricia Díaz Cayeros, 105–120. Mexico City: Universidad Nacional Autónoma de México, 2007.

Nunn, Charles F. *Foreign Immigrants in Early Bourbon Mexico, 1700–1760.* Cambridge: Cambridge University Press, 1979.

Nutini, Hugo G. *The Mexican Aristocracy: An Expressive Ethnography, 1910–2000.* Austin: University of Texas Press, 2004.

Nutini, Hugo G. *The Wages of Conquest: The Mexican Aristocracy in the Context of Western Aristocracies.* Ann Arbor: University of Michigan Press, 1995.

Olmos, Viridiana. "Manuel de Sumaya en la catedral de México." *Palabra de Clío: Blog de la Asociación de Historiadores Mexicanos Palabra de Clío* (July 16, 2010). http://palabradeclio. blogspot.com/2010/07/manuel-de-sumaya-en-la-catedral-de.html.

Olmos, Viridiana. "El magisterio de capilla de Manuel de Sumaya en la catedral de México (1715–1739)." Licentiature thesis, Universidad Nacional Autónoma de México, 2009.

Ortiz, Mario A. "La musa y el melopeo: Los diálogos transatlánticos entre Sor Juana Inés de la Cruz y Pietro Cerone." *Hispanic Review* 75, no. 3 (Summer 2007): 243–264.

Oxford English Dictionary (December 2013). http://www.oed.com/view/Entry/53985?rskey=u QrRoT&result=1#eid.

Palisca, Claude V. *Humanism in Italian Renaissance Musical Thought.* New Haven, CT: Yale University Press, 1985.

Paz, Octavio. *The Labyrinth of Solitude.* New York: Grove Press, 1985.

Peña Muñoz, Margarita. "El teatro novohispano en el siglo XVIII." *Biblioteca Virtual Miguel de Cervantes* (2005): 1–31. http://www.cervantesvirtual.com/obra/el-teatro-novohispano-en-el-siglo-xviii 0/.

Pollin, Alice M. "Towards an Understanding of Antonio Eximeno." *Journal of the American Musicological Society* 10, no. 2 (Summer 1957): 86–96.

Ramos-Kittrell, Jesús A. "Music, Liturgy, and Devotional Piety in New Spain: Baroque Religious Culture and the Re-evaluation of Religious Reform during the Eighteenth Century." *Latin American Music Review* 31, no. 1 (Spring–Summer 2010): 79–100.

Ramos-Kittrell, Jesús A. "Dynamics of Ritual and Ceremony at the Metropolitan Cathedral of Mexico 1700–1750." Ph.D. diss., The University of Texas at Austin, 2006.

Reyes Acevedo, Ruth Yareth. "El testamento de Francisco López Capillas: Un testimonio histórico." In *Primer coloquio Musicat: Música, catedral y sociedad,* ed. Lucero Enríquez and Margarita Covarrubias, 93–101. Mexico City: Univeridad Nacional Autónoma de México, 2006.

Robles Cahero, José Antonio. "Inquisición y bailes populares en la Nueva España ilustrada: Erotismo y cultura popular en el siglo XVIII, 1760–1829." Licentiature thesis, Universidad Autónoma Metropolitana, 1989.

Roubina, Evguenia. *El responsorio "Omnes Morienmini . . ."de Ignacio Jerusalem: La primera obra novo-hispana con obligado de violonchelo y su entorno histórico.* Mexico City: Escuela Nacional de Música, 2004.

Rubial García, Antonio. *La plaza, el palacio y el convento: La Ciudad de México en el siglo XVII.* Mexico City: Consejo Nacional para la Cultura y las Artes, 1998.

Rubio Mañé, José Ignacio. *El virreinato, IV: obras públicas y educación universitaria.* Mexico City: Universidad Nacional Autónoma de México—Fondo de Cultura Económica, 1983.

Ruiz Torres, Rafael Antonio. "La música en la Ciudad de México, siglos XVI–XVIII: Una mirada a los procesos culturales coloniales." Ph.D. diss., Instituto Nacional de Antropología e Historia, 2011.

Russell, Craig H. "Zumaya, Manuel de." *Grove Music Online* (2007–2011). http://www.oxfordmusiconline.com/subscriber/article/grove/music/31064?q=sumaya&hbutton_search.x=0&hbutton_search.y=0&hbutton_search=search&source=omo_gmo&search=quick&pos=1&_start=1#firsthit.

Russell, Craig H. *From Serra to Sancho: Music and Pageantry in the California Missions.* New York: Oxford University Press, 2009.

Russell, Craig H. "The Splendor of Mexican Matins: Sonority and Structure in Jerusalem's Matins for the Virgin of Guadalupe." *Institute of Sacred Music—Yale University, Colloquium Journal* (Autumn 2007). http://ism.yale.edu/sites/default/files/files/The%20Splendor%20of%20Mexican%20Matins-1.pdf.

Russell, Craig H. "Manuel de Sumaya: Reexamining the a cappella Choral Music of a Mexican Master." In *Encomium Musicae: Essays in Honor of Robert J. Snow,* ed. David Crawford and Grayson Wagstaff, 91–106. Hillsdale, NY: Pendragon Press, 1997.

Russell, Craig H. "The Mexican Cathedral Music of Ignacio de Jerusalem: Lost Treasures, Royal Roads, and New Worlds." *Revista de Musicología* 16, no. 1 (1993): 43–77.

Russell, Craig H. "Newly Discovered Treasures from Colonial California: The Masses at the San Fernando Mission." *Inter-American Music Review* 13, no. 1 (Fall–Winter 1992): 5–9.

Saavedra, Leonora. "Chávez, Revueltas, and the Myth of the Aztec Renaissance." Essay presented at the Colloquium Series, Music Department, Northwestern University, Fall 2006.

Salazar Simarro, Nuria. "Música y coro en el convento de Jesús María de México." In *Keyboard Music in Female Monasteries and Convents of Spain, Portugal and the Americas,* ed. Luisa Morales, 29–48. Almería: Asociación Cultural LEAL, 2011.

Saldívar, Gabriel. *Historia de la música en México*. Mexico City: Secretaría de Educación Pública, 1934.

Sánchez Flores, Ramón. "José Ignacio Bartolache: El sabio humanista a través de sus bienes, sus libros e instrumentos de trabajo." *Boletín del Archivo General de la Nación* 2, no. 13 (1972–1976): 187–216.

Sánchez Menchero, Mauricio. *El corazón de los libros. Alzate y Bartolache: Lectores y escritores novohispanos (s. XVIII)*. Mexico City: Universidad Nacional Autónoma de México, 2012.

Sánchez-Navarro Peón, Carlos. *Memorias de un viejo palacio (la casa del Banco Nacional de México)*. Mexico City: Compañía Impresora y Litográfica Nacional, 1951.

Sánchez Reyes, Gabriela. "Oratorios domésticos: Piedad y oración privada." In *Historia de la vida cotidiana en México, volumen III: El siglo XVIII: Entre tradición y cambio*, ed. Pilar Gonzalbo Aizpuru, 531–554. Mexico City: El Colegio de México, 2005.

Sánchez Rodríguez, Ingrid. "Los infantes de la catedral metropolitan de la Ciudad de México: Primeras notas." In *Autoridad, solemnidad y actores musicales en la Catedral de México (1692–1860)*, ed. Lourdes Turrent, 167–210. Mexico City: Centro de Investigaciones y Estudios en Antropología Social, 2013.

Schwaller, Frederick. *Orígenes de la riqueza de la iglesia en México: Ingresos eclesiásticos y finanzas de la iglesia 1523–1600*. Mexico City: Fondo de Cultura Económica, 1990.

Seed, Patricia. "Social Dimensions of Race: Mexico City, 1753." *Hispanic American Historical Review* 62, no. 4 (November 1982): 569–606.

Seminario de Música en la Nueva España y el México Independiente. "Presentación." http://musicat.unam.mx/v2013/index.html.

Seminario de Música en la Nueva España y el México Independiente. "Proyecto Musicat: Libros de coro, polifonía." http://musicat.unam.mx/nuevo/polifonia.html.

Seminario de Música en la Nueva España y el México Independiente. "Proyecto Musicat: Catálogo del archivo de música de la catedral de México." http://musicat.unam.mx/nuevo/adabi_dg.php?sig=2-A2161–1&busquedas=YToxOntzOjEwOiJjb21wb3NpdG9yIjtzOjMwOiJJKRVJVU0FMRU0sIElnbmFFjaW8gKDE3MDctMTc2OS0=.

Sigüenza y Góngora, Carlos. *Triunfo parténico*. Mexico City: Ediciones Xochitl, 1945.

Small, Christopher. *Musicking: The Meanings of Performing and Listening*. Middletown, CT: Wesleyan University Press, 1998.

Spell, J. R. "The Theater in New Spain in the Early Eighteenth Century." *Hispanic Review* 15, no. 1 (January 1947): 137–164.

Spell, Lota. "Music at the Cathedral of Mexico in the Sixteenth Century." *Hispanic American Historical Review* 26 (August 1946): 293–319.

Spiess, Lincoln and Thomas Stanford. *An Introduction to Certain Mexican Musical Archives*. Detroit, MI: Information Coordinators, 1969.

Statuta ecclesiae mexicanae necnon ordo in chorus servandus. Mexico City: Mariano de Zúñiga y Ontiveros, 1748.

Stevenson, Robert Murrell. "Ignacio Jerusalem (1707–1769): Italian Parvenu in Eighteenth-Century Mexico." *Inter-American Music Review* 16, no. 1 (Summer–Fall 1997): 57–61.

Stevenson, Robert Murrell. "Sor Juana Inés de la Cruz's Musical Rapports: A Tercentenary Remembrance." *Inter-American Music Review* 15, no. 1 (Winter–Spring 1996): 1–21.

Stevenson, Robert Murrell. "The Last Musicological Frontier: Cathedral Music in the Colonial Americas." *Inter-American Music Review* 3, no. 1 (Fall 1980): 49–54.

Stevenson, Robert Murrell. "Baroque Music in Oaxaca Cathedral: Mexico's Most Memorable Indian Maestro." *Inter-American Music Review* 2, no. 1 (1979): 179–204.

Stevenson, Robert Murrell. "Sixteenth and Seventeenth Century Resources in Mexico: Part III." *Fontes Artis Musicae* 25, no. 2 (April–June 1978): 156–187.

Stevenson, Robert Murrell. *Christmas Music from Baroque Mexico*. Berkeley: University of California Press, 1974.

Stevenson, Robert Murrell. Review of *El Melopeo Tractado de Musica Theorica y Pratica*, by Pedro Cerone. Facsimile reproduction in two volumes of *El Melopeo y Maestro*. Introduction by Alberto Gallo. *Journal of the American Musicological Society* 24, no. 3 (Autumn 1971): 477–485.

Stevenson, Robert Murrell. *Renaissance and Baroque Musical Sources in the Americas*. Washington, DC: General Secretariat—Organization of American States, 1970.

Stevenson, Robert Murrell. "The First New World Composers: Fresh Data from Peninsular Archives." *Journal of the American Musicological Society* 23, no. 1 (Spring 1970): 95–106.

Stevenson, Robert Murrell. *Music in Aztec and Inca Territory*. Berkeley: University of California Press, 1968.

Stevenson, Robert Murrell. "Mexico City Cathedral Music: 1600–1750." *The Americas* 21, no. 2 (October 1964): 115–135.

Stevenson, Robert Murrell. "From Archive to Print: Problems and Premises." *Inter-American Music Bulletin* 36 (July 1963): 1–4.

Stevenson, Robert Murrell. "Latin American Archives." *Fontes Artis Musicae* 9, no. 1 (January–June 1962): 19–21.

Stevenson, Robert Murrell. *The Music of Peru: Aboriginal and Viceroyal Epochs*. Washington, DC: Pan American Union, 1960.

Stevenson, Robert Murrell. "Early Peruvian Music." *Inter-American Music Bulletin* 20 (November 1960): 6.

Stevenson, Robert Murrell. "Sixteenth and Seventeenth Century Resources in Mexico (Part II)." *Fontes Artis Musicae* 2, no. 1 (1955): 9–15.

Stevenson, Robert Murrell. "Sixteenth and Seventeenth Century Resources in Mexico (Part I)." *Fontes Artis Musicae* 1, no. 2 (1954): 68–78.

Stevenson, Robert Murrell. *Music in Mexico: A Historical Survey*. New York: Thomas Y. Crowell, 1952.

Tanck de Estrada, Dorothy. "Tensión en la torre de marfil: La educación en la segunda mitad del siglo XVIII mexicano." In *Ensayos sobre la historia de la educación en México*, ed. Josefina Zoraida Vázquez, Dorothy Tanck de Estrada, Anne Staples, and Francisco Arce Gurza, 25–113. Mexico City: El Colegio de México, 1981.

Taruskin, Richard. *The Oxford History of Western Music*, volume 2. New York: Oxford University Press, 2010.

Tate Lenning, John, ed. *Reales cédulas de la Real y Pontificia Universidad de México de 1551 a 1816*. Mexico City: Universidad Nacional Autónoma de México, 1946.

Taylor, William B. *Magistrates of the Sacred: Priests and Parishioners in Eighteenth-Century Mexico*. Stanford, CA: Stanford University Press, 1996.

Tello, Aurelio. *Misas de Manuel de Sumaya: Archivo musical de la catedral de Oaxaca: Revisión, estudio y transcripción*. Mexico City: Instituto Nacional de Bellas Artes—Centro Nacional de Investigación, Documentación e Información Musical "Carlos Chávez," 1996.

Tello, Aurelio. *Cantadas y villancicos de Manuel de Sumaya: Archivo musical de la catedral de Oaxaca: Revisión, estudio y transcripción*. Mexico City: Centro Nacional de Investigación, Documentación e Información Musical "Carlos Chávez," 1994.

Torres Medina, Raúl Heliodoro. "¿La solución al problema? El administrador de las obvenciones a partir de 1758." In *Autoridad, solemnidad y actores musicales en la Catedral de México (1692–1860)*, ed. Lourdes Turrent, 211–240. Mexico City: Centro de Investigaciones y Estudios Superiores en Antropología Social, 2013.

Torres Medina, Raúl Heliodoro. "La capilla de música de la catedral de México durante la segunda mitad del siglo XVIII." Ph.D. diss., Universidad Nacional Autónoma de México, 2010.

Turrent, Lourdes. "Los actores del ritual sonoro catedralicio y su ámbito de autoridad: El prelado, el deán y el arcedeán en la Catedral de México." In *Autoridad, solemnidad y actores musicales en la Catedral de México (1692–1860)*, ed. Lourdes Turrent, 23–54. Mexico City: Centro de Investigaciones y Estudios Superiores en Antropología Social, 2013.

Valdivia Sevilla, Francisco Alfonso. "Usos y prácticas musicales en la *Cytara de Apolo I Parnaso en Aragón* de Ambrosio Bondía (Zaragoza, 1650)." *Revista de Musicología* 36, nos. 1–2 (2013): 93–140.

Van Young, Eric. *La crisis del orden colonial: Estructura agraria y rebeliones populares de la Nueva España, 1750–1821*. Mexico City: Alianza Editorial, 1992.

Ventura Beleña, Eusebio. *Recopilación sumaria de todos los actos acordados de la Real Audiencia y Sala del Crimen de esta Nueva España, tomo primero*. Mexico City: Felipe de Zúñiga y Ontiveros, 1787; facsimile ed., with prologue by María del Refugio González. Mexico City: Universidad Nacional Autónoma de México, 1981.

Ventura Beleña, Eusebio. *Copias a la letra ofrecidas en el primer tomo de la recopilación sumaria de todos los autos acordados de la Real Audiencia y Sala del Crimen de esta Nueva España, tomo segundo*. Mexico City: Felipe de Zúñiga y Ontiveros, 1787; facsimile ed. Mexico City: Universidad Nacional Autónoma de México, 1981.

Villalobos Jaramillo, Javier. *Los 100 sitios y monumentos más importantes del centro histórico de la Ciudad de México*. Mexico City: Matesis Asociados, 2012.

Viqueira Albán, Juan Pedro. *¿Relajados o reprimidos? Diversiones públicas y vida social en la ciudad de México durante el Siglo de las Luces*. Mexico City: Fondo de Cultura Económica, 2001.

Viveros, Germán. "El teatro como instrumento educativo en el México del siglo XVIII." *Estudios de historia novohispana* 12 (January 1992): 172–180.

Vizarrón y Eguiarreta, Juan Antonio. *Escuela de música en que perpetuamente hallen las niñas más desvalidas del Recogimiento y Casa de San Miguel de Bethlen de esta Ciudad de México dote y título para poder ser religiosas*. Mexico City: Doña María de Rivera, 1746.

Wingell, Richard. "Medieval Music Treatises: *Speculatio* versus *Institutio*." In *Paradigms in Medieval Thought. Applications in Medieval Disciplines: A Symposium*, ed. Nancy van Deusen and Alvin E. Ford, 157–171. Lewiston, NY: Mellen Press, 1990.

Winter, Cicely and Ryszard Rodys. "Sor María Clara del Santísimo Sacramento and her Family: A Dynasty of Organists and Organ Builders in Eighteenth and Nineteenth-Century Oaxaca, Mexico." In *Keyboard Music in Female Monasteries and Convents of Spain, Portugal and the Americas*, ed. Luisa Morales, 109–132. Almería: Asociación Cultural LEAL, 2011.

Zamora, Fernando and Jesús Alfaro Cruz. "El examen de oposición de Ignacio de Jerusalem y Stella." *Cuadernos del Seminario Nacional de Música en la Nueva España y el México Independiente* 1 (2007): 12–23.

INDEX